D1565937

Death of an Industry

Garment manufacturing can be singled out for its pivotal role in the economic development of countries across the globe during different periods in world history. Especially since the 1970s, this industry has been crucial in ushering in the era of industrialization in Asia and Africa. The global enactment of a series of American policies on the international trade of clothing, including the Multi-Fibre Arrangement (MFA), have given shape to a postcolonial landscape of industrial spectacle which is inextricably intertwined with the webs of social transformation and political regime change. This book studies the relationship between the turmoil of the garment industry and the People's War in Nepal. It revisits how the expiry of the MFA led to a major politico–economic reshuffling in Nepal, and examines the formation of a new industrial working class thereafter. Resisting the abstractism of aid policy, it proposes a new lens for examining the garment industry's embeddedness in local and global politics during a very long period of national transition.

Death of an Industry is an outcome of multi-sited research. Drawing on ethnographic and policy research, it captures the tensions between subaltern workers and disillusioned capitalists, as well as the legal frameworks of the global trade diplomacy and aid advisory bodies which engineered the readymade garment industry in Nepal under a depoliticized framework of market competitiveness. It foregrounds the stories of the factory owners and workers, for whom the rhetoric of export competitiveness involving garment manufacturing initially brought a new way of earning a living and then abruptly took it away.

This monograph explains the anti-politics of export competitiveness which made the wave of industrial destruction a necessary (yet painful) chapter for capitalism and development to prevail. It shows how the class activists that emerged from the crumbling empire of garment manufacturing built a resistance that led to a regime change and eventually ended monarchy in Nepal.

Mallika Shakya teaches in the Department of Sociology at South Asian University, New Delhi. She completed her PhD in anthropology and development studies from the London School of Economics and Political Science. She has also taught at the University of Pretoria, South Africa and has been an advisor to the World Bank's International Trade Department between 2004 and 2012.

Death of an Industry

*The Cultural Politics of Garment Manufacturing
during the Maoist Revolution in Nepal*

Mallika Shakya

CAMBRIDGE
UNIVERSITY PRESS

CAMBRIDGE
UNIVERSITY PRESS

University Printing House, Cambridge CB2 8BS, United Kingdom

One Liberty Plaza, 20th Floor, New York, NY 10006, USA

477 Williamstown Road, Port Melbourne, vic 3207, Australia

314 to 321, 3rd Floor, Plot No.3, Splendor Forum, Jasola District Centre, New Delhi 110025, India

79 Anson Road, #06–04/06, Singapore 079906

Cambridge University Press is part of the University of Cambridge.

It furthers the University's mission by disseminating knowledge in the pursuit of education, learning and research at the highest international levels of excellence.

www.cambridge.org
Information on this title: www.cambridge.org/9781107191266

© Mallika Shakya 2018

First published 2018

Printed in India by Thomson Press India Ltd.

A catalogue record for this publication is available from the British Library

ISBN 978-1-107-19126-6 Hardback

for
ffinlo, sheetal, abha

Contents

Figures and Table

Abbreviations

ADB	Asian Development Bank
AGOA	African Growth and Opportunity Act
ANTUF	All Nepal Trade Union Front
ATC	Agreement on Textiles and Clothing
CA	Constituent Assembly
CBPTA	Caribbean Basin Preferential Trade Act
CMP	cut-make price
CMT	cut-make-and-trim price
CPDCC	Constitutional Political Dialogue and Consensus Committee
CPN/M	Communist Party of Nepal (Maoist)
CPN/UML	Communist Party of Nepal (United Marxist-Leninist)
CSR	corporate social responsibility
DOI	Department of Industries
FIT	Fashion Institute of Technology in New York
GAN	Garment Association of Nepal
GEFONT	General Federation of Nepalese Trade Unions
ICT	Information and Communication Technology
IFIs	International Financial Institutions
ILO	International Labour Organization
IMF	International Monetary Fund
ISIC	International Standard Industrial Classification
JNU	Jawaharlal Nehru University
L/C	Letter of Credit
MFA	Multi-Fibre Arrangement
NC	Nepali Congress
NIDC	Nepal Industrial Development Corporation
NSE	Nepal Stock Exchange Limited
NTUC	Nepal Trade Union Congress
NTUI	New Trade Union Initiative

SAP	Structural Adjustment Programs
SCI	Social Capital Initiative
SPA	Seven Party Alliance
UNDP	United Nations Development Programme
WTO	World Trade Organization

Key Names

FACTORY 1

Arya-Nepal	A mass manufacturing factory and the first of three whose ethnographies form part of this book
Navin Sharma	One of three owners of Arya-Nepal II who later became the CEO and main actor in Arya-Nepal III
Sameer Lamichhane	Son of the owner of Arya-Nepal I who worked as the Production Manager for Arya-Nepal II and III
Ram Lamichhane	Sameer's father and one of the three owners of Arya-Nepal II; he retired before Arya-Nepal III was launched
Mr Jain	One of the three Jain brothers, financiers of Arya-Nepal III based in Ludhiana
Ajay	A young line-supervisor in Arya-Nepal who went on to become the face of the union when they mobilized labour protests anticipating closure of the factory

FACTORY 2

Adam & Eve Boutique (A&E Boutique)	A culturalized (or 'niche') factory owned by the Rauniyar family, manufacturing ethno-contemporary garments drawing on a rich weaving industry spread in various regions of India, and the second of three factories whose ethnographies form part of this book
Chhote Lal Rauniyar	Proprietor of Adam & Eve Boutique
Gayatri Rauniyar	Wife of the A&E proprietor Chhote Rauniyar
Shukra Pariyar	The oldest of the tailors in A&E Boutique
Raju	One of the three embroiders that Chhote and Gayatri worked with, recruited along with another embroiderer from the Nepal-India border town of Rautahat

FACTORY 3

Swakan-Chhemu	A culturalized (or 'niche') factory, owned by a Shakya family, manufacturing ethno-contemporary garments drawing on the symbolism of the Himalayas, and last of the three factories whose ethnographies form part of this book
Samyak Ratna Shakya	Oldest of the three Shakya brothers who own Swakan-Chhemu; he was well known for his community activism and later became part of celebrity writer Heinrich Harrer's network in Kathmandu
Pratyak Ratna Shakya	Middle of the three Shakya brothers who own Swakan-Chhemu who initially started the garment business
Vivek Ratna Shakya	Youngest of the three Shakya brothers and a graduate from the Fashion Institute of Technology of New York
Rubi	Fashion Specialist in Swakan-Chhemu based in Kathmandu
Clair	The Europe-based fashion designer who visited Kathmandu on regular stints to design Swakan-Chhemu products
Rana	A migrant from the Kumaon hill region in India who initially worked as a contractor in Swakan-Chhemu and later joined Arya-Nepal as a labour supervisor

OTHER FACTORIES AND GARMENT BUSINESSMEN

Varun	Owner of the factory in Gwarko which initially had a stand off with the Maoists before they joined mainstream politics, but later successfully negotiated its working terms through community mediation
Ankur Kabra	A Marwari garment businessmen from Kathmandu who I interviewed after he had moved to Kolkata following the garment industry crisis in Nepal

OTHER EMINENT PERSONS

Bishnu Rimal	President of the UML-affiliated trade union GEFONT in 2018
Rameshwor Khanal	Former Secretary of Finance who later took a stint with the new left-leaning party Naya Shakti led by former Maoist leader Baburam Bhattarai
Kiran Sakha	President of the Garment Association of Nepal in 2003
Hari Datta Joshi	A full-time trade union activist and leader now the Vice President (Union Council) of the UML-affiliated GEFONT in 2017

Acknowledgements

The idea for this book began with a vague chat with Professor John Harriss about what is it that I wanted to study that took place a little before I formally joined the PhD programme in LSE but after I had already quit my job with UNICEF. My response was that every society is different but I do not see a meaningful way in which development practitioners tackle this societal difference other than to speak of culture in ways that smack of orientalism, and that I wanted to pursue this question vis-à-vis industrial development in Nepal. John agreed, and thus I embarked on a scholarly journey from international development to economic anthropology. I have never asked John whether he remembered that, a few years back, I had turned down an offer to study for a Masters degree at LSE to go to the University of Glasgow which I ranked 'better' because it was there that Adam Smith the father of economics had taught, and also because I worried that LSE called itself a 'school' whereas Glasgow called itself a 'university'. I think John knew that teaching me was going to be a very long journey, and I am grateful that he still took me on.

Choosing a research topic is one thing, materializing an ethnography on that topic is another. I was hoping my ethnographic experience to be similar to that of others before me who had worked on Nepal. Perhaps one of the strongest impressions etched into my mind about doing ethnography were the ones written by Professor David Gellner, whose fieldnotes I sometimes sneaked a peek at when he lived with my maternal family when I was about seven years old. I must say, whatever little I learned at LSE about doing shop floor ethnography prepared me well in advance that my experience was going to be different. Even so, David's wise advice, that the best question an anthropologist can ever ask in the field is a simple one, 'what are you doing, and why?' grounded my work from beginning to the end. It implies that an anthropologist must always be present in the field to gauge what is normal and worthy of asking about, but also be attentive as to how this dichotomy keeps changing with time.

Despite being situated just a few kilometres from the locality I grew up in, the garment shop floor initially proved inaccessible for me. After being denied access by a whole slew of garment factories, for suspicion of being an undercover reporter or just a nuisance distracting workers from their work, I finally got introduced to Chhote Lal Rauniyar who gave me access to his world of garments, and without his generosity and kindness, this study could never have happened. Chhote *dai* and Gayatri *bhauju* welcomed me into their homes and put me in touch with their friends in the industry, and the rest as they say is history.

It is only after the field unfolds on you that you begin to think about the complexities of doing an ethnography, and the favours bestowed on you by so many people from so many different walks of life. I learned from Dinesh Sharma that a good businessman is also a thorough gentleman and that generosity is built into business acumen. Prakash Lamichhane, with whom I exchanged a homely way of addressing as *afu* (the self) thus avoiding any honorary kinship or even an honorific *tapain*, became a friend with whom I was able to share several of the ups and downs of our careers, his from garment to tourism and mine from aid to scholarship. The tip he gave me early on in my fieldwork that, I should look less pedantic and drop all my multi-syllabi words if I wanted people to be relaxed about being interviewed and thus open up to me, could have easily come from an LSE doyen. Later, Rahul and Ashok Shakya taught me about the logistics of trading fashion garments while Rupa, Mukta and Samika let me further into the world of fashion designing in Kathmandu. My immersion into fieldwork would not have been complete without a cool and tranquil pad I was provided in the house of Bhaskar and Juna Maya Panday Koirala whose friendship sinks deeper in me as I grow older and hopefully wiser in life. What Dinesh *dai*, Chhote *dai*, Prakash, Bhaskar and Juna Maya all had in common was our love for labradors, two to be precise – Ffinlo and Sparky, which were around almost every hour spent with them, their friendly barks constantly interrupting conversations and offering opinions about the flavors of my fieldwork.

Bishnu Rimal explained to me the complex history of union movement and the even more complex structure of GEFONT that had been painstakingly forged under his leadership since Nepal democratized. Hari Datta Joshi was my 'go to' man for all questions about garment unionism. Salik Ram Jammarkattel shared with me the Maoist take on garment. I cannot thank enough the shop floor unionists and ordinary garment workers who made all three of them into national union leaders. Much of my insights about garment unionism came from discussions with Narayan Man Manandhar, Bijendra Man Shakya, Hari Roka, Rajendra Maharjan, Michael Hoffman, Fraser Sugden, and Dhruba Raj Adhikari. However, it was the shop floor workers like Shukra Pariyar, Deepak Karki, Jeena Kusma, Bina Das, Suhail Ansari, Pramod Mandal, Keshav and Rana who made me see what laboring and unionizing actually means on the ground. My reflection on the union movements in Nepal would have not been complete without reminiscing about it in Pretoria, which could have looked out of place but it never was thanks to the generous friendship and collegiality of Andries and Irma Bezuidenhout, Sakhela Buhlungu and Eddie Webster. I owe Jonathan Hyslop almost everything I know about the social history of South Africa.

Doing fieldwork is one thing, writing it up is another. John Harriss was right that the drafts of my thesis began to make sense only after I joined the World Bank and had a concrete everyday filter through which I could interpret my 'data'. It was the tension between advisory aid business and reflexive anthropology which finally gave me a dialectic voice through which to convey my disagreements with macroeconomic assumptions about industrialization and argue for alternative propositions that are necessarily paradoxical and counter-intuitive. I thank Sudhir Shetty and Paul Cadario for continuing to mentor me not only when I was a naïve Young Professional (YP), but worse yet, as I later began to increasingly adopt Global South views about democracy and development. Uri Dadush and John Panzar were liberal managers who gave me freedom to experiment with ideas. I respect Vincent Palmade, Mark Dutz, Papa Demba Thiam, Yevgeny Kuznetsov and Vandana Chandra for persistently articulating alternative views on industrialization. Mona Haddad and Jose Guilhermo Reis continued to help with my curiosities about competitiveness. Fernando Hernandez Casquet, Monica Alina Antoci, Yolanda Strachan, Faezeh Foroutan, Aurora Ferrari, Weenarin Lulitananda, Uri Raich, Nuru Lama and Gayane Minasyan offered friendship. Anthropologists in the Bank Ranjit Nayak and Lynn Bennett, but also Juliana Oyegun who led the Bank work on diversity, almost always made me see something new about being an anthropologist and an 'other' in the Bank world of economists. Laurie Zivetz always opened her doors for me to discuss everything under the sun but also this aspect of my job. In borrowing the business school concept of industrial clusters, I want to thank Christian Ketels, Jorge Ramirez-Vallejo and Amit Kapoor for scholarly engagement and collaborative field work while I was still affiliated with the World Bank. Outside of work, I found retreat in the home of Robert and Sarah Levine throughout my residence in the United States, a privilege which continues to date.

The story of the 'death' of the garment industry, which was beyond the scope of my PhD dissertation completed in 2008, would not have been possible without going back to the university. Barbara Harriss-White not only encouraged me to take that major step but also housed and fed me when I moved to Oxford. I thank the Queen Elizabeth House, Contemporary South Asian Studies Programme, and Wolfson College for offering me platforms from where to manage my transition back into academia. Kate Meagher inspired me tremendously and Cyril Fouillet was a very generous fellow postdoc in the department. The 'Nepal crowd' consisting of Bal Gopal Shrestha, Uma Pradhan, Mitra Pariyar, Shrochis Karki, Chiara Letizia, Anna Stirr and Sir Sam Cowan were always there when I needed help or inspiration. Also, having been away from LSE during the writing-up phase, I was glad that I could finally reconnect with LSE's Anthropology of Work team led by Jonathan Parry. Later, discussions about 'work' morphed into a discussion about economic anthropology with Patrick Neveling, George Baca and Winnie Lem.

I finally 'became' an economic anthropologist only after I joined the Human Economy Global South programme with Professor Keith Hart. Juliana Braz-Dias, Doreen Gorden and I explored South Africa together from Venda to Cape Town. Rehana Valley-Ebrahim was always fun to chat with and I miss Elaine Salo for her generous academic companionship. John Sharp and Innocent Pikirayi helped me settle into the Department. Delicia Pillay and Nadia Barnard came up with a solution every time I got stuck. Upon leaving Pretoria and moving to Delhi, I was shocked to lose my friend from Oxford, Nandita Sahai, whose devoted care for her ailing labradors and elderly parents was something I valued most about South Asia. I owe gratitude to the friendship of my students Kumud Bhansali and Shray Mehta who continuously updated me on emerging literature on industry and work. The Department of Sociology at South Asian University allowed me the time and space to finalize this book. I am grateful to the Martin Chautari team in Kathmandu and especially Pratyoush Onta for having me as a part of their Nepal team outside country.

For someone who speaks English as her fourth language, this book could not have been written without help from a very kind editor, Justin Shaffner. The thesis which became the basis for writing this book was finalized in 2008 and edited by Sue Redgrave. I am grateful to Qudsiya Ahmed in CUP for her friendship and the professional support received from her team throughout the production of this book.

Finally, I wrote this book for my daughter Abha who brought the joy of creative chaos that stirred me so deeply. Singing Newa rhymes for her finally brought me back 'home' while I probably owe much of what I have experienced about the 'world' to Juan, Ffinlo and Sheetal. I love my sisters Sudarshana and Ujwala along with my three brothers. My aunt Dhammavati Guruma was my inspiration for growing up to be a public intellectual. My father Moti Kajee Shakya introduced me to Marxism long ago, a reference point that has helped me navigate through the ebbs and flow of becoming an economic anthropologist later in life. My quiet but fiercely independent mother Ratna Shakya has always been there for me, and understood me without ever having to explain.

1

Situating the Idea
Industry, Society and Development

Until our paths crossed again in California in 2009, Navin and I had
not seen each other for several years, not since 2004 in Kathmandu
just before he migrated to the United States and I stayed on to continue my
fieldwork. As we exchanged a warm embrace, I was struck by the irony of the
encounter. The contrasts of our life trajectories could not have been starker.
I was looking for a quiet retreat, having just quit my job at the World Bank
and saying goodbye to an American life to go back 'home'. Navin Sharma,
who moved to the United States from Nepal five years ago, was manning a
sixteen-hour shift job in order to keep his new petrol pump franchise afloat.
America may be the land of dreams but it comes with its own occasional
setbacks. Talks about the Sharma family struggles got lost in the barking of
two retrievers chaotically running around the small house they had bought
in a peripheral suburb of California. Their son had an accident which left his
skin scarred but spared his life and physical abilities. With a tinge of nostalgia
and suffering, they spoke with pride about having finally found a foothold in
America. I could hear the lull in the room when I announced to them I was
leaving to resume my earlier research on the garment industry in Nepal. The
garment industry is dead, they told me, there is nothing more to say about it.
I said that I wanted to understand what that meant.

After arriving in Kathmandu, I went to see Chhote, a mutual friend of ours.
His garment business had remained profitable some time after the industry had
lost steam, which he attributed to his designing talents and ability to retain
the loyalty of buyers and consumers. Emboldened by the retention of sales,
Chhote initially went ahead and built a modern garment-making facility, but
later changed his mind about continuing after sensing the brewing hostility
against businesses in general. It was much later that he learned that his own

workers, away from his watchful eyes, had begun to turn up at the protests called by the new trade union formed by the Nepali Maoist rebels. Chhote was offended by his own workers' participation in the unions but workers maintained that owners [*malik*] will have their interests to consider just as the workers also have obligations to look after their own. As the working class bifurcated from the capital while the former embraced solidarity and the latter weighed on pragmatism, Chhote then shut down his factory and looked for a different line of work.

Workers' ordeals were of course harsher than that of the factory owners' when the industry collapsed. The death of the garment industry led to an exodus of workers to a wide range of work, almost a *déjà vu* of Henry Mayhew's *London Labour and the London Poor* (1850): From jobs like running tea stalls on pavements and selling cheap clothing and accessories in the local flea market to porter jobs in construction sites, manning as security guards, driving micro buses transporting commuters in and around Kathmandu, and acting in films and dancing in *dohori* restaurants; but also non-jobs such as loitering around the offices of political parties and homes of eminent citizens 'waiting' for any opportunity, or helping people do paperwork and figure out procedures in government offices for everyday tasks such as renewing driving licenses, registering enterprises and renewing passports, facilitating priests and crowds in temples and mosques, even haphazardly piggybacking onto already crowded teams of *dalals* (go-betweens) as Nelson (2015) described, half-efficiently looking to pair up buyers and sellers in real estate business. Whatever lives they lived now, every (former) garment worker I met in and around Kathmandu shared their views on the common experience of having botched careers (*karobaar bigranu*), drowned savings (*ghar baar dubnu*), social jilts (*samajma tamasha bannu*), spoiled reputations (*kalo dhabba laagnu*), and no future prospect in sight (*bhavishya andhakar hunu*). They all spoke of the garment industry as something that came and went like a mighty tsunami.

Such a sea of stories about how a tempestuous garment industry left people in a lurch forced me to reflect on Nepal's way of industrialising for development. How common is it for industries to 'boom and bust' so ephemerally? Or, can industrialization be more steadfast? And what can such stories of industrial wavering and steadfastness tell us about what industrialization means for the societies and nations where they are situated, both in terms of their individual losses and gains but also their overall being beyond their roles as labourers and leaders of production? Within the sphere of production, in addition to the examples cited above, we must remember that the garment industry is also populated by other actors: service providers, policy makers, political activists and international aid advisers, among others. I investigate the garment industry as a part of an industrial ecosystem, a concept I introduce at the tail end of Chapter 2 and expand on in Chapter 3. My theorising of the Nepalese garment industry is drawn from empirical data from a variety of field sites including the review of the ebbs and flows of the garment shop floors, of the surrounding service and regulating bodies, of the unionism that emerged later, and also of the international trade diplomacy in Washington, DC which dictated much of the global garment flow in the late last century as I describe in detail later. Outside the sphere of production, I am interested in understanding the colours and textures of the socio-political backdrop on which industrial projects are sketched.

The fruit of multi-sited research, this book narrates the tensions between subaltern workers and disillusioned capitalists as well as the legal frameworks of the global trade diplomacy and aid advisory which engineered the readymade garment industry in Nepal under a depoliticized framework of market competitiveness. My decade-long journey through the rise and fall of the garment industry in Nepal – as an ethnographer, activist, policy adviser, and academic – gave me insights into both the obvious and subtle about this industry, and the community of people who populate it as factory owners, workers, policymakers, donors of development aid as well as the amateur and professional observers who played their own roles in the making and circulating of garment narratives. For factory owners and workers, the rhetoric of export competitiveness involving garment manufacturing initially brought a new way of earning a living and then abruptly took it away. For policymakers and aid donors, this rhetoric was about the creative destruction deemed necessary for capitalism and development to prevail. For the class activists who built the resistance movement that staged a regime change and eventually brought an end to the monarchy in Nepal, the fall of the garment industry was a promising new beginning on class formation among the new precariat labour. Media and *buddijivis* (intellectuals) produced their own understanding about garment, industrialization, development and democracy. In entangling my own life with that of my ethnographic kin and friends in this industry, I expose the inherent human imperfections within idealized notions of individual rational choice, market efficiency and class uprising.

This first chapter situates the research topic within scholarship on industrial development and its embeddedness in society. The last chapter before the one on the Aftermaths will discuss the complexities of class and cultural politics that coincided with Nepal's extended political transition, which was part radical and part status-quoist. These two constitute the bookends. Between the two, I reflect on how industrial failures are implicated in the everyday lives of Nepalis populating the industrial ecosystem around the readymade garment industry and how industrial fluctuations are situated within the politics of development and democracy. How do these turbulences look from the eyes of enterprising Nepalis seeking to join the global modernity? The readymade garment industry was an important social movement whose foundations lay on aspirations and efforts towards prosperity. At one level, this movement involved cultural and political elites altering their traditional vocations in bids to seize new developmental opportunities. At another level, this entailed the wholesale migration of unskilled youth from rural to urban industrial districts looking for a foothold in the neoliberal state and economy. This was neither the story of class bifurcation nor teleological development, but of the life cycle of an industrial ecosystem *per se*. I examine the rhetoric on trade and aid while uncovering the global politics of developmental policymaking that underpins the garment ecosystem. My lens of seeing the garment industry's embeddedness in local and global politics allows me to resist abstractism both in comprehending neoliberal industrialization and class uprising.

Industry and development

Enterprise is something most people are familiar with. Human history revolves around acts of material production, be it for subsistence, patronage, or profit. Of these, the enterprise of producing things for profit, ranging from needles to skyscrapers, is a central tenet of modernization. Europe embraced commodification of the material sphere as part of its modernising venture, but its construction of 'self' remained human and thus uncommodifiable (Kopytoff 1986). This distinction was entangled when Europe experienced an expanding colonial geography, an extreme version of which was captured in discussions of why enterprises such as slavery, though legitimized in their colonial territories by Europeans, continued to cause discomfort within metropolitan Europe because of their conflation of two contradictory value systems. This tension was not overcome and so led to a double standard when the colonial era ended: it was assumed, by both the former colonizers and the colonized, that the new states could achieve modernization only by emulating European systems of material production and socio-political organization (Shils, 1960; Geertz, 1963).

Hann and Hart (2011) remind us of how the former colonizers' commitment to help the newly liberated states, in the wake of the anti-colonial revolution, was commonly described by the term 'development.' However, over the course of the few decades following the global euphoria of the postcolonial moment, the First World commitment to Third World development faded, triggering a fundamental transformation of meanings and motives. If the rapid growth of the world economy in the 1950s and 1960s encouraged brief hope about a 'teleology' of development, the oil crisis and 'stagflation'[3] of the 1970s thwarted it, and turned it into a 'status' (Ferguson, 2005).[4] In the 1980s, as the Anglo-Saxon world recovered from depression, paving the way for the ascendancy of monetarism and what Mcwandawire (2001) called the 'neoclassical counter-revolution', even more pronounced alterations emerged in the way developed nations shirked their commitments of pursuing development in postcolonial geographies. Previously encouraged to emulate the Anglo-Saxon Keynesianism of the 1970s, Third World countries now came under pressure to withdraw regulatory and welfare functions and focus on fiscal tightening to facilitate servicing of their debt to the First World (Toye, 1987; Harvey, 2007; Krugman, 1992; Baca, 2004).

Entwined within the postcolonial politics of development is a discourse on industrialization. In the 1960s, the developmental proposition for late industrializers was that states should take on the initial 'big push' to trigger entrepreneurial spirit (Rosenstein-Rodan, 1943),[5] either by incubating a set of key industrial sectors or by building spatial 'growth poles' (Perroux, 1950). In this scheme, industrial development could be essayed either in a balanced way (Nurkse, 1953), such as holding multiple industrial sectors on par with one another, or by disrupting the sectoral equation so that one growing sector puts pressure on another, thereby stirring a sustained (if chaotic) growth trajectory (Rostow, 1960; Gershenkron, 1962). Stocktaking in the 1980s showed varied industrial trajectories across countries in Asia. Japan, an early industrial nation, was an example of how states could selectively promote industries that show better export potential (Komiya, Okuno and Suzumura, 1988). Late industrializers – Korea, Taiwan, Singapore, and Hong Kong – also provided state support, but their method was to anticipate market failures and develop pre-emptive strategies to counter failures (Lindauer, Kim, Lee et al, 1991; Pack, 1992).

The role of the state diminished in the late 1980s, with the rise of Structural Adjustment Programs (SAPs) under the directive of the World Bank and the International Monetary Fund (IMF hereafter). SAPs justified economic liberalization through claims that domestic deregulation of industries would pre-empt 'rent-seeking' by elites, thereby allowing the release of resources from less to more productive applications, and that the removal of barriers to international trade would enhance overall competitiveness by exposing domestic industries to competition from rivals abroad (Krueger, 1974).[6] The economic liberalization discourse unleashed a new wave of global geopolitik, so much so that Francis Fukuyama (1992) called this 'the end of history' because the alternative – state-guided – path to industrialization was now considered decisively outmoded, and the neoliberal spirit of this discourse further defended it against those who questioned its distributive implications (Cornia et al, 1987; Stiglitz, 2004; Harvey, 2003; Mirowski, 2013).[7]

Economic liberalization was never free from criticism. Even before neoliberalism reached this far, Nobel Laureate Paul Krugman (1992) called it a 'counter-revolution' against the residues of the developmental agenda from half a century ago. Criticism of neoliberalism intensified further when economic liberalization failed to deliver growth in most places. Ha-Joon Chang (2002) argued, for example, that all major developed countries had subsidized their own industrialization; thus, the IFIs' policy conditionality of state withdrawal reeked of hypocrisy, even conspiracy. Rodrik (2004, 2006) and Sabel (1984, 2001) questioned the boundless faith, displayed by the Washington Consensus, in the anonymous and universal forces of the market, and proposed case-specific analyses that may identify the 'binding constraints' hindering growth. Their analyses were anchored in the notion that trajectories of industrialization necessarily vary across the globe. For example, American systems such as Fordism and Taylorism[8] are substantially different from the Japanese system of 'lean manufacturing'. Work teams in Japanese production plants might be as large as those in American plants, but the central bureaucracies in Japan do not disempower workers as much as they do in the United States (Sabel, 2001; Sabel and Zeitlin, 1997). Japan can further be contrasted with China, which has a 'centripetal' industrial configuration, of loyalty to superiors and long-term collaborative tendencies (Tam, 1990; Fukuyama, 1995; Hamilton and Biggart, 1988). Such notions of collective capitalism are in contrast not only with American managerial capitalism but also with European proprietary capitalism, which is organized around loose groups of specialized firms which coordinate their inputs and outputs through short-term market contracting around long-term strategy (Maurice, 1979; Lazonick and West, 1998; Sorge, 1991; Hollingsworth, 1997).

The variety of industrial experiences gave rise to the notion of divergent capitalisms. Whitley's (1999) study of comparative business systems in East Asia focuses on four parameters: capital providers and users; consumers and suppliers; competitors and alliances; and employers and employees. A growing body of literature on South Asian industry concerns itself with industrial clusters, which is a business school term used to pair up spatial coordination with the depth of business alliances and networks (Porter, 1990), but it has also been expanded to mean alliances among small and medium enterprises with common social justice and environmental concerns (Schmitz and Nadvi, 1999; Cadene and Holmstrom, 1999; Schmitz, 2000; Schmitz and Knorringa, 1996). The concept of industrial clusters has been taken up by sociologists and social geographers to analyse overlaps between industrial organizations, social institutions, and politics (Sabel, 1984; Chari, 2004; Tewari, 2008). The argument in this book is premised on the position that, while the framework of the industrial cluster is a useful one, it needs to be situated within the large-scale politics of society and development.

Industry and society

Economies do not function in isolation but within societies, situated within world systems (Strathern, 1985; Wallerstein, 1974). The question is: How? An obvious starting point in Nepal has been to question the commodification of democratic values under neoliberal economic reforms. Policymakers have pieced together fragmentary projects to conjure development as an abstract object while letting go of the political impetus for tempering corporatism with social justice (Panday, 1999 and 2011). The 'anti-politics' of development actually necessitates a critique of the de-socialized account of industrialization we read in the books on Nepal by aid agencies that preach development. In contrast, Nepal's National Archives are replete with accounts of ethnic politics regulating trade and industry, both in medieval and modern times (Shakya, 2013b). An ethnic mapping of Nepali businesses shows that the ruling elite are disproportionately represented in state-supported industrial sectors, while traders from marginalized ethnicities remain confined to their traditional businesses even after they are no longer viable (Zivetz, 1992; Quigley, 1984). An ethnographic unpacking of the neoliberal tenet that market access equals social opportunity, shows how development in Nepal is deeply rooted in the cultural politics of the market (Rankin, 2004). I follow this line of inquiry about socio-economic embeddedness, with regard to two related concepts, trust and social capital, placing them within the broader ambit of what economic sociologists have called institutional studies (Harriss et al, 1995).

Quintessential economic institutions such as business firms have intrigued economists. If a collective pool of buying and selling activities inevitably leads to a 'general equilibrium' in the market, why don't businessmen function individually? What makes them choose to collectivize themselves under the administrative and financial structures of corporate firms? Indeed, the scale and specialization of firms and corporations become more sophisticated as they are more deeply rooted into the market forces intensifying competition between firms. Coase (1937) explains this with the idea of transaction costs: it takes money to obtain transaction-relevant information, to negotiate and conclude contracts, and to monitor and enforce contracts. There are costs to use the price mechanism, and we can possibly think of these as equivalent to 'friction' in physical systems (Arrow, 1969 in Williamson, 1986: 176; Williamson, 1975). Coase concludes that producers and traders act individually as long as they can internalize transaction costs. When such costs surpass internalization, bureaucratic institutions such as firms come into being.

Organizational studies have borrowed from Coase and Williamson to show that industrial bureaucracies such as firms and corporations are embedded within broader cultural and political systems. At the micro level, such institutions affect leadership, ethics, and structures within and between firms; at the macro level, they work to diversify industrial systems across societies. Take the example of Fordist and Taylorist capitalism: while these are established as the quintessential systems of production in America, and their hegemony in the rise of global capitalism cannot be ignored, what remains unanswered is the inevitability of their universal application. Examining the economic downturn of the 1970s, Piore and Sabel (1984) ask whether the American adherence to mass production might have been more of a historical accident rather than a destiny worthy of being prescribed globally, as the natural path to economic success. Considering the divergence of capitalisms across the globe, they suggest that a 'flexible specialization' – craft and technological alternatives to mass production, involving a loose network of independent producers in place of large-scale producers – exists, and accounts for inconsistencies in classical economic forecasts based on mass manufacturing as an ultimate universal solution (Sabel and Zeitlin, 1997).

There is a growing literature on the specificity of industrial trajectories in developing countries. A classic book edited by John Harriss et al (1995) argues that social institutions do not always follow economic rationality. Instead, they are a collective of common-sensical and public-ideological concerns, ranging from colonial hegemony (Clarence-Smith, 1995) to caste principles and patriarchy (Harriss-White, 1995; Bernal, 1994). Social institutions can be likened to a kind of 'scaffolding' through which individuals and communities evaluate their surroundings and negotiate their ways through the systems and structures in place (North, 2005). The way this manifests in societies is in the guise of the 'rules of the game', which inhere to the collective meanings generated by particular groups of people over time (Harriss, 2002). Countering the neoliberal claim that long-lasting institutions are those that make profit out of social networks, it has been argued that social institutions have evolutionary contributions in constructing markets (Harriss, 2006).

Let me conclude this section by recapturing two recent debates on the society/economy dichotomy to clarify why the profit-motive needs to be contained within the market and not beyond. Although he did not invent the term, Robert Putnam popularized the notion of 'social capital' two decades ago by tapping into nostalgia about 'loss of community'.[9] His argument – that trust-based networks can improve the efficiency of society by facilitating a co-operative spirit that can trigger economic and developmental success even in the face of adversarial rule (Putnam, 1993; Putnam, 2000) – offered economists a new explanatory variable, readily usable in topics relating to social, cultural, and political studies. The World Bank even launched an ambitious Social Capital Initiative (SCI) and brought on board Nobel Prize-winning economists Kenneth Arrow and Robert Solow to work on it (Dasgupta and Serageldin, 1999). But the Bank sought a quick exit after the concept came under attack from both economists and anthropologists (Fine, 2001). John Harriss (2002) argued, for example, that Putnam's oversimplified definition of social capital conveniently singled out 'horizontal, voluntary associations' – such as neighbourhood clubs and choirs – for policy interventions, while keeping the 'dark side' of social capital – such as criminal mafia, political Unions, and communal organizations – at bay. As Bourdieu (1986) had put it, conceptualization of social capital was rooted in variability of access to durable social relationships, and the unevenness of the benefits derived from it, that stretched across generations.

The World Bank and social capital aside, engagement with the sociology of the market and its rationality also leads us to Karl Polanyi's (1944) classic *The Great Transformation*. The problem of (over)attribution concerning Polanyi arises from the fact that the 'embeddedness' fetish of the 1980s – revolving around Granovetter's (1984) dichotomy of 'over-' and 'undersocialized embeddedness' – conveniently overshadowed what Polanyi was centrally concerned about: the pendulum-like motion of 'double movement' (Neveling, 2011; Blyth, 2003). The central premise of Polanyi's book was that an opposition will eventually gain momentum if the state takes an extreme position, which embraces material prosperity while compromising social justice. Seen from this perspective, Polanyi was more concerned about the issue of 'disembedding' rather than 'embeddedness' per se. He argued that a disembedding process was triggered during the early stages of the industrial revolution in England, not only by the market-centric behaviours of individual actors, but also by the state's refusal to acknowledge the popular mobilization against public policies which endorsed the extreme commodification of land, labour, and money. One can see something of a Malthusian nemesis operating in Polanyi's anticipation of political uprisings that would punctuate and reverse the individualistic-materialistic drive. The emerging anthropological discourse, that Keith Hart, Laville, and David Cattani (2010) have called 'the human economy', has made Polanyi again relevant to the neoliberal crisis at the turn of the millennium.

A note on research, methodology and chapterization

My entry into the world of garments, in 1997 as a graduate student pursuing my Masters, was as an economist. Upon learning that garment manufacturing was by far the largest industry in Nepal throughout the 1990s, comprising as much as one quarter of its total exports to the world, I set out to understand its suitability and promise for Nepal. When I arrived in Kathmandu for my doctoral fieldwork in 2002, I encountered two contradictory views: one view was that the industry was Nepal's first step towards modern industrialization, while the opposing view was that it was 'doomed' from the start and destined to die. Examples from Bangladesh, China, India, Lesotho, and Mauritius were drawn upon to substantiate both viewpoints in the debate. While trying to make sense of this conundrum, I learned that these two viewpoints, in reality, referred to two entirely different ways of making and trading garments prevalent in Kathmandu and elsewhere. This divide seemed increasingly important to me even if it was entirely lost on the national and global policymakers who supposedly understood and regulated this industry. The task of 'disaggregation of data' in mainstream economics essentially means going down to the higher digits of the national account statistics, from single to two and then three digits and henceforth. In this case, the concerned database is the International Standard Industrial Classification (ISIC) as prescribed by the United Nations. I quickly learned that this did not allow me to make the distinction I was beginning to apprehend from what my informants told me; a distinction rooted neither in the final *outcome* of their toil nor the destinations of their products, but rather in *the way* they chose to toil and the people they chose to *associate* with.

My method of disaggregating the manufacturing of readymade garments in Nepal was to separate the specialized garments, which I would call the 'craft' type, from the everyday garments, or the 'mass' type. The work of the people involved in the manufacture of both types of garments was enmeshed with their lives, and drew heavily on their social surroundings. The distinction between the two could not be overlooked, especially with regard to the irony inherent in it: those with access to capital and political connections were part of the 'mass' subsector, while those without either carved out a space for themselves in the 'craft' subsector. The former achieved efficiencies of scale and precision by securing deals from the American brands that ruled the market. The latter, much smaller in number and all members of minority ethnic groups, developed networks that were based on craft and culture, and penetrated lucrative niche markets in far-flung corners of the United States. I decided to divide my time in the garment industry between the 'mass' and the 'craft' subsectors.

Acknowledging the ethnic aspects inherent in the mass/craft dichotomy of the garment industry, I selected three factories to be my initial ethnographic field sites, where I would position myself as an unskilled labourer on the shop floors. In Arya-Nepal's mass manufacturing shop floor, I initially worked as an unpaid 'thread-cutter'; my task was to cut off hanging threads after the garments had been stitched, but before they were sent for finishing. I enjoyed socialising with other workers doing the same job, while the factory owner was pleased that I had apparently taken to heart the principle he said he was trying to advocate among his employees that 'no job is too big or small'.[10] After my blue-collar credentials were tested for a few months, I was given a temporary desk in the office of the Production Manager, which was adjacent to, and overlooked, the main stitching floor. I would flit between the office and the shop floor, keeping my ears open for the circulating news and brewing gossip, among both the owners and workers. Occasionally, I undertook minor work such as the time measurement of each task and sub-task of production, the data later being fed into the planning of their assembly lines. At other times, I was an obedient observer, simply taking notes while owners, supervisors, and workers discussed operations.

While working at Adam and Eve Boutique (A&E Boutique hereafter), a specialized 'craft' producer, I divided my time between the office of the owners on the first floor and the workshop of the designers on the second floor. For the owners, I was merely an observer who would listen as they negotiated the prices and purchases of fabrics with weavers, traders, and prospective fabric suppliers. Among the designers, who were always experimenting with colours and designs, I was sometimes a live mannequin, modelling and commenting on their ideas, and sometimes a messenger, running to and fro between them and the tailors, embroiderers, and storekeepers. At another manufacturer, Swakan-Chhemu, I shared a room with the fashion designer and the graphics designer, adjacent to the owners' rooms on the top floor, and I undertook tasks such as designing brochures and commercial advertisements. When European fashion designers and buyers came to Kathmandu, I took them on tours and facilitated their conversations with tailors and embroiderers. These tasks still left me with plenty of time to both formally interview people, when specific issues came up, and also to socialize with workers and owners.

My shop floor research spanned the entire period of my doctoral fieldwork, beginning in November 2002 and ending in April 2004. Towards the end of this period, as people got to know me better, they came to expect that I would always be present on the shop floors, as much as a salaried worker would be, sharing tasks and gossip alike. As my friendship with the people in these few factories flourished, I began to accompany them on their chores in and around town, buying raw material and accessories, negotiating processing and other services, and helping with paperwork both at the customs office in the airport and at border check posts. What turned out to be especially important for me were the long hours I spent at the Garment Association of Nepal, mingling with the crowd of factory agents who would visit the Association office to obtain export permits and quality-clearance documentation. Over time, as I immersed myself deeper in the world of garments, my information base expanded. Though I was primarily seen as an affiliate of Arya-Nepal, I later developed contacts and friendships among people from other garment factories and service providers. Because of my connections with Arya-Nepal, I was not a complete outsider to most people in the garment business, and hence, people were not only more forthcoming in what they shared with me about their business, but more importantly, this common acquaintance saved me from being suspected of being a media spy looking for an exposé on issues of child labour, worker abuse or environmental hazards, as occasionally happened in the industry. These credentials as a 'garment person' certainly helped me conduct in-depth interviews of the factory owners and managers of thirty-three factories, focusing on the nature and scope of garment making. I also interviewed officials at the Ministry of Industries and Commerce, as well as at the Garment Association of Nepal, on the national industrial policy.

In April 2004, just as I was wrapping up my fieldwork and preparing to head back to London to finish writing my PhD thesis, I found myself witnessing a serious crisis that forced most garment factories to shut down. Chaos had engulfed the entire industry in Nepal. Every week there would be a report of yet another factory being shut down. My field notes of this time speak of the despair among garment workers and owners alike. The notes also speak of the general sense of confusion because, despite its significance as the largest exporter and employer just half a decade ago, the condition of the garment industry was little reported in the national media, as the country found itself in the middle of a civil war, especially after 2001. Economists and industry analysts kept an eye on the turbulence in the garment industry, but through a neoliberal lens which either interpreted the garment crisis as a necessary 'hiccup' or blamed the garment workers for the industry's failure. It initially seemed that the mass sector within the garment industry would die, but that the craft sector might survive. I decided to extend my fieldwork to not only continue my investigations into the still-surviving craft factories, but also to better understand the implications of the failure of the industry for the leaders of the Garment Association. At one point, I joined the policy-lobbying effort coordinated by the Garment Association of Nepal, which sought help from American legislators to table a bill in the American Congress and Senate that would give Nepal privileged access to the American market, and thus help the garment industry cope with the ongoing crisis. The bill remained under consideration for a long time, especially as American parliamentarians seemed willing to be persuaded that an industrial development 'carrot' might weaken the rise of the Maoists in Nepal. Eventually, however, the bill was dropped.

I was aware that the context of aid hegemony in the making of the garment narrative could not be overlooked. Even as Nepali garment businessmen lobbied with parliamentarians in Washington, DC for preferential treatment for garment imports from Nepal, the policy analysts at the World Bank and IMF maintained that the Nepalese garment industry deserved to die if it could not compete with other countries on price, quality, and speed of production. These two competing global narratives created a policy conundrum for Nepal, such that the country both acknowledged the importance of the garment industry, and dismissed it in the same breath. The contradictory politics of admission and omission seemed to permeate this industry, and is clearly something that informed my research, and furthered my understanding of the paradox of 'aid' substantially. Drawing on my initial training as a development economist, I read the economic policy analyses commissioned, through donor agencies and think tanks, by the Ministry of Industry and Commerce. As my interest developed further on the question of whether or not it made sense to argue that the crisis in Nepal's garment industry emerged from its lack of productivity, I spent six comfortable years in Washington, DC (2004-2010) working as an industry and trade specialist for the World Bank, travelling periodically to East and South Asia, Africa, and Eastern Europe to analyse garment industries there. Essentially disillusioned by the promises of 'aid', and the hollowness of its logic for development, I left the World Bank and 'headed home' as I have recounted at the beginning of this chapter.

After several years of uncertainty, it seemed that the decline of the garment industry was accelerated when Nepal carved its way out of the civil war that had caused the deaths of over ten thousand Nepalis in a decade. The decline of the industry was accelerated by a militant union uprising, which became the focus of my research during my three visits to Kathmandu between 2005 and 2008. As it became clear that the industry had no future, protests among the garment workers in Nepal intensified, with their early demands for fair compensation being eventually replaced by a call for a reversal of neoliberal industrial organization. In 2009, when I returned to Kathmandu after quitting my aid-funded life in Washington DC, I conducted research on labour union politics among workers affiliated with the garment industry. This project allowed me, more than had been possible during the shop floor research, to focus more specifically on class politics and on the way it is implicated in the economy of a country in political transition. My research took a different turn as Nepal lingered through a very long transition, initially basking in the euphoria of the 2006 uprising, but later sinking into a status-quoist situation after the first Constituent Assembly failed. From 2010 onwards, I began to study the lives of my informants beyond the world of garments, exploring their ethnic and regional identities. From being a shop floor and a union ethnographer, and finally an analyst of ethnicity, national transition, and development, my research methods have been stitched together from various roles to create an eclectic patch-worked whole.

This book engages with Anthropology's debate with Economics on methodology and content. I argue that the garment industry in Nepal was never merely a construct of the anonymous forces of supply and demand, as the neoliberals would have it, but a densely coordinated industrial ecosystem, deeply rooted in the culture and politics of the space it inhabited (see Chapter 3). I break with the capital-labour dichotomy, which dominates the study of industries, to make explicit the tensions between the voices of people from the industry on the one hand, and, on the other, the political and legal frameworks of the global trade diplomacy which regulate this industry while they preach depoliticized market competitiveness. In Chapter 4, I consider the extent to which making garments is a human activity where the materiality of production is deeply embedded in the culture and politics of craft. I argue that the culturally coded social organization nudges some businessmen to develop market niches for themselves, while leaving the rest to compete within the mass-manufacturing subsector. The 'normality' of garment production in Chapter 4 is contrasted with an analysis of the crisis, or the 'death', of the industry, in Chapter 5. The collapse of the garment manufacturing industry was certainly a lot more painful than the statistics in the national accounts and economic surveys can convey. Garment people fought a perceived cosmology of bad spirits, or '*dasha*' as they called it, with suave management reforms that sought to deploy scientific software aiming to cut factory costs and locate market niches, thereby generating a new language to speak about the paradoxes of modernity and development. This new conscience took a decisively political turn as it morphed into a militant Union movement after merging with an ongoing Maoist People's War that sought footholds in the cities, especially Kathmandu (see Chapter 6). The outcome was the unlocking of a Pandora's box of questions involving the politics of development, as well the nation and its reconstitution (see Chapter 7). By unfolding these multiple layers within the common narrative of the boom and eventual bust which the Nepali garment industry experienced, and analysing the resettlement strategies of rich businessmen and the rootlessness of poor workers, this book probes the global and local contexts of the failure of development in Nepal.

Endnotes

1. *Dohori* is a repertoire of folk songs in Nepal where men and women exchange romantic couplets with a fixed rhyme scheme often accompanied by playing of folk instruments.
2. See Jeffrey (2014) for an ethnography of lower middle class young men in Meerut in India which theorizes waiting as a social experience and basis for mobilization within the micro-politics of class.

3. 'Stagflation' denotes a slow economic growth scenario complicated by an unusual combination of high inflation and high unemployment, thus posing the policy dilemma as to whether to curb one or the other, since addressing one problem would force deterioration of the other.

4. Ferguson (2005) argues that developmental aspirations and assurances of the 1960s – that Third World countries can achieve the prosperity of enjoyed by the First World if they made efforts – have now been lost, thus turning the ranking of development from a 'telos' to a 'status'.

5. In sync with Rosenstein-Rodan is Rostow who argues, in his much acclaimed thesis on the 'non-communist manifesto' published in 1971, that traditional societies must internalize a profit-motive enterprise culture before an industrial 'take-off' could be attained.

6. The ten tenets of economic liberalization were later inscribed as a 'Washington Consensus' or a standard set of policy prescriptions to be applied on developing countries seeking loans from IFIs (Williamson, 2004). These tenets include: (i) end of budget deficits; (ii) reallocation of public expenditure from politically sensitive areas to those with high economic returns; (iii) tax reform; (iv) financial liberalization; (v) unified exchange rate; (vi) end of quantitative and tariff barriers; (vii) abolition of barriers on foreign direct investment; (viii) privatization of state enterprises; (ix) abolition of regulations impeding the entry of new firms; (x) secure property rights, especially in the informal sector.

7. See Bhagawati (2008) for his summary of criticism directed against economic liberalization. He argues that the grassroots-level NGOs need not be taken seriously while the advocates of a 'human face' of Structural Adjustment could be persuaded that the Adjustment already had a human face. He then targets macro-economists such as Dani Rodrik and Paul Collier in an attempt to inflict more damage on the cause of liberalization by critiquing the central tenets of economics. See Rodrik (2006) and Collier and Page (2009) for further substantiation of the latters' views.

8. Fordism entails systems where large managerial bureaucracies and semi-skilled workers are mobilized to scale production in a cost-effective way, while Taylorism adds specialized machineries to this set up (Taylor, 1947; Drucker, 1972; Boyer et al, 1997; Braverman, 1998).

9. Robert Putnam's (1993) book *Making Democracy Work* was an immediate bestseller and formed a pair with another bestseller by Francis Fukuyama (1995), *Trust: The Social Virtues and the Creation of Prosperity*. President Bill Clinton even used the term 'social capital' in a State of the Union address. In his book, Putnam briefly acknowledged the work of James Coleman (1988) but not Pierre Bourdieu.

10. The factory owner, Navin, had also assigned a relative of his to do this thread-cutting task. Invoking the example of her and me, Navin often told other workers that he treated everyone equally based on their capacity to work, regardless of their personal connections and, clearly, degree certificates.

2

Nepal and Garments

In Nepal, as elsewhere, the past influences the present, and individual actions are rooted in collective trajectories. Drawing on interviews and archival materials, this chapter situates the Nepali readymade garment industry within a span of economic history stretching from Nepal's pre-Unification (or Conquest)[1] era to its interface with the British colonizers, as well as postcolonial South Asia. The historical reconstruction of the changing relations of industrial production and cultural practices in Nepal allows me to demonstrate how the decline of the Nepali garment industry is not an isolated crisis but rather a failure of development, situated within the country's transition from a mono-ethnic Hindu neoliberal state to a federal republic with alternative aspirations for prosperity.

The story of the Nepali garment industry also needs to be situated within the global industrial landscape. In being both export-oriented and import-driven, garment manufacturing is inextricably woven into the international politics of trade, and its apparati such as the World Trade Organization (WTO), the World Bank, the International Monetary Fund (IMF) and the Office of the United States Trade Representative (USTR). The negotiated trajectory taken by the Nepali garment industry within this global institutional set up is a deeply localized one, and needs to be differentiated from its global and regional counterparts, even if it shares with some of them a common point of origin of an American Multi-Fibre Arrangement (MFA) for international trade. This chapter will tell the story of the 'Nepalization' of the garment industry in terms of who populated it and what kinds of imaginations fuelled its designs while it lasted (Shakya, 2004).

Nepal

Having been, for long, a relatively isolated Himalayan kingdom, Nepal has undergone radical economic expansions more than once in its recent history.

From the mid-seventeenth century up until the beginning of the twentieth century, the ancient kingdom of Nepal in Kathmandu Valley functioned primarily as a gateway to Tibet. The Buddhist Newar traders enjoyed the privilege of unlimited residential rights as well as a monopoly over minting Tibetan coins, secured through a treaty brokered in 1650 which built on earlier exchanges, including a marriage alliance between Kathmandu's princess Bhrikuti and the Tibetan emperor Songtsan Gampo in the seventh century (Slusser, 1982; Rankin, 2004). Even while they remained protected against the growing influence of the British East India Company in the south (Bista, 1980; Regmi, 1971), the political status of Buddhist Newars waned after the Hindu Shah kings defeated them in 1769 as part of a greater Unification (or Conquest) project.

As the British rule in India consolidated into the 'Raj' after the mid-nineteenth century, it waged a vicious war against the Shahs of Nepal, ending only with the annexation of much Nepali land. This was followed by the rise of a regime loyal to the British: the Ranas. The Ranas launched the first wave of industrialization in Nepal in the 1930s in collaboration with Indian Marwari traders who, at that time, were already serving the British in Kolkata (Gaige, 1975; Hardgrove, 2004, Kudaisya, 2003). This first wave – manifested in the rise of industries producing not only fast moving consumer goods like matches and cigarettes, but also those processing agricultural commodities like jute widely used for bulk packaging before plastic was invented – was just one component of the broader Rana-Marwari alliance rooted in Hindu nationalism.

The earliest Marwari traders entered Nepal in the 1850s through individual invitations from the Rana court, immediately following the Indian rebellion in 1857 when Nepal's Prime Minister Jung Bahadur Rana not only supported the British but also provided military aid in defeating the rebels. Just when the Marwaris had established themselves as a trusted local trading ally for the East India Company, Jung Bahadur Rana also established himself as a political ally of the British. In recognition of Jung Bahadur Rana's unconditional loyalty throughout the testing times of the Indian rebellion, the British gave Nepal substantial territories in the far west of the Nepal-India border, which later came to be known as the *naya muluk* (new nation). It was unclear from the official treaty whether this land was a British gift to the Rana family or an addition to the territories of the Nepali state. This ambiguity led the Ranas to invite the first cohort of Marwaris to set up businesses in the Nepal-India border towns.

A new system of government was put in place in the new territories, which among other things, opened up contracts and jobs as commercial bidders and state economic supervisors to people of non-hill and valley descent, as well as providing Marwari traders with necessary land and logistical services for the new tier of manufacturing and trade. This new alliance between the Ranas and the Marwaris in Nepal under the patronage of the British colonials, juxtaposed the benevolent capitalism of the merchant caste with the royal duty of the warrior caste (Shakya, 2014).

The second wave of industrialization came during the rule of King Mahendra, who assumed power in 1960, ending a democratic regime that had been operating after a popular uprising had ended the Rana regime in 1951. A new constitution was promulgated in 1962 launching a one-party 'Panchayat rule' under the king. This constitution formally replaced the caste-based penal code (*muluki ain*), institutionalized by the Rana regime, but continued to turn a blind eye to entrenched caste and ethnic hierarchies that continued to discriminate against marginalized people. King Mahendra's Panchayat regime was noted for embracing the postcolonial wave of development, albeit to launch new oppressive regimes, in contrast to its neighbor states, such as India and Sri Lanka, where development embodied democratic victory and independence from colonial powers. This paradoxical 'development' involved turning a blind eye to the contradictions inherent in the so-called 'soil-suited' political structure of developmental practices (Panday, 2011). For example, the king consistently held Panchayat representatives accountable for all developmental goals, while himself holding supreme political power, and regularly interfering in everyday governance to impose his own feudal patronage, which he interpreted as development. Not surprisingly, the three national economic plans covering the period between 1956 and 1970 failed to trigger industrialization, while raising grave concerns about the 'clustering' of Bahun-Chhetris, all from Kathmandu, in industrial sectors that enjoyed privileged access to state resources (Goodall, 1978). Concerns were occasionally raised that this 'clustering' effect diluted the rigour of economic planning, as planners tended to prioritize caste and ethnic interests over developmental concerns (Wildavsky, 1972; Schloss, 1980).

The caste and ethnic interests of the elite became more firmly entrenched as the state promulgated new industrial policies privileging certain groups of people and businesses over others. The fourth national economic plan, launched in 1970, continued to ensure a proactive role for the state in industry, and is especially known for its generous protection of manufacturing industries (Thapa, 1967 cited in Wildavsky, 1972). The Nepal Industrial Development Corporation (NIDC), a government body designated to provide financial and technical support to industries, was mobilized to such an extent that its portfolio quadrupled during the fourth plan (Pradhan, 1984). After the two Industrial Acts of 1974 and 1981 formalized lucrative licenses and issued generous tax holidays for select industries, a Nine-Point Export Promotion Programme was introduced in 1984, allowing exporters access to concessional credit. The elite Bahun-Chhetris, no longer forbidden from seeking profit ventures as they had been under the *Muluki Ain*, emerged as the primary beneficiaries of this state-sponsored industrialization. Zivetz (1992) has shown how parastatals and corporations in lucrative state-supported sectors, such as the National Salt Trading Private Limited, were controlled by ruling elites. Emerging industrial opportunities were quickly occupied by the privileged. Despite not being culturally associated with most sites of tourist interest, the Bahun-Chhetris owned over a quarter of the travel agencies registered during the fourth plan. The Sherpas and Gurungs, who lived in the sites that became the primary tourist destinations, and the Newars, who had built the cultural heritage of Kathmandu, had much smaller shares in the tourism businesses launched with government support (Zivetz, 1992).

The third wave of industrialization, which continued the international aid leverage for development, is associated with the popular uprising of 1990, that ended the king's one-party Panchayat rule and embraced multi-party democracy under constitutional monarchy. This wave opened the doors to economic liberalization leading to privatization of state resources, the removal of business subsidies, and the dismantling of barriers to international trade (Mahat, 2005). Although Nepal had signed two policy-lending contracts with the World Bank and IMF in the late 1980s, it was not until the new Industrial Enterprise Act of 1992 was enshrined as law that an ambitious programme of structural reform was unleashed. All import licenses were scrapped by 1993, peak tariff rates were more than halved within just two years into the Act, and the license requirement for setting up industries was abolished, except for those with direct implications for defence, public health, and environment. The Foreign Investment and Technology Act of 1992 allowed foreign investment up to 100 percent in large industries, and a 'one-window system' was put in place, to facilitate tax and foreign exchange services. The privatization of banks increased the availability of money for starting new industries, while strengthening and reform of business associations ensured broader dissemination of information about business opportunities.

On the ethnic front, the popular movement of 1990 gave rise to what Gellner (2003) called an 'ethnogenesis' similar to what happened in India during the time of independence, and for rather similar reasons. The formerly marginalized castes and ethnicities felt that they had been liberated by the demise of the Panchayat ideology that had favoured the ruling Bahun-Chhetri culture and polity. Some efforts were made by the Nepali state to end ethnic exclusion but the new constitution gave little room for the much-hoped-for ethnic liberation and Nepal remained a Hindu kingdom. Since the civil service was still dominated by Bahun-Chhetris, policy liberalization failed to achieve ethnic neutralization in the new economy even with the intent to do so.[2] Both financial and social capital remained in the hands of the ruling elite, and most business associations continued to be dominated by them at the top, even as the membership base of these associations widened and became more diverse. Most of the lucrative businesses remained in the hands of elite social groups, such as the Bahun-Chhetris, along with a few old merchant groups, such as the Marwaris and the Newars. This period of democracy and liberalization is the context for my ethnography of the rise of the garment industry in Nepal.

Democracy and liberalization triggered an economic boom in the early 1990s, but it was short-lived, and the economic downturn coincided with an armed insurgency that gained momentum at the turn of the century. The Communist Party of Nepal, Maoist (CPN/M hereafter) launched a violent civil war (or People's War) that held Nepal captive over the next decade. Political instability deepened, especially after the royal massacre of 2001 that saw King Birendra and his entire family wiped out. His brother, King Gyanendra, assumed power but pushed the country further into instability by dismissing the parliament. Finally, a 'twelve-point agreement' signed in November 2005 between CPN/M and an alliance of seven major democratic political parties (SPA) formally ended the People's War, which had claimed more than ten thousand lives in over a decade. The democrats and revolutionaries, who united to confront King Gyanendra, later went on to declare Nepal a secular republic in 2008, as an elected Constituent Assembly set out to write a new constitution. This raised hopes of a fundamental restructuring that would address old grievances held by people at the country's social and political periphery. The popular aspiration was that a 'new Nepal' would offer rigorous affirmative action for historically marginalized peoples, including the indigenous population of the hills (the Janajatis), some of whom are not Hindus and do not subscribe to caste in the way the Hindu elites do, the low castes (Dalits), the borderland people who differentiate themselves from the hill-Hindus in terms of the language of communication as well as the politics of regional identity (Madheshies), and women. The previous rhetoric of modernization and economic liberalization gave way to an identity- and class-based politics calling for social justice. What this meant for businesses was that a new activism swept through the shop floors, with workers demanding better working conditions on the one hand, and giving rise to new ethnic clusterings on the other. The readymade garment industry, whose collapse coincided with this new political context, offers a lens through which to probe varied responses from those situated at different ends of the spectrum of the Nepali political economy.

Garments

Garments are one of the most globalized manufacturing industries in the world. Since the United States is the largest consumer of garments manufactured in much of the so-called Third World, I will briefly discuss the changes the industry underwent in the past in the United States so as to anticipate the more recent turmoil that this book investigates.

As early as the 1880s, the American garment industry welcomed a wave of Yiddish-speaking Jewish immigrants from Eastern Europe, who worked for German Jewish employers (Soyer, 2005),[3] and, after the Second World War, some articles of clothing being sold in the American market began to be produced in Japan and Hong Kong. Although the share of garments imported from Asia was small, American labour Unions took notice of the emerging phenomenon and exerted pressure on the government to protect domestic workers by imposing a quota to limit imports. The American government later used this quota system, earlier issued to calm Union protests, as ammunition in a massive trade war. The 'Multi-Fibre Arrangement' (MFA hereafter), as it came to be known, was first formalized in 1974, and its validity was extended four times to last through 2004. The MFA not only spelled out precisely how many pieces of garment each country could export to the United States, but also developed an elaborate enforcement mechanism for its monitoring on a day-to-day basis. These country-quota levels sought to reduce increased rates of East Asian and Indian garment exports to its market, intending thereby to encourage exports from smaller and poorer countries whose share of exports into the United States market had earlier been very small. Within South Asia, for example, Indian exports were curtailed by the MFA, while Bangladesh, Pakistan, and Sri Lanka found their exports encouraged. Nepal was given the highest South Asian 'quota per capita' of 2.3 pieces per head, on the grounds that its garment industry was the most nascent compared to all its neighbours in the region.

The readymade garment industry under the MFA is one of the best reminders for Nepal that industrialization is hardly linear and unidirectional. Its trajectory was not easily anticipated because it was dependent on a complex set of events connecting everyday shop floor activities with international politics. Nepal's garment manufacturing industry began in the late 1970s, and eventually grew to be the largest employer of unskilled labour and contributing up to a quarter of national exports in the late 1990s. But the industry almost vanished into thin air within a few years after the MFA expired in 2005. An agreement signed in Marrakesh in 1994 gave birth to the World Trade Organization (WTO) that soon dictated that the MFA would be replaced by the Agreement on Textiles and Clothing (ATC) on January 1, 2005. This agreement was intended to rid the international garment flows of American trade politics, which meant that Nepal was set to lose implicit cost subsidies, of up to 43 per cent, which had made it competitive in the American market (Birnbaum, 2000). Indeed, more than a fifth of the garment companies in Nepal left the field by 2002, fearing the expiry of the MFA, and a majority of the remaining followed suit soon after the MFA expired.

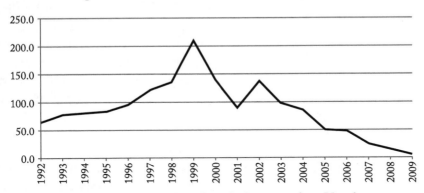

**Figure 1: Exports of Readymade Garments from Nepal
(in US dollars in millions, 1992–2009)**
Source: Garment Association of Nepal data sets. x-axis shows the year

The running joke among the garment-trade people was that the trend data on the garment industry in Nepal resembled the zigzag of a Himalayan range. As Nepal was liberalized in the early 1990s, its garment exports reached a steady level of sixty million US dollars, or thereabouts. As the effects of market liberalization took root, Nepal's garment exports grew a peak of over 200 million US dollars in 1999. As political turmoil erupted in the following years, especially as Maoist rebels began to attack urban areas and disrupt national highways, garment exports began to dwindle, initially in 2000 and steadily after 2002. In 2005, the year after the MFA expired, Nepal exported only 50 million US dollars' worth of garments, just half of what it had exported years before. In the subsequent year, the trend of annual halving of exports continued. In 2009, Nepal exported just under 5 million US dollars' worth of garments, and in 2010, garment exports were just over 2 million US dollars.

The accounting books in the Garment Association of Nepal, which diligently tracked garment trends, marked July of 2010 as the month when the garment export was zero. Soon after, the country saw a bitter spat erupt between the Trade Unions and policymakers about the closure of one of the last remaining large garment factories in 2011. Although some of the craft producers continued manufacturing, policymakers marked the closure of Surya Garments as the end of an era for the Nepal garment trade, which I discuss at length in Chapter 6. The data in the national accounts continued to record garments being exported out of Nepal, and that trend seemed to somewhat increase as the business environment stabilized in the years before Nepal promulgated its new constitution in 2015. But those garments were different, both in terms of how they were being produced and to whom they were being sold. Neither did the MFA-era garment factory owners join these new ventures nor did the Garment Association of Nepal (GAN) give them membership. Ironically, the emerging enterprise of clothes-making seemed to resemble what individual quilters and tailors were doing in the 1970s to cater to the 'hippy' tourists, before the tumultuous MFA saga began in Nepal, as if the industry had come full circle, back to its roots.

The quilters and tailors of the 1970s had been hidden in the dense neighbourhoods of the inner city, even if they had sold their clothes to shops in the tourist hub of Thamel. It was only in the heydays of the 1980s and 1990s that haphazardly built garment factories became a ubiquitous feature of the lower-middle-class neighbourhoods sprawled around the Ring Road. Ironic as it may be, the first generation of garment mass-manufacturers were located in the relatively well-off neighbourhood of New Baneswor, situated conveniently between Nepal's only international airport and the centre of Kathmandu. This part of town became a hub of Indian businesses. All garment ventures in Nepal at the time were run by Indians who had moved to Nepal to benefit from the MFA quotas, especially after Nepal liberalized. Since the Indians brought all the investments and technical know-how at this time, their Nepali partners did not have much of a role in running factory operations (Zivetz, 1992). They were mostly there to serve the bureaucratic purpose of having to list a Nepali partner to be registered as a Nepali business. Almost all of these partners – called 'sleeping partners' as they had a dormant role – were either Bahun-Chhetri or Marwari businessmen, who had privileged access to the state bureaucracy which closely regulated businesses at this time.[4]

From the mid-1980s, as Nepali partners began to take a keen interest in the opportunities offered by their industry, some significant changes began to appear in both capital and labour. Over the years, Nepali businessmen had become familiar with the way garments were produced and traded; they were able to do this quickly because the industry focussed on basic and homogenized products which involved the repetition of a set of tasks that could be learnt by simply watching and doing. The size of the industry grew exponentially, as more and more Nepalis began to take an interest in this emerging field of business. From just ten or twenty garment companies in Kathmandu in the 1980s, the number skyrocketed to 700 in 1990.[5] After Nepal became a democracy, business registration procedures were simplified to allow greater access for common Nepalis, while the Foreign Investment and Technology Transfer Act of 1996 scrapped the earlier requirement for foreign investors having to have a Nepali partner. Further, the Garment Association of Nepal, established in 1988, was reformed substantially in 1992 and was delegated the powers of supervising the task of distributing MFA quotas and clamping down on quota-hoarding by the elite. Owing to all of these, the number of garment companies in Kathmandu is said to have reached over a thousand in the mid-1990s. They could be seen scattered in and around the north-western suburb of Gongabu, the north-eastern suburb of Jorpati, the western suburbs of Balaju and Sitapaila, and the southern suburbs of Satdobato, Hattiban and Gwarko (See Illustration 2 on the Spatiality of Garment Industry Cluster in Kathmandu).[6]

The politics of business registration and know-how now addressed, the garment industry moved on to tackle issues of machinery and organization. On the one hand, the Indian-made and manually-powered *tullu* machines were replaced with Japanese (mostly a brand named 'Juki'), German (mostly a brand named 'Brother'), and Taiwanese machines ('Falcon', 'SeaSir', 'Justta', etc.). On the other hand, main stitching was physically synchronized with specialized stitches such as 'over-locking', 'flat-locking', or 'button-holing', which, in turn, meant that factories could no longer subcontract machinery from ragtag contractors (*thekedars*), who rented out both machinery and labour, but had to now commit substantial capital themselves to acquire expensive machinery and operational know-how (see Chapter 4). In financial terms, while Indian machines cost no more than 40 USD each, the Japanese machines cost about 400 USD, and the machines for specialized stitches cost more than 900 USD. As far as labour organization was concerned, factories began to hire workers directly, on a piece-rate wage on a weekly basis, making *thekedars* redundant. The social contracts between the workers and the *thekedars* were eliminated as the recruitment process became anonymized, and the new rhetoric about 'productivity' re-interpreted labour precarity as a new autonomy of work, while construing commodification of labour as a necessary aspect of modernity and business competitiveness.

Deregulation of both market and trade unleashed cut-throat competition, based on costs and productivity, leading to a race to the bottom, forcing factories to either merge and scale up, or leave the field altogether. From over 1000 factories in 1994, the number of registered garment factories declined to 323 a year later, to 212 after two years, and fewer still thereafter. While the number declined, the surviving businesses grew larger in size. While an average business, in the 1980s, owned 90 or so machines and employed 150 or so workers, it owned over 300 machines and employed over 400 workers in the late 1990s. The businesses now not only diversified their products and markets but also the sourcing of the inputs used for production. Equipped with better machines and a larger pool of workers, Nepali garment factories no longer confined themselves to the production of the two staple garment items, trousers and shorts, but expanded to include a wide range of other garments, which were more demanding on production but reaped better rewards in the end. The size of their purchase orders also increased four-fold within the same duration, while the turnaround time between order and delivery (or 'lead' time) improved significantly. But even then, prices went down globally and profit margins shrank: while more than 60 per cent of their production fetched over 4.00 US dollars in the 1980s, only 45 per cent managed to keep costs below this price threshold in the 1990s.

Mass-manufacturing businesses do not tell the whole story of the Nepali garment industry. It is also necessary to look at the select factories producing ethno-contemporary 'craft' garments for global niche markets along the lines of what Comaroff and Comaroff (2009) called 'ethno-preneurship'. The factories manufacturing Nepali ethno-contemporary garments – all of them owned by persons belonging to the cultural identity that they cashed in on – were smaller, slimmer and more cost-effective than mass-manufacturing and were often envied by them. A quick comparison between the two showed that mass manufacturers, on average, invested over 20 times the capital in comparison to craft producers but still earned only half the profit that the craft producers did. Craft manufacturers manufactured in smaller quantities but commanded higher prices and profits. But craft manufacturers were few and far between: there were only five in 2001 and, from what my informants told me, only seven in 1994, at a time when there were 1,087 mass manufacturers. All the craft garment exporters specialized in ethno-contemporary garments, specifically ones where the ethnic materials and symbols came from the producers' own cultural traditions. In other words, all of the craft producers tapped into their own culturally inherited skills and identities, to acquire expertise and legitimize their claim over the niche captured.

What initially distinguished the craft garment producers, from their mass manufacturing counterparts, was that the former seemed better equipped to outlive the latter. When the garment industry collapsed, following the expiry of the MFA in 2004, and coinciding with political instability in Nepal, mass manufacturers shut down one after another. Contrary to the mainstream narrative about business productivity, which valued scale of production over the originality of design, craft garment businesses prolonged their operations beyond the MFA. However, these immediate 'islands of success' were soon engulfed by 'an ocean of failure' once the tide of national political turmoil ran high. I discuss the particularity and order of this last phase of the Nepali readymade garment saga in Chapters 4, 5 and 6.

Situating Nepal within the regional and global discourses on garments

A reading of the literature on South Asia's garment industries affirms that the garment industry's trajectory in Nepal diverges from that of the industry in its neighbouring countries, let alone those in other countries, both in the way it evolved after the introduction of the MFA and in how it collapsed after its expiry. It is true that the industry evolved alongside the MFA in the 1970s and its trajectory then was similar to those seen in Bangladesh and Sri Lanka in South Asia, Cambodia and Vietnam in East Asia, Mozambique and Lesotho in southern Africa, the islands of Madagascar and Mauritius, and Mexico and Ecuador in Central and South America, to mention just a few. It can be argued that the way this industry is regulated by the centralized global bureaucracies of the United States of America, the World Trade Organization and the International Financial Institutions, including the World Bank and IMF, makes it a legitimate claim that the readymade garment industry is a singular giant manufacturing hierarchy, eclectically spread across a vast geography of Third World capitals (Blokker, 1989). This global-macro perspective emphasizing the politics of international trade and foreign aid, however, conceals more than it reveals, at least for those who are interested in the everyday experiences of the common people on the ground who insert themselves in myriads of ways into the bureaucratic operations of national and regional institutions steering development.

I begin by situating Nepal within South Asia, and argue for a differentiation on two counts: development and revolution. On the development front, Nepal was long considered an ideal expatriate destination by international aid professionals. In addition, because of its strategic location as a frontline state against communist China, Nepal received development assistance from an extraordinarily large number of countries and agencies during the cold war (Mihaly, 2009). This gave rise to a paradox: policymakers were fixated on dealing with the bureaucracies of foreign aid to such an extent, that achieving productivity and competitiveness on the ground – let alone concerns for social justice and human dignity – became secondary concerns. With reference to the garment industry, while almost every aid advisory report on Nepali garments preached productivity as a yardstick for industrial success (World Bank, 2008; ILO, 2008), the country has not seen the kind of detailed productivity analyses offered by, for example, Banerjee and Munshi (2004), for the Indian garment industry, or Teal and Baptist (2008), for the Korean.

The domain of aid and development for Nepal is bleakly opaque and outdated. While there has long been a proliferation of haphazardly-put-together benchmarking and advisory routines, very few or none have used specialized techniques that have been applied elsewhere to inform industrial development policies. As a cursory example, we see that the aid discourse on industrial growth does not draw on the frameworks of 'global value chains' or 'binding constraints diagnostics', two ideas that have lately become popular among those who study industries elsewhere (Islam and Rana, 2012; Fernandez-Stark, Frederick, Gereffi, 2011; ADB, 2016). The question of specialized techniques aside, the schema of depoliticized development that the aid community in Nepal seems to have so unquestioningly internalized (Panday, 2011) has left little room for probing the global politics of the garment trade and its implications for Nepal. This is an industry that was born out of American trade politics and came to a halt as soon as that politics changed. Nepal was the biggest victim of MFA trade politics, but even so, we hardly see the analysts of international trade take Nepal as a case study for investigating the MFA-related legal apparati, as was done for Bangladesh and elsewhere (Dowlah, 1999).

Further, scholars investigating the effectiveness and meaning of the politics of labour standards have not made Nepal their case study either. The global divide between manufacturing and consumption, combined with the rise of individualist concerns about ethics and corporatized consciousness on social responsibility, has led to a proliferation of both scholarship and activism in the disciplines of sociology and business studies on labour standards of garment manufacturing (Dickson et al, 2009). Ethnographies of health and safety of the garment workers have proliferated within South Asia, with foci on Bangladesh, India and Sri Lanka (Prentice and De Neve, 2017; De Neve, 2009; Ruwanpura, 2013; Kabeer, 2004). Global and local activism, operating within the frameworks of corporate social responsibility (CSR), has seen unprecedented mobilization of garment workers, along with policymakers who regulate their work and consumers who wear their products, on the question of labour and environmental standards, of which the Alliance for Garment Workers Safety in Bangladesh, ILO's Better Work programme in most countries in South Asia, and new trade unions like NTUI in India, are just a few examples. As controversial as the claims of the frameworks on corporate social responsibility may be, such activism is missing in relation to the Nepali garment industry. Accordingly, the scholarship on corporate social responsibility as well as the compliance on environmental and labour standards proves to be only tangentially relevant for Nepal, and CSR scholars have certainly not made Nepal their case study.

Let me now turn to the question of revolution. What made me socialize with rebels and radicals – as well as reactionaries – while researching the garment industry was the fact that it became increasingly difficult and, later, impossible to write about garments without acknowledging and analysing the effect of its path crossing with the Maoist-led People's War. Here, a running joke on Nepal among professors in the prestigious Jawaharlal Nehru University (JNU) in Delhi comes to mind. JNU is known for its radical student, and faculty, activism. When I once asked about the quality of Nepali students, a respected JNU professor replied, 'See, Indian students in JNU complete their PhDs because they never leave campus fearing they might miss a revolution if it ever came their way in Delhi; in contrast, Nepali students never quite complete their PhDs because a revolution erupts in Nepal every decade or so, and students are needed back home to people the movement.' During my field research, the People's War seeped into the garment industry shop floors in so many different, but clear, ways that I realized I had started distancing myself not only from the frameworks of industrial productivity and labour standards, but also those that looked at exploitation within the dichotomized frames of capital and labour (Mezzadri, 2014; Banaji, 2003; Barrientos et al, 2010; Carswell and De Neve, 2013). Instead, my approach to the questions of exploitation and resistance – in fact, rebellion – was to situate these within the broader national and social *dispositifs* and look at them in the light of everyday words and actions of protest, that highlighted the multiple layers of the proletariat condition on the Nepali garment industry shop floors (Shakya, 2016b; Beckman, 2004; Bezuidenhout and Buhlungu, 2008).

Notwithstanding the garment industry's developmental and revolutionary contexts within Nepal, I further differentiate it from regional garment narratives on gender. The global discourse about the readymade garment industry features gender as a core dimension of the garment workforce, thus invoking a gender paradox of development. Mainstream development discourse has explained the gender paradox in these terms: women are a hidden labour resource of the Third World, but their entry into the workforce may help them acquire a new agency towards empowerment. This claim has been contested by scholars of several disciplines.[7] Garment industries in and around South Asia have provided convenient case studies for both camps to illustrate their claims. However, even this scholarship has not made the Nepali garment industry its field of inquiry, a fact which I take as an implicit endorsement of my claim that the degree of engendering is relatively low for the Nepali garment workforce.

Despite a few factories having attempted to capitalize on gender as a cheaper workforce, with varying success and failure, women constitute a much less significant workforce in the garment industry in Nepal, compared to Bangladesh and Sri Lanka. Even so, studies that look into gender's liminality between tradition and modernity, and those that probe the changing notions of morality among working women, do seem relevant for Nepal. What Lynch (2007) said about the paradox of 'Juki girl stigma' of faux or immoral modernity, that female Sri Lankan garment workers live through, or what Hawamanne (2008) said about the poetics of everyday alienation, is relevant for the women garment workers of Nepal. As Brooks (2007) suggested, the paradoxes of gender and modernity may trigger changing modes of disciplining labour as factories shift from Fordist to flexible modes of manufacturing. But Naila Kabeer (1991) is right on the mark when she argues that Bangladeshi women garment workers rely on both fictive and real kinship, even more so when they face shop floor crises, and entrenched power struggles, without having any institutionalized means of support at their disposal.

Beyond studies on productivity, value chain, labour standards, and gender, can the world of the garment business be theorized to confront its complexities more directly? Soyer's (2005) analysis of New York garment capitalists has much in common with Sehata's (2009) observations about garment workers in Egypt; both situate production within broad frameworks of social identity and solidarity. Even so, neither of their approaches is about class consciousness *per se* but more about the entwining of the everyday lives of workers and entrepreneurs, so much so that their theorization of the industry verges on the theorization of social relations. Others have emphasized the spirit of resistance, especially when discussing labour rights and environmental considerations (Brooks, 2007; Phelan, 2007; Hensman, 2011). Resistance is central to my own work on the garment industry in Nepal and I have sought to situate it within the broad contexts of state restructuring, rather than confining it within the limits of industry, class, gender, and ethnicity. In doing so, I am informed by what Sharad Chari (2004) documented about the complexities of social reform and reproduction in the case of the Gounder peasants who metamorphosed into the new garment capitalists of Tirupur in South India in the 1970s. For Chari, the study of capital involved 'a politics of work' rooted in local configurations of capital, labour, and state. The formation of what Chari called 'fraternal capital', is about 'decentralized capitalism' out in the *mofussils*. This necessitates analysing the ensemble of relations that draw on 'histories of practices and practices of recollection', but also compels the analyst to think about shifting hegemonies in the anarchy that capitalism is. That chaotic phase in the late 1970s, which Chari captured in his ethnography, was notably over in southern India within two decades, as De Neve (1999) informed us, but its ethos seemed to still encapsulate the garment industry in Nepal in the 1990s.

From shop floor ethnography to an ecology of work

It was my concern for the complexity of the garment industry paradox, of its abrupt rise and demise in Nepal against a steadier trajectory seen in the rest of South Asia region, and a desire to understand the myriad ways in which the garment industry microcosm in Kathmandu Valley was inserted within the changing political economic milieu while being influenced by it, that led me to explore frameworks beyond productivity and competitiveness, wage and working conditions, corporate social responsibility and labour standards, gender, and global value chains. Towards this purpose, this chapter introduces the garment shop floor, situating it within the political and economic history of

Nepal while also extending the discussion to cover global and regional concerns, involving those who run and regulate this industry. I have explained that most analyses of the scale and scope of the garment enterprise seem to privilege class concerns about those who constitute its workforce while the mainstream (and depoliticized) rhetoric of market supremacy cloaks the complexities of international trade politics. After stating these methodological concerns, however, it is less clear what conceptual devices exist to proceed with a line of inquiry that embraces anthropology for its concerns for universal humanism.[8] I am proposing the idea of 'industrial ecosystem' as a way forward, even though it has to be said that this takes me into uncharted waters within the discipline of economic anthropology.

I am aware of the possibility that the idea of an 'industrial ecosystem' might mystify more than it clarifies, especially if it loses sight of the scale of the 'human', and and then still leaves the problems of social justice 'depoliticized' as John Harriss (2002) put it. On the front of politicization, however, the frameworks that dichotomize those who (wo)man the shop floors as capital owners and labourers might help narrate the accounts of class resistance, it has its own methodological constraints when dealing with questions of intersectionalities. Without a doubt, the manner in which owners and workers relate to each other, through a myriad of nodes and go-betweens, needs to be made explicit in our attempt to sketch out a trajectory of collective action that concerns human dignity. 'Politicizing' certainly requires a deeper reflection on the everyday concerns and behaviours of those who populate the garment shop floors and/or influence these floors, in order to comprehend the negotiations through which policy and popular decisions are arrived at, and how social justice takes priority – or is brushed aside when a trade-off is inevitable – over other variables.

The idea of an industrial ecosystem is also an attempt to address how problematically anthropology compartmentalizes work into social and economic, human and machine, everyday and deliberative, and ethnographic and aggregate. A compartmentalising approach may be convenient in that it offers clarity for theorising and documenting a case study, and hence may facilitate academic advocacy and activism. But, as this analysis reveals, compartmentalization is convenient only because it gives the illusion that a piece is whole or that a model is real. As Chris Hann (2017) put it poignantly, methodological individualism led economists to dismiss the thoroughly political character of how economy gets 'disembedded' from society, in terms of both consolidation of the state power and societal response through counter-movements. We should also recall Isaac's (2006) account of how the unwillingness on part of the substantivist school to recognize the Marxianist intentions of the framework of embeddedness – attributed to Karl Polanyi – led to its 'demise' in economic anthropology in the 1980s.[9] Even more problematic was the substantivist school's later admission that substantivism as a concept was applicable only for 'aboriginal (pre-colonial) economies in tribal kingdoms', because their orientalized ethnographies documented cultures without situating them in national and global politics (Dalton 1990:166-7, cited in Isaac, 2006).

My proposition of an industrial ecosystem is informed by these methodological and political concerns. I have found it necessary to venture in and out of several disciplines, including not only development economics, business studies, anthropology, and sociology, but also human geography and social history. My research subject has pushed me to engage with a diverse set of interlocutors: toiling workers, elite businessmen, fashion designers, revolutionaries calling for a regime change, auditors brooding over factory files, craftsmen and artisans inhabiting the nooks and crannies of the Nepali and Indian weaving industry, policy lobbyists on K Street in Washington DC, aid bureaucrats, politicians, and poets. My approach to the framework of an 'industrial ecosystem' is as follows: I track the evolution of the idea in the chapter that follows, beginning with a nod to Michael Porter's concept of the industrial cluster, but placing it within a Polanyian discourse on socio-economic 'embeddedness' that has acquired its own etymology in the anthropology of resistance. I then elaborate on this in relation to my case study of the readymade garment industry cluster in Nepal, which constitutes a mapping of commercial and social entities animating this cluster, which leads to the documentation of some of the core elements of garment-making. As I do so, I first demonstrate how this spatial cluster is implicated in the institutional ecosystems of policy making, business networking, and labour solidarity, and then proceed to consider alternatives which recognize the complexity of human relations beyond class dichotomies, as I unfold the multiple dimensions of sociality and commerce in the garment industry.

Endnotes

1. The region of current-day Nepal was divided into more than fifty small states and principalities until King Prithvi Narayan Shah, from the small principality of Gorkha, conquered them all and created the kingdom of Nepal in 1768.

2. Dixit (2001) shows how the proportion of Bahun-Chhetris in public service referral commissions for jobs increased from 80 to 97 per cent between 1993 and 2000, while that of Newars reduced from 11 to 1 per cent.

3. The New York garment industry went on to employ other immigrant groups such as Italians, Dominicans, Chinese, Koreans, Puerto Ricans, Afro-Americans and many others over the next century and a half.

4. I have argued that culture and religion provided a source of commonality and cooperation between the Indians, hill-based Nepali Bahun-Chhetris and Nepali Marwaris, allowing them to form and sustain business partnerships through which to access support of the Hindu kingdom amid state-led industrialization (Shakya, 2007).

5. The were several more garment companies who ran manufacturing houses but had no registration, because they did not have the necessary social capital that would help them deal with the cumbersome bureaucracy that oversaw business regulations. Those with no registration did not qualify for public subsidies for enterprise and trade.

6. Within Kathmandu, the Town Development Act of 1988 had prohibited construction of commercial buildings inside the Ring Road. Outside Kathmandu, it was considered convenient to have them near the highways connecting Kathmandu with the Kolkata port. But only few businesses chose to operate outside Kathmandu, and even fewer were able to sustain themselves, because these remote locations required large capital for being able to internalize necessary services which were readily available in Kahmandu but not in the remote towns on the border.

7. Naila Kabeer (2000) has dismissed the idea of gender paradox in labour market arguing that the 'paradoxical element' evaporates once these are explained in an integrated eco-sociological framework, based on in-depth analyses that look into the everyday concerns of the female worker as she moves in and out of the home- and work- fronts.

8. See Hart (2015) for a pragmatic point of view about anthropology being a subject that should work towards achieving the goals of universal humanism along the lines of what Immanual Kant argued for.

9. Rhoda Halperin (1975, 1984) had documented the Marxian origin of Karl Polanyi's basic ideas but was unable to get her interpretation published for almost a decade, because the surviving Polanyi supportesr were against a Marxian interpretation (Isaac, 2006).

3

A Garment Industry Ecosystem

In this chapter, I map the industrial ecosystem within which garment workers and their various counterparts live and work. The industrial spatiality I discuss here sets the stage for what follows in chapters 4 and 5: a shop floor ethnography of garment manufacturing from apparent normalcy to crisis. My proposition of the industrial ecosystem draws on Michael Porter's (1990) idea of industrial clusters – spatial coordination underpinning business networks and alliances[1] – and its curious overlap with anthropology in acknowledging that every society has its own characteristic sets of rules, norms, and concepts; or in other words, culture. From this acknowledgement emerges a policy proposition: programmes of industrial development should build on societal rules about trust and entrepreneurship, instead of blindly relying on abstract hypotheses about the supply–demand equilibrium, which do not acknowledge human agency in industrialization.[2]

Porter's idea of 'industrial clusters' triggered two sets of responses from global economic thinkers. One set of responses, largely negative, was from a group of economists, including those linked to the International Financial Institutions (IFIs), who protested the notion that 'micro' issues, such as firm coordination, mattered more than the all-encompassing 'macro' forces of supply and demand. At the heart of this debate lay the tricky notion of 'rent-seeking', or the phantom value generated by entities with lobbying power, where resources are channelled to specific entities and sectors even when the market rationale for doing so does not exist (Krueger, 1974). After all, the IFIs' Structural Adjustment programs of the 1980s and 1990s had drawn on the concept of rent-seeking to prescribe an entrenched public policy position for governments in developing countries: their job was to dismantle the barriers of entry and exit for capital to enter any industrial sector, in order to ensure that scarce resources could move freely to the best industrial sectors, and, within those sectors, to the best firms.

The other response to the idea of the industrial cluster was a positive one, and gained support from some unexpected quarters of social science – such as anthropology – among those looking for ways to counter the neoliberal hegemony of free markets, which advised states to withdraw from industry regulation to let the anonymous forces of supply and demand take charge. For example, Cadene and Holmstrom (1998) used clusters as an anthropological tool for investigating how modern industrial districts in South India emerged by building on their distinct cultural roots. Michael Piore and Charles Sabel (1984) had already laid the foundation for a proposition on 'flexible specialization' as an alternative coordinative system that, they argued, co-existed globally, even if the Anglo-Saxon discourse[3] only highlighted the pursuit of mass manufacturing under the Keynesian influence in the 1930s. Several others took a cluster-based approach in calling for an active role of the state in regulating industries for development (Schmitz and Nadvi, 1999; Sabel and Zeitlin, 1997; Zeng, 2006; Collier and Page, 2009), and were later joined by those who took issue with the World Bank and the IMF, with respect to the economic liberalization paradigm being inadequate because it had failed to deliver industrial success in developing countries since its adoption in the 1990s (Rodrik, 2011; Rodriguez-Clare, 2005; Chang, 2002).

In theory, the idea of industrial clusters echoed scholarship that problematized the economy-society dichotomy and overlap, looking at relationships between a myriad of agents constituting the spheres of social and political economies. The lens on the society-economy nexus lent itself to a charged debate on 'embeddedness', revolving around contestation of Mark Granovetter's (1985) definition of it. The idea of the cultural scaffolding of economic structures is represented in the literature on institutional theory, reflected in works such as that of Nobel Laureate Douglass North (1990, 2005) who probed the role of institutions as mental models and societal norms in the ways markets and economies evolved. Under a dual premise of 'old' and 'new' institutional economics,[4] two approaches emerged: on the one hand, the transaction-costs approach of the formalist school, that measured the economic value of ostensibly non-economic institutions such as friendship, caste and trust (Coase, 1937; Williamson, 1975), and, on the other, the diversity studies of the substantivist school, which argued that rationality varied across societies differing in values and social systems, thus giving rise to society-specific capitalisms (Clegg et al, 1990; Harriss, et al, 1995; Harriss-White, 2003).

My own take on embeddedness is different from both schools of thought. I agree with Karl Polanyi (1944) that the 'economy is an instituted process', and that the formal understanding of economy, as a 'means-end' relationship, has been conflated erroneously with the substantive meaning that concerns economy with the morality of the provisioning of material wants in society (Narotzky, 2005). The idea of provisioning can be traced as far back as the 4th century BC when Aristotle coined the term '*oikonomia*' to signify the 'household management' of the semi-fortified great houses of the agrarian empires. The modern understanding of economy, as a 'means-end' relationship, actually took root over a millennium later, with the victory of mercantilism over agrarianism, initially in England and, later, carried over to its colonies in the United States. Mercantilism's co-optation of *oikos* manifests best in Adam Smith's (1776) claim that society would only benefit from the individualistic, rationalistic ideas of supply and demand forces which offered a mechanism – he called it 'an invisible hand' – through which private vices (like greed) get mobilized to generate a veritable public order. A similar co-optation is manifest in the way the formalist school of post-cold-war liberalism absorbed Karl Polanyi into the rational choice framework.[5] In this, I agree with Krippner (2002) and Isaac (2005) that, for Polanyi, markets were not networks of producers, let alone value-neutral sites for equipoising anonymous forces of supply and demand, but rather full social institutions reflecting 'a complex alchemy of politics, culture, ideology'.

In taking issue with the formalist school's reduction of the idea of embeddedness to an audit of profit-value of morality or social-value of commerce, I agree with Beckert (2009) that markets and industries must be taken in their entirety – what he calls the level of 'macro-social' – along with the inevitable criss-crossings between major and minor elements of society, culture, and politics. This echoes Geertz's view about how the Balinese socio-political order, including the bilateral agreements negotiated between feudal lords and their moneymen, acquired legitimacy only with the mustering of the grand theatricality of the state *dispositif*, and not *vice versa*. I take a similar view, that industrial coordination needs to be understood in its entirety and not in parts. My proposition about industrial ecosystems requires considering industry in its relation to all of the complex links it has with society and state.

In mapping Nepal's readymade-garment industrial ecosystem, one has to admit that the sheet is almost blank since there is hardly any literature that discusses the societal aspect in Nepal's industrialization, especially the garment sector. Almost a poster child for the drive of the IFIs for economic liberalization, the government in Nepal relied extensively on macroeconomists without giving much policy-making space to industry thinkers, anthropologically minded or otherwise. If there were exceptions that took up cluster-based development programs, they were small players, and certainly outside the limelight of mainstream policy (Shrestha, 2003). Even so, garment businesses, as well as their social and business counterparts, did forge alliances, depending on the nature of externalities and complementarities, while being guided by social norms and political necessities. Further still, the cluster of garment factories and their contractors were situated within a broader industrial ecosystem comprising financiers and transport operators, service providers and designers, policymakers and politicians, as well as buyers of the global market, whose motives and interests were aligned with the values and norms within which they operated.

The readymade garment cluster in Nepal

I flipped through the Members' Business Directory for 2004, an annual publication of the Garment Association of Nepal (GAN hereafter), which probably offers the best snapshot of the garment industry cluster. Its first page showcased an official *shubha kamana sandesh* (a message conveying auspicious wishes) from the Minister of Industry and Commerce, which stated his hope that the garment industry would attain competitiveness (*pratispardhatmak kshyamata*) within the newly liberalized economic set-up (*khula bazar*) in Nepal. This was followed by another letter from the Secretary of the same ministry, which advised that the garment industry should diversify its market (*bazar vividhikaran*) in order to be more competitive. His call for diversification was taken up by the President of the GAN who stated, in his own message, how GAN had recently established a cell to study the likely impacts of diversification as Nepal joined the World Trade Organization (WTO) the same year. Based on the trade analyses prepared by that cell, it was claimed that the United States would continue to be the primary market for Nepali garments, although efforts were being made to reach out to other markets in Europe and Canada.

Then followed the main body of the Directory with short profiles on the 155 garment factories operating in 2002. Several of the larger factories paid for additional space for colourful advertisements showcasing glamorously dressed models advertising how competitive their prices were and how advanced their methods of production were. The newest garment manufacturer, Surya Nepal, had bought an entire page in the directory, where it prominently displayed that it had already exported over a million garment pieces in its first 300 days of operation. Accompanying this announcement were images of its ultra-modern machines, but even larger than the photographs of the machines was a group photograph of an early morning yoga session in the factory, with the caption, 'Discipline and yoga improve dexterity, and relieve monotony on the shop floor.' Another factory, Arya-Nepal, had its production manager, Sameer, pose alongside a fashion model – a niece of the CEO – wearing t-shirts and trousers stitched in Arya-Nepal. Three or four similar advertisements featured individual factories, and several others featured individual fabric suppliers in Delhi and Shanghai. These were followed by an alphabetical listing of all GAN members, each allocated a small text box to list the name of the contact person, along with essential information such as factory location, production capacity, and areas of specialization.

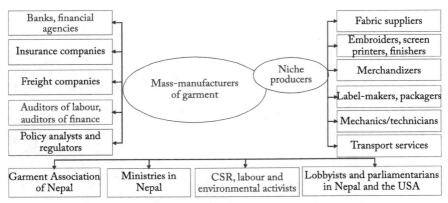

Figure 2: Readymade Garment Industry Cluster in Kathmandu

The members list was followed by another list, double the length of the first, offering information on courier and cargo service providers, followed by a much smaller third list, of embroiderers and screen-printers. The directory then went on to list suppliers of finishing equipment and accessories, label makers, packagers, and technicians. This sub-cluster of service providers were further followed by a featured list of business brokers who could connect Nepali garment manufacturers with the organizers of the garment mega-shows in Las Vegas and California. Finally, the back cover of the directory displayed an advertisement for a Chinese sewing machine, 'Gemsy', featuring a blonde model with Caucasian features, supposedly expressive of its 'world-class' quality. Listed within the Directory, though not prominently, were the general contact lists of banks and other capital providers, of key officials and relevant cells in the ministries in Kathmandu, of Nepali diplomatic missions in key export locations abroad, and of legal intermediaries who may help businessmen in resolving disputes both in Kathmandu and overseas.

The spatiality of factories and markets

A city that grew from being a fertile agricultural precinct to the bureaucratic capital of a hyper-centralized state, and later turning into an industrial hub, Kathmandu has kept city planning at bay throughout it growth. It was only in 1996 that the government came up with a law that large factories must move outside the inner city; a law with which most complied but a few didn't. Smaller workshops were not required to move outside town, even though increasing rents pushed them deeper and deeper into the spatial pockets of inner city poverty. A few of these workshops, for example, were located on the edge of squatter settlements occupying public land, reclaimed after the Bagmati river effectively shrank to a smelly drain flowing right through the middle of Kathmandu Valley.

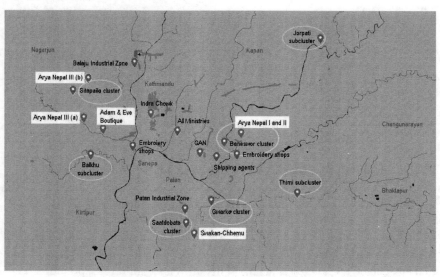

**Figure 3: A Spatial Overview of the Readymade Garment
Industry Cluster in Kathmandu**

The garment cluster of Kathmandu had its origins in New Baneswor (see Figure 3: The Spatiality of Garment Cluster in Kathmandu), a colony at the east end of the valley adjoining the international airport, and an extension of what has now come to be known as Old Baneswor. As the garment industry boomed in the 1980s, the paddy fields behind Baneswor quickly gave way to multi-storey houses accommodating the *nouveau riche* from within and outside the valley. Upper class Indians and Madheshis constituted a large demographic section in New Baneswor at that time, and almost half of the garment businesses in Nepal were operating from there in the late 1980s and early 1990s. The residents in this neighbourhood are known for their loyalty to democracy and liberalism, as in the following popular joke about Nepal's first democratic election of 1991. Having gained immense popularity during the public uprising, and certain that New Baneswor was a party stronghold, Nepali Congress stalwart Krishna Prasad Bhattarai had decided to stand for elections from this constituency. But to everybody's surprise, he lost the election to the candidate from the Communist Party of Nepal, United Marxist-Leninist (UML hereafter). It transpired that Bhattarai's upper class followers had simply not bothered to step out of the comfort of their homes since it had been raining a little, thinking Bhattarai would win anyway. This election drama aside, the residents of New Baneswor did remain loyal to the Nepali Congress, and the ideals of free market and liberalism, throughout the 1990s.

Most of the garment factories in New Baneswor, housed in the concrete buildings along the maze of its alleys, had been relocated from mud and brick houses in inner Kathmandu, following the municipality's city planning rules. The garment ecosystem quickly adapted as they congregated in this new locality: transport operators and cargo handlers moved to the main road on the way to the airport; embroiderers and accessorizers located their shabby workshops on the side lanes off the main road; a prominent hotel and a bank were located just a block away from the building of the Garment Association of Nepal (GAN) which stood on the major road junction; a Chinese business-restaurant, owned by the former President of the garment association and popular among the garment businessmen and their foreign buyers, stood just a block away; and the Department of Industries office was not far away from all of this.

Around the year 2000, some factories moved out of New Baneswor, giving rise to garment factory clumps in and around the government industrial zones in Saatdobato and Sitapaila in the northwestern suburbs of the Kathmandu Valley. Although some businesses did rent factory shells within public industrial zones there, the common wisdom among owners was that private buildings allowed more flexibility than public industrial zones. People who owned land in the grids neighbouring the public industrial zones began to construct their own factory shells and then rent them out. As more factories sprung up in Sitapaila and Saatdobato, quite a few garment factory clumps came up on the other side of the Valley in the Boudha-Jorpati sector, just off the ring road. Not many businessmen dared to run factories outside of Kathmandu Valley because of the centralized pooling of infrastructure and services within the capital, as well as the deteriorating security situation in the rural areas as the Maoist People's War gained ground at this time. There were just two or three who did, in the southeastern border region of Biratnagar and Jhapa, though they were much larger in scale and had higher quality standards and better technology, as well as internalized systems of handling transport and logistics.

The Nepali garment cluster was connected with other clusters around the world in more ways than one. Since the Nepali garment industry relied almost exclusively on the United States garment market, there were several spatial connections between the two ends of the earth. I will discuss three specific channels of connections between Kathmandu, Washington DC and the United States West Coast: (i) the logistics of transporting finished products from Kathmandu to ports of the West Coast; (ii) global activism on labour standards connecting the First World with the Third; and (iii) policy lobbying which steered the course of American diplomacy on international trade.

Let us look at the first channel of connection. Generally, it took two to three weeks for a container load of garments from Kolkata port which is the closest port from Kathmandu to land on the West Coast of the United States via sea. The queues at the ports, and delays in security clearance at the Nepal-India borders, could add days to the waiting period, even if the merchandise managed to avoid political strikes (*chakkajam*) or accidents on the road. At the rate of 3.60 US dollars per kilo for a 500kg container from Kolkata to Los Angeles, businessmen estimated about a third of their final price would go in transport. Of course, longer delays at ports and borders would add to godown, or warehouse, fees. Further still, it was the responsibility of the manufacturer to pay for expedited shipping or air cargo if he missed the production deadline at his end. Not just the transport charges but all of the input and production costs were the responsibility of the manufacturer. Funds for these would be generally raised against the guarantee of the Letter of Credit (L/C), signed by the buyer when the purchase order was finalized. Reputed global buyers, such as GAP, would pay the L/C amount on sight of the shipment at the designated United States port, whereas others would not necessarily be so prompt. It was generally agreed that those who designed their own garments were able to negotiate a much better deal with their buyers, compared to those who simply replicated the designs which buyers provided them. Most of the businessmen who designed products received full or partial payment in advance. Some even had their buyers co-funding the sampling, or co-distributing the finished products. Furthermore, since these designer garments were higher in price and lower in quantity, many would choose to simply send them by air directly to their final destination, avoiding all the problems of shipping and L/C payment.

The second channel of connection between Nepal and the United States was through the inspection of labour standards. Although discussions on ethics date back to the writings of Durkheim and Weber, its neoliberal avatar calls for a shift of social responsibility from the state to business (Salmon, 2010). While some claim that the demand for better standards of work on the overseas shop floors of multinationals is a call for global solidarity on business ethics, what we also see are practices being used to justify the carefully calculated welfare responses of companies whose activities lack transparency. An even bigger problem here is that a narrow individual outlook lies at the heart of the neoliberal discourse on the ethics on labour: What can an individual consumer do to solve the corporate crisis of job-offshoring? It should then not come as a surprise that, however complex its moral and intellectual foundations might be in the cosmopolitan capitals, on the ground it is often reduced to a farcical cat-and-mouse game between First World inspectors and Third World inspectees.

Factories were almost always tipped-off about the arrival of *chhadke* (unannounced) inspectors, as soon as they landed in Kathmandu airport. The airport immigration staff would call their friends in garment factories to warn them of oncoming danger; these factory people would then pass on the word to others in the business. By the time the inspector turned up on the shop floor, everything was already tidied up to the inspector's taste: excess machines were whisked away to make sure each tailoring desk had as much space as designated by the rule book; broken needles were collected and removed; emergency exits were cleared out and unlocked; fused bulbs were replaced and hanging wires tucked away; toilets were cleaned, water supplies were refilled, and first aid kits were replenished. Anyone wearing clothes from the factory needed to quickly change into something else, so that global buyers would not think their products were leaking into the local market. Anyone younger than eighteen needed to exit through the back door, including those who were adult but looked younger – why risk it with the buyers? And above all, the managers would hide away their real files on labour and wages and share the sanitized versions meticulously maintained for this very purpose. Once the inspection was over, a generous meal was offered to the guests, even though they almost always turned it down. And, as the inspector left satisfied, everybody patted each other on the back. What was either party to do other than to put up with this meticulous, though farcical, show of compliance? Did anybody really believe that a factory earning three dollars a t-shirt from the inspector's employer would pay its workers four dollars to do the job?

The third channel of communication between the Kathmandu garment industry cluster and its American counterparts involved legislators in the United States Congress and the Senate. Trade regulations dictating the flow of merchandise, the MFA, had been agreed upon through 2004, but nobody knew what would happen after that. While South Asia had been told in no uncertain terms that the 2004 expiry was final, and that its days of duty-free entrance to the American market were over, sub-Saharan Africa was granted the same status through another trade regulation that came into being in 2001, the African Growth and Opportunity Act (AGOA). Coverage widened the following year when another law, the Caribbean Basin Preferential Trade Act (CBPTA), was formalized. The neoliberal school had heralded the dismantling of the MFA as victorious in persuading the United States to stop being the godfather of international trade, but the rise of AGOA and CBPTA showed what a farce their claim of market dehegemonization was. Amid this acrimonious saga, some countries in South Asia decided to try their hand at lobbying for an AGOA-type patronage for their own products. Along with Bangladesh and Sri Lanka, Nepal also had a go at lobbying in the United States Congress and Senate for trade preference for its garments.

The first step towards lobbying in the United States was to pass a resolution within the Garment Association of Nepal (GAN), which then approached its contacts among the ruling and opposition Nepali parties in order to push it through the government system. The Ministry of Foreign Affairs, rather than the Ministry of Commerce and Industry, was deemed more powerful to lead a delegation on this, and, after a round of briefings, a delegation under the Joint Secretary left for the United States in April 2003. Mobilizing Nepal's contacts in the United States, this delegation persuaded Democratic Senator Diane Feinstein from California to table a bill asking for duty free access for Nepali garments. Her husband, Richard Blum, was an investment banker and philanthropist interested in Tibet and Tibetan Buddhism. He had attempted, unsuccessfully, to climb Mount Everest from the Tibetan side with Sir Edmund Hillary, and later founded a charity, the American Himalayan Foundation, to help schools in Tibet and Nepal.

For the proposed trade bill to become law, it had to be seconded by another Senator, and two Congressmen. With the limited connections Nepal had in the United States, the delegation had to be realistic about its strategy and considered it best to appoint a lobbyist to push the case further. But the two registered lobbyists the delegation met demanded fees Nepal could not afford. The next best alternative was to find someone who would be willing to take on the task on a voluntary basis. An obvious candidate was Mary Carroll, an amateur trekker and professional fundraiser, who was popular among the embassy staff and the Nepali diaspora, and enjoyed the status of Nepal's honorary Trade Representative for the United States East Coast. Carroll considered the proposal but turned it down. The delegation's initial success, in having the trade bill proposed in the Senate, was rapidly being undercut by their inability to recruit an effective lobbyist and carry out the necessary follow-up. Their timing, too, turned out to be especially bad. Even before a formal discussion could be initiated on the bill in the Senate, it came under attack from a Texas-based hydropower company, Panda Energy International, over a pending compensation claim related to its forced premature withdrawal from a project in Nepal due to Maoist-induced security threats. A second foreign policy blunder, which nipped the garment industry lobbying efforts in the bud, concerned Tibet. In May 2003, as part of King Gyanendra's efforts to win Chinese support for his assumption of state power after the royal massacre, Nepal arrested, and handed over to China, eighteen Tibetan refugees who had just escaped Tibet and were on their way to Dharmashala to meet the Dalai Lama.[6] The pro-Free-Tibet activists launched a massive campaign against this move in California where they had a powerful presence. With protests brewing among people of her own constituency and faced with opposition from a powerful US company, Senator Feinstein withdrew her support for the Nepali preferential trade bill in July 2003, effectively killing it even before it was officially proposed.

A second delegation on Nepali garments went to Washington, DC, in October 2003. This delegation met, and brought on board, Republican Congressman James Walsh from Syracuse – who had a special connection with Nepal in that he had spent two years in Nepal's Tarai region in the 1970s as an American Peace Corps Volunteer – to sponsor and introduce the bill in the US House of Congress. Despite his help, the bill could not be pushed, although the Nepali Embassy continued its lobbying efforts with other prominent Americans with Nepal connections. About a year later, it even tried to form a multinational alliance with Bangladesh, Cambodia, Sri Lanka, and four other small island states from the Pacific. Despite Bangladesh and Cambodia having strong lobbying experience, Sri Lanka having a pressing case for support in the aftermath of the tsunami, Nepal having been ravaged by the Maoist civil war, and the island states evoking much sympathy in the US, the proposed bill was never approved.

The spatiality of textile and fabric

Acquiring fabric is the logical first step in the making of garments, but the business directory published by GAN was marked by the conspicuous absence of a textile sub-cluster within Kathmandu. Notably, this glaring absence of the textile industry within the country did not generate a policy discourse around the need for one. Instead, the government chose to offer increasingly attractive incentive packages for those importing textile into Nepal. On the advice of the World Trade Organization, Nepal reimbursed the standard textile import duty of 20 per cent to those businesses which imported textiles, turned them into finished garments, and exported those within three months.[7] The policy rationale here was that textile imports should be made easy, because fashions change fast in the West, and to keep up with it, developing countries would need to diversify their sourcing through imports, rather than depend on local production.

Notwithstanding a few exceptions that I discuss later, the general practice in the garment business is that First World buyers tell their Third World manufacturers exactly which fabrics to import and from which company. Manufacturers situated in the lowest tier were those operating on '*dhyadu*' (or bulk rate), where they collected CMP ('cut-make-price') and let the buyer supply necessary textiles with each purchase order. More upscale manufacturers worked on CMTP ('cut-make-and-trim-price'), where they sourced their accessories independently but still took detailed instructions from buyers when sourcing fabrics.[8] Very few sourced their own fabrics. Among the six companies that independently sourced their fabrics in Nepal was Swakan-Chhemu, which could only do so by personalizing its relationship with a textile company in Shanghai. This company had a label appealing to consumers with an environmental conscience, and the company sourced organic fabrics made out of hemp, which is considered fertilizer-free. Swakan-Chhemu cultivated a friendly relationship with its Chinese fabric supplier over many years. The company owner's son interned with the Shanghai company one summer, and the two sets of businessmen visited each other in Shanghai and Kathmandu despite the challenges of language. Neither of them spoke the other's language and especially the Chinese counterparts' communication in English was patchy at best. In additon to such challenges, their relational contracting could work only because Swakan-Chhemu could persuade its buyer, a London-based Jewish company which campaigned for Free Tibet even if they approved of sourcing fabrics from China, to co-design garments (see Chapter 4).

One glaring exception to the garment industry rule of thumb, about buyers dictating manufacturers' sourcing of fabrics, was how producers of craft garments sourced their fabric – a concept I elaborate on further in Chapter 4. Here, I discuss my ethnography of a small craft producer, A&E Boutique. This factory drew on the vibrant textile cluster across the border, in India, and, by doing so, it successfully tapped into a niche of ethno-contemporary garments within the United States market. A&E Boutique designs emerged from a close collaboration between its Kathmandu proprietor and a Seattle-based buyer. The buyer visited Kathmandu each year, having identified the colour and fabrics being forecast for a given fashion season for the market on the US West Coast. Then began the curious project of imagining which of the fabrics available in the Indian textile sub-cluster could be improvized to imitate samples featured in the US fashion magazines. For their 2004 summer collection, for example, they first shortlisted six fabrics including velvet, brocade and cotton. Then, they set out on a massive hunt in the nooks and crannies of Indian cities, trying to persuade traditional weavers to weave something comparable, and at a much cheaper price. The key figure in facilitating this massive exploration was a young Delhi-based merchandiser whom the Kathmandu manufacturer had groomed over the years. Fabric merchandising was seen as not just a job but almost a personal commitment, in that the team needed to work closely to keep track of a complex web of orders, payments, and transport logistics involved in mobilizing weaving sub-clusters in the far-flung corners of India and bringing the fabric to the Kathmandu factory.

The density of the network between the weavers and fabric merchants was impressive. The map of India had a thematic layer of fabrics, in the way they were reproduced verbally in everyday conversations on the manufacturers' shop floor in Kathmandu. For example, Ahmedabad is famous for its brocades, as *amrus* in pure silk, *kimkhwabs* (little dreams) on a mixture of silk and cotton, or *asavali* with richer and bigger patterns. Benaras is also famous for brocade but for *zari jamdani*, weaved through a play on weft using gold or silver thread, or cut-work *jamdani* and jacquard silk. Amritsar is famous for tweed and woollen fabrics; Bengaluru for *dupian* silk; Mumbai and Chennai for leather; Jaipur for tie-and-dye fabrics; and Karnataka for fabrics like *ilkal* and *narayanpeeth*, produced from a cotton and silk mix. The process of acquiring fabrics from these cities was even more complex than the composite web of fabric-distribution itself. For example, the Benares brocade sub-cluster offered three options for buying fabrics. The most expensive way was to buy it from a local *gaddi* (counter), or established commission agent in the local *sutti* (market), but one could get it slightly cheaper, and made to order, from a *grihashtha* (textile weaver and trader) who owned and managed up to a hundred looms. But the most cost-effective way was to know a community of good weavers, and then place an order through a reliable *gaddi* associated with them, who would ensure quality, while guaranteeing the transaction. For this, one would supply the raw materials to the weaver in advance, and the balance would be paid on delivery. This would bring the costs down by about 40 percent.

In Karnataka, for example, where the weaving industry operated under a more horizontal set-up, price variation came almost entirely from the financial system in place. There were weavers, or village-level co-operatives of weavers, who worked under a system called *rokda*, where they bought their own raw materials and, thus, were in a position to bargain strongly. The second system, *satta*, involved the buyer paying for the raw materials in advance, and then waiting for the finished product to be delivered. The final option was *mungada*, whereby the buyer provided the weaver with raw materials on a rolling basis. An outsider dealing with this market would often have no choice but to buy from the *rokda* system, whereas someone with local connections would be able to access the second or third options.

A&E Boutique revelled in this chaotic world, where weavers worked under half-collapsed roofs and with very complicated cultural patronage, and took a certain pride in the fact that only it – and no another garment house from Kathmandu – could swim like a fish in the waters of artisanal weaving in India. 'Modern systems are good, but not here; not among these wonderful artisans,' Chote, the owner of A&E Boutique told me once. 'Here, we deal with artisans as artisans, not businessmen. That is how we save a few pennies, and they get theirs in time. Now imagine A, B and C [garment] businessmen ordering fabrics from these people without knowing them and their *maal* [material]. That would be a flat business, and these outsiders will be cheated on day one. After one round of buying they are sure to catch their ears and say, "No, baba, never again, never again!" …' This fits in well with what he had told me earlier about the cloth bazar of Indrachok, within Kathmandu, where he initially learned his trade, that businessmen dealing with craft people had to speak the language of craft but also be very thrifty with every penny in hand, with every stitch on the cloth and with every friendship in the market.

Despite not being utilized by garment manufacturers exporting abroad, the old clothing cluster of Indrachok, situated right in the heart of Kathmandu city which has been inhabited by generations of immigrants from North India, was the place where Chote met his future wife. They got married, lived, and worked there, until they moved to Kalimati to their new house and with a new factory aimed at exports. Indrachok consists of roughly a quarter of a square kilometre with a thick web of narrow alleys, and it was while selling saris and other fabrics in retail that Chote met all of his future buyers, who later helped him launch A&E Boutique to cater to the US market. Indrachok is not only a shopping district, but a centre of material culture, of sorts, where women shop and socialize, especially when creating their wardrobes for festivals and rituals. A substantial shopping trip to Indrachok is a must for every would-be bride in Kathmandu and her entire entourage of friends and relatives. Almost all of the merchandise in the shops of Indrachok comes from various corners of India, Pakistan, and Bangladesh. Most things are handmade, or are the products of cottage industries. The Indrachok economy in Nepal, like that of its counterparts in various parts of India, is at the periphery of the formal economy; trade is conducted through informal channels, often avoiding taxes and duties, yet the clientele is from the elite of the formal economy.

At Indrachok, the shopkeepers and suppliers not only exchange fabrics and accessories but also build business and social alliances. Business networks are not constrained within the *Chok* (square) itself; Indrachok businessmen must develop multiple trustworthy alliances with traders from far away, who supply the stores here, if they are to survive the cut-throat competition in the market. An understanding of the business alliances is especially important, because all production orders and financial transactions are conducted verbally, and over a long time span, legitimized only by sketchy paper receipts, which serve more as memory-joggers than any real legal purpose. Shopkeepers develop their expertise from early childhood, through apprenticeships with parents or kin. Knowledge of product quality is especially important because, on the one hand, the market is abuzz with a vast diversity of choices with no codified standardization to distinguish original from fake, while, on the other hand, the clientele largely consists of experienced shoppers who also know the Indrachok market very well, are able to bargain for the best quality, and want value for money.

The spatiality of accessories

While fabrics almost always came from abroad, embroidery and accessories were a subcomponent of production and had to be located within Kathmandu. Many complained that the garment ecosystem was handicapped due to an insufficient input of accessories and a virtual absence of high quality service providers for embroidery work: there was just one computer-aided embroiderer in Kathmandu that had the approval of global buyers. Although there were other embroiderers – not computer-aided but often with better skills – they could not be employed because they lacked international recognition and buyers objected to them. The craft producers were not caught in this quagmire, and they developed their own circles and patronages for managing the embroidery and accessorizing services necessary for their production.

Although craft garment producers preferred that their embroiderers join as staff, the latter preferred to work freelance, which made it a constant struggle for factories to retain the loyalty of embroiderers. Most craft garment manufacturers in Nepal, including A&E Boutique, eventually developed relational (or long-term) contracting[9] with select groups of embroiderers that had to stand the test of time on loyalty and trust. A&E Boutique's experience is a good case in point. Its owner, Chhote, sent out embroidery work to two subcontractors, one from Kashmir and the other from Rautahat in the western plains of Nepal. But a sudden crisis loomed for the Kashmiri embroiderer: he was a widower in his fifties and was keen to remarry even though his adult children from the first marriage opposed it. As this family tussle continued, it drained him of energy to work, caused fissures in his social and business networks, his working capacity was reduced, and much of his business went to other embroiderers. Especially after the embroiderer's adult children approached A&E Boutique to 'do something about it' – meaning that their father was too caught up in family feuds and hence he cannot serve effectively as before – their *sahu* (patron and client), Chhote, began to look for someone new to replace the Kashmiri embroiderer.

Chhote then discovered a new embroidery artisan from Kolkata, who operated from Kathmandu. The new embroiderer, Raju, was introduced to Chhote through one of his trusted staff members. Raju was, at this time, working for other retail clients. Impressed by Raju's work and shaken by his own crisis of having lost a regular embroiderer, Chhote not only offered Raju work right away, on rates that were *mage bhanda badhi* (more-than-was-asked) with a full advance, he even visited Raju at his workshop a couple of times. That Chhote personally made a trip all the way to a shabby corner of town made a big impression on Raju and his fellow artisans. Of course, before showering Raju with such favours, Chhote had carried out a rigorous background check on his kinship and business networks in the market. He had also sought feedback from his buyer on Raju's *iman-jaman-saman* (character and performance). Assured of Raju's potential as a loyal artisan, Chhote then introduced Raju to his other regular embroiderer from Rautahat, in a bid to ensure that Raju could assure himself of Chhote's ability and willingness to reward loyalty.

The Rautahat embroider had been working for Chhote for almost two decades, and had seen the rapid expansion and increasing sophistication of production in the A&E Boutique factory. Though Nepali, his family had roots in the Indian embroidery district of Lucknow which is famous for its traditional *chikankari* embroidery. When the embroiderer had first come to Kathmandu, he had not known if there were embroidery jobs in town. He certainly had not brought his machines with him. So he offered himself as a tailor in the garment assembly lines where he could easily manage straight stitches under the detailed division of labour. After trying his hand at a few such factories, he came to know of Chhote who was looking for better-skilled tailors. He made an impression on Chhote who, liking his embroidery skills, gave him a loan to buy his own machine and took him on as a subcontractor with the implicit assumption that Chhote would be his sole client. The embroiderer paid back his loan within six months, and then took another to buy two more machines and employ more workers. After about ten years, he owned twenty-five embroidery machines, and employed thirty-two artisans, most of whom were his kin from Rautahat and Lucknow. Although Chhote paid him more or less the market rate, and though other businessmen tried to poach him, the embroiderer kept his word that Chhote would remain his sole client.

The spatiality of business networking: Garment Association of Nepal (GAN)

Beyond the networks of individual garment factories and their subcontractors and buyers, a business association lay at the heart of the Nepali garment community, which mediated the businessmen's interface not only with policymakers within Nepal, but also with American policymakers who had considerable clout in matters affecting industrial development in Nepal. The Garment Association of Nepal (GAN) was established in 1987 with less than thirty business members, but had come to represent over a thousand dues-paying business members by 1995. It was not only that the industry had grown in size but also that the Association had become more useful and had opened its doors to a wider network over time. In the 1980s, GAN was a leisurely club of the elite few who had the right connections in government to obtain business licenses, entitling them to the MFA quota through which they gained subsidized entry into the American market (see Chapter 2). At that time, GAN membership was not only a status symbol but also a rent-seeking device, in that membership allowed a business to forge a partnership with foreign investors in the protected business climate of Nepal at the time.[10] Those without GAN membership, even if they were Nepali and had substantial production, were not eligible for MFA quotas and, hence, could not export. The era of industrial protectionism ended with the regime change in 1990, and that opened the way for the Nepali economy to be liberalized (Dahal, 1998). The de-licensing of business registration brought the so-called 'fabricators'[11] into the government books, while pro-FDI policies did away with the provision that foreign investors mandatorily needed a *bona fide* local partner to register their factories, thus doing away with the 'sleeping' partners.

The early 1990s and 2000s saw GAN evolve into a vibrant business association, increasing in size and stature. Not only did its income increase through membership dues, it also began to offer paid services, including not only those I discussed earlier, but also of maintaining business directories and market databases. A watershed moment for GAN came in 1992 when the Department of Industries (DOI) delegated to GAN the complicated job of MFA quota distribution. GAN reformed its by-laws to scrap the last remaining restrictions on its membership, and then went on to commission sophisticated software compatible with the American MFA accounting system. This software monitored MFA quota usage among GAN members, while automatically feeding information into the national export monitoring system. Investing the resources it generated by handling MFA paperwork on behalf of the American government, GAN constructed an office building within its premises where DOI representatives, responsible for approval of MFA quotas, could be stationed. Through the MFA monitoring software, GAN was able to track exactly how much revenue the government was raising from the garment industry in taxes and levies. Both its physical proximity to the DOI as well as its access to detailed data on industrial revenues enabled GAN to emerge as a powerful advocacy and lobbying group on garment-related issues (see earlier discussion on garment lobbying in Nepal and America).

As it grew in stature and size, GAN began to levy a certain percentage for every dollar exported through its MFA database, which amounted to a substantial sum as revenue. It utilized this new income by taking upon itself responsibilities towards improving the competitiveness of Nepali garments, involving three possibilities: (1) that GAN should help the garment community cut the time and costs of its production; (2) that subsidies should be provided to members towards attaining aesthetic distinction for their products so that they could capture an upper tier of the market; and (3) that GAN should help the industry diversify its markets. While individual businesses worked to reduce the time and cost of production, it was considered that GAN should offer policy incentives to improve distinctiveness and diversification.[12] Representing a community long aware of the success of the craft garment producers who designed their own products, GAN initially demanded that the government help build a fashion-designing centre within proximity of the garment cluster. But the Ministries[13], clearly under the influence of the neoliberal hegemonic perspective of markets being a self-regulated system whose zero-sum interpretations meant any government involvement in industry development would 'distort the market' by encouraging rent-seeking behaviour among the businessmen, told GAN that the state would not 'pick a winner' among industries, and would act only on those schemes that had cross-industry appeal. GAN then took it upon itself to develop and implement its own policy incentive schemes, mobilizing its own funds where necessary.

One such scheme was based on rewarding garment makers who were already exporting 'non-quota items' or were exporting to 'non-quota countries' thereby indicating possibilities of life beyond the MFA quotas. Non-quota producers were few and far between in Nepal. There were just nine factories out of 212 in 2000, just four years before the MFA was scheduled to expire, when GAN was considering its policy incentives. The group of factories exporting non-quota items to the MFA-regulated US market was a mixed bag: some exported products considered to be low in value, such as bed sheets and towels, while others exported the high-value items, such as ornately designed jackets and accessories for women. Three factories exporting to non-quota markets focussed on the UK, Europe, and Japan. In the first year when GAN began its work on diversification, generous cash refunds were awarded to all nine factories. Some of the factories expressed their gratitude by donating part of the award back to GAN.

This happy incentivizing was repeated the following year as well, but only for some of the earlier awardees. GAN abruptly issued a directive that only the exporters of 'non-quota' items would continue to receive cash refunds, and not the exporters to 'non-quota' markets. This led to allegations and counter-allegations among businessmen, where the losing party felt they were being discriminated against on the grounds of ethnicity. Later GAN explained that breaking into non-quota markets was turning out to be more difficult than exporting non-quota items, and that it wanted to put its money where possibilities were more realistic. The unrewarded businessmen maintained, nevertheless, that GAN's policy reversal showed its ethnic bias.

In personal conversations, one of the disgruntled garment businessmen, a Newar, drew my attention to the double sword of ethnicity, and pointed out how ethnicity had a different significance in communal business politics compared to state and business relations. Newars and other Janajatis were visibly a minority within the GAN leadership. Only about 20 per cent of GAN's executive committee members came from this group, whereas the remaining 80 percent were either Bahun-Chhetris or Madheshis, most of whom had earlier been in business partnerships with Indians even if the factories 'Nepalized' in the 1990s (Shakya, 2008). GAN Presidents were almost always either Bahun-Chhetri or Madheshi, save for two exceptions, both Newars.[14] Despite complaining of being discriminated against in GAN's business promotion programmes, the Newars, and other ethnic minorities I met in GAN, maintained that it benefited everybody if GAN had a President, either from the ruling elites among the Bahun-Chhetris, or from the Marwaris[15] who have a distinct identity among the Madheshis for being close allies of the rulers. One businessman from the Newar community remarked: 'The job of GAN President is not to please businessmen or to be "revolutionary" [in terms of social inclusion]; his job is to deal with the government effectively. That is why we need a man with "men in government" [signifying social capital]… Newars do not have this; nor do other Janajatis. They may have money and skills but not "men in government." There might be one or two exceptions but the reality is that only Bahun-Chhetris or Marwaris have this, in today's Nepal.' This commentary came as a surprise; despite being disgruntled about his own treatment in GAN, this businessman recognized the need to be led by an individual from the ethnic and social elite, thus indicating how deeply entrenched is the view that modern Nepali state is ethnic.

It is an irony that the businessmen and policymakers who embraced the neoliberal rhetoric of 'not picking winners' and 'not distorting the market' could not overcome ethnic bias when it came to business promotion and policy lobbying. The tension inherent within this ethnic paradox surfaced on several occasions. For example, when the Maoists caused havoc in the garment industry in 2003, and GAN came forth to negotiate a collective settlement for all its members, the ethnic reasoning was all too clear (see Chapter 6 for details on the Maoist disruption of garment industry). This was one occasion when the Bahun-Chhetri and Marwari leaders of GAN went to their Janajati members seeking help, because it was widely considered that the Maoists were much more lenient towards the Janajatis, while the Bahun-Chhetris and Marwaris were perceived as the 'feudal and expansionist elements' (*saamanti ra bistaarvaadi*) that were hand-in-glove with the 'old regime' (*purano satta*) which the Maoists had vowed to uproot. Although the final deal was kept secret, it was common knowledge – within and outside the garment community – that a group of Bahun-Chhetri and Marwari businessmen within GAN had agreed to pay a collective sum in return for peace on the shop floors. Most Janajati businessmen stayed out of the deal and negotiated individually with the Maoists, because they felt they could fare better by handling the matter on their own. The greater elites among the Bahun-Chhetris and Marwaris, who had closer ties with the conservative faction of the Nepali rulers, also stayed out of this deal, thus taking a hard line against the Maoists. Soon after concluding this deal with amenable GAN group, the Maoists planted a home-made 'socket bomb' in one of the garment factories owned by a hardliner Marwari who had refused payment to the Maoists. Following this incident, and also owing to a deteriorating business environment and the imminent expiry of the MFA, a large number of Marwaris and Madheshis left Kathmandu, while the Bahun-Chhetris retired from the business but remained in town.

Endnotes

1. In introducing the concept 'industrial clusters,' Michael Porter (1990) argued that the competitive advantage of nations comes from successful coordination and alliance-building among businessmen and associated public institutions, towards achieving business sophistication as well as improving the business-enabling environments within which they operate.

2. Alfred Chandler, a noted business historian, had argued, as early as 1977, in his book 'The Visible Hand' that the business empires in neoliberal America did not anonymously emerge from the functions of demand-supply equilibrium, but from careful engineering of businesses by a few financiers, statesmen and business giants.

3. Hart, Laville and Cattani (2010) argue that Anglophone discourses on neoliberalism needs to be differentiated from alternative economic thoughts from France, Latin and South America, and Scandinavia. Their call for a 'human economy' implies that alternative economic thoughts – often lost in translation in the increasingly anglicized world – should be brought back to the global mainstream.

4. See Harriss (2002) for a discussion on why the so called 'new' institutional economics failed to explain not only why the same institutions function differently in different societies, but also why some institutions remain relevant for societies even if they are materially 'inefficient'. Contesting the rationalist takeover of institutional studies, Harriss argued that there was merit in reverting to older traditions, such as the German historical school and early American institutionalism.

5. See Hann and Hart (2011) for a discussion on the 1960s' debate between the formalists and substantivists, ranging from Herskovits' ([1940] 1952) call for

a dialogue between anthropologists and economists to Fredrick Barth's (1969) transactionalist proposition that even complex institutions such as ethnicity could be analyzed through a utilitarian framework.

6. King Gyanendra ascended the throne on 4 June 2001, following the royal massacre of 1 June 2001. In October 2002, King Gyanendra had dismissed the elected government led by Sher Bahadur Deuba to appoint a royalist, Lokendra Bahadur Chand, as the new Prime Minister. The change of regime also meant the intensification of the royal campaign for Chinese support, especially because India was not very supportive of the King's removal of political parties from the rule.

7. The customs reform of 1996 made textile import especially easy because the duty drawback system was computerized through a system called ASYCUDA++, or Automated System for Customs Data ++ such that importers no longer needed to deposit any money but they only needed to offer a bank guarantee of the equivalent duty amount for the duration in which imported textile was utilized for garment manufacturing and exported thereafter.

8. My informants expressed the terms CMP and CMTP in English and their understanding was that these are standard terms internationally, but a reading of the garment trade literature suggests these to be local variations. Instead, De Neve (2014) and Mezzadri (2017) refer to similar concepts as 'cut-make-trim (CMT)' and 'full package pricing'.

9. See Knorringa and Nadvi (2014) for discussions of relational contracting among businessmen in Brazil, China and India.

10. A landmark move towards allowing foreign investment in local enterprises in Nepal, was the enactment of the Foreign Investment and Technology Act of 1992 which allowed hundred percent foreign ownership of businesses with a fixed capital over 20 million Nepali Rupees. The Foreign Technology and Transfer Act of 1996 further widened the doors for the entry of foreign investors into Nepal. Before these, foreigners needed to have one Nepali business partner, a condition met by many by registering a partnership with any elite Nepali family who could mobilize their connections in the state bureaucracy to facilitate the paperwork, even if they did not bring capital or business knowhow to the table. It was common to refer such Nepalis as the 'sleeping partners' in business (See Chapter 2).

11. Fabricators were those factories that functioned well on the ground but remained hidden from the government books. This meant that these factories had no claims on the export-related public incentives including MFA quotas, so its primary function was to do jobwork for other factories who had the right network and hence access to quotas. Most fabricator factories belonged to the middle class while the elites took the moral high ground as the 'registered' factories. Ironically, however, it was common that the fabricators had larger and more genuine operations on the ground and paid more (indirect) taxes than the so called 'registered'.

12. GAN actively lobbied with the government to fine-tune garment and trade policies; for example, to design a complex Duty Drawback System (DDS) to regulate the

import of fabrics to manufacture exportable garments. It also worked with the Federation of the Chamber of Commerce and Industries (FNCCI) to determine minimum wage, and to design safety regulations for factory buildings, as well as to facilitate the participation of Nepali businessmen in trade fairs abroad.

13. The three Ministries, with whom the Garment Association of Nepal engaged, were the Ministry of Finance (for macroeconomic policies including tariff and non-tariff regulations as well as issues involving exchange of foreign currencies but also the practice on customs), the Ministry of Industry, Commerce and Supplies (for industry-specific policies on tax and subsidies as well as practices on business regulation including those affecting the supply chain), and the Ministry of Foreign Affairs (for diplomatic efforts especially between Nepal and the United States for MFA-related logistics and reporting).

14. The first three Presidents of GAN were the from the Kathmandu elite, probably explained by the fact that the Panchayat regime, which had lasted until 1990, had nurtured a select few families and ethnic groups into positions of power. It was Chandi Raj Dhakal, the fourth President of GAN, who stirred things a bit, but not necessarily towards steering it to a better direction. A dashing young man of the Bahun community from the hills, who did not come from the narrow circle of state elites he built what was once the largest garment factory in the country, and went on to win the best practice awards in few years in a row, but eventually ended up being mired in several corruption scandals.

15. I have argued in Chapter 2 that Marwaris relate themselves to be part of the Madheshi community from the Nepal-India border towns even though they have a history of working in close alliance with the Rana rulers until the 1950s and then later with the Shah kings (Shakya, 2014).

4

The Normality of Garment Making

Entrepreneurship requires human agency and Nepal's readymade garment industry cannot be an exception. In 1981, Shah Safari, a Seattle-based distributor of Indian ethno-contemporary garments, entered Nepal looking for a cheap franchise. The company was owned by two ethnic Gujarati brothers from Kenya, Raj and Akhil Shah. They decided to not set up their own factories in Kathmandu. Instead, they opened a purchasing house that contracted a dozen or so Nepali businessmen to manufacture garments following their designs. This venture was an instant success, and, within a few years, quite a few garment factories had sprung up in Kathmandu to take orders from Shah Safari. Shah Safari designs combined casual American styles with Indian fabrics and silhouettes. Public curiosity about the spiritual retreat of the Beatles in Hrishikesh, near Nepal, helped set a new fashion trend among Westerners for loose oriental garments, such as 'Madras' plaid shirts and festooned clothes with oriental screen-print graphics. Riding this new wave of celebrity hipsterism, and working for patrons like Hollywood icon Kevin Costner who once bought everything left on their shelves, Shah Safari went on to capture as much as a quarter of the market share on the US West Coast, for the basic clothing item of young men's woven tops. They went on to set up buying houses in Korea, China, Bangladesh, and, of course, Nepal.

Although Shah Safari was a designer label, it followed a production model associated with mass manufacturing: of strictly disconnecting design from production. All of its designing work was done in-house in Seattle, while the suppliers abroad simply replicated the samples provided. The central feature of this production model was that most of the profit remained in the hands of those who copyrighted the designs rather than those who manufactured the products. This new fetish of design gave the impression of a new economic order connecting opposite ends of the world, even if production was fragmented across the boundaries of state and class (Dale, 2010). Manufacturers in the

Third World, including those in Nepal, tried to break into the designing side of production, but it turned out to be lot more difficult than envisaged. Below, I narrate this problem from the perspective of a young garment businessman who I came to know well during my fieldwork in Kathmandu.

Sameer, a teenager from the priestly class of Bahun-Chhetris in Nepal, was apprenticed to his father's garment factory in the 1980s. Decades later, he would reminisce how his youth was wasted on garments, as he burned the midnight oil studying for a college degree while working full-time at an age when his peers were mostly 'fooling around and having fun' (*hallera hidnu*). Especially telling was his experience during the national hardship that began in March 1989, when India had blocked Nepal's only access to the sea, following disputes on renewal of a certain trade and transit treaty between the two countries.[1] The blockade unleashed an unprecedented crisis as Nepal ran out of most of its daily necessity goods. There was an acute shortage of not only petrol and kerosene that had to come via India, but also fresh vegetables, fruits, sugar, and everything else. The supplies in local markets simply dried up. Making do with no sugar in his morning tea, Sameer queued up every day to collect his ration of petrol and ferry it on his bicycle to the factory, so that there was enough fuel to run the generators. The blockade eased off thirteen months later, in April 1990, by which time the new democratic regime was in place.[2] Democratization eased the cross-border traffic but also marked the beginning of an ambitious economic liberalization programme in Nepal, which benefited factories like Sameer's, thus triggering a new wave of hope among the youth for better entrepreneurial opportunities and material prosperity.

Although Sameer made considerable progress in scaling up production and upgrading technology, as the wave of democracy and liberalization engulfed the garment industry (see Chapter 2), the one final barrier he could not breach was that of design. I discussed in Chapter 3 how the association of garment businessmen identified fashion designing as the way forward for Nepal's garment business. Like several other garment businessmen, Sameer experimented by hiring designers in the factory, but learned the hard way that Nepali designers did not know enough about Western tastes about fashion, nor could they anticipate the rapid changes in global market trends. He even made an effort to learn designing by enrolling himself in a formal diploma course run by a fashion-designing institute in Kathmandu. He obtained the degree but discovered it was of no use to him. The more he delved into it, the more he became aware what an impossible task it was to try to compete with the West in its own disposition. He put it this way:

> How can we design Western clothes better than westerners themselves? That is impossible. What is possible is that we can design 'our' type of clothes that would appeal to their sense of fashion. … After all, fashion designing in today's world is all about 'mixing' ours [Eastern] with theirs [Western]. That is the secret. We happily buy Western clothes because that is what is fashionable for us, but what they want to buy from us is clothes with our designs that took to their fitting. That is the fashion that sells today. We buy clothes from each other. We both buy clothes that are supposedly *about* each other, *for* each other.

What Sameer was pointing to was the fact that Nepali designers who were selling well in the Western markets were all selling Nepali ethnic designs, often adapted to suit Western tastes in clothing, but essentially creating a global value of materiality out of an orientalized notion of 'Nepali-ness'. Sameer made several efforts to set up business partnerships with design houses who had cracked these market niches, but none were prepared to share with him the jealously guarded secrets of their success. Even those he considered close friends would not let him peek into their design studios, even if they spent entire evenings together drinking or chatting. After trying hard and failing to persuade his friends, it eventually dawned upon him that his friends had all learned their designing skills through life experiences (*parera janne*), while he himself was merely a classroom learner (*padhera janne*) of manufacurturing.

The distinction Sameer made between the 'two kinds of people' populating the garment industry in Nepal deserves closer attention, especially in the charged context of the 'death' of the industry that this book problematizes. All analyses of the garment industry in Nepal – commissioned by government policymakers, but mostly carried out by donor agencies – portray it as an anonymous industry, where a large swath of faceless workers toil on tailoring machines on assembly lines to manufacture mass products lacking in character or design (van Heerden et al, 2002; Zeng, 2006). Outside the domain of aid and development, Marxist scholars like Alex Perry (2010) and Naomi Klein (1999) have called garment manufacturing the penultimate satanic mill of faceless proletarianization. Industrial sociologists, including those who follow frameworks such as global value chains and global commodity chains, and who have dissected garment into endless subcategories and a cascade of subsectors, still do not differentiate garments on the basis of their human intentions about design (Gereffi, 2002). I argue that a close inspection into the world of Nepali garment businessmen necessitates differentiating between 'mass' and 'craft' garments if we are to understand how two different ways of working and living coexisted within the sphere of the Nepali garment industry.

Classroom learners and scientific mass manufacturing

In Nepal, garment manufacturing is associated with modernity. Burghart (1984) reminds us how King Mahendra pledged to push modernization (*adhunikikaran*) as development (*vikaas*) when he assumed power in 1961, ending Nepal's first democratic stint that had lasted a decade. I have discussed elsewhere how Nepalis, especially the elite, began to abandon their caste occupations in the 1980s as part of a national aspiration towards modernity, but still under state patronage (Shakya, 2011).[3] Among those who changed vocations was Ram Lamichhane, Sameer's father, who nudged me towards thinking about the flux between the 'mass' and the 'craft' types, in the way the readymade garment industry evolved in Nepal.

Ram grew up in a priestly, Bahun, family in the Kathmandu Valley, and went on to seek occupations outside his caste-designated role. The youngest of six sons from two co-wives in a large joint family, Ram moved to India and joined the Indian army after earning a college degree in the humanities. Unfortunately, his choice to join the army – scorned as a *marne-maarne pesha* (a profession of dying and killing) among his Bahun kin – brought him into such direct confrontation with his family, that he was forced to desert after just a few years into service. Upon return, his parents gave him his *ansha* (a son's share of inheritance in ancestral property), but then dissociated from him socially. Ram used this inheritance to start a readymade garment factory in 1982, which I call here 'Arya-Nepal I'.

The Panchayat regime considered industrialization to be a state-controlled affair. Business regulations were so tight in the 1980s, that the simple task of registering a factory was a privilege available only to those who had 'source force': access to patrons, relatives, and friends in key positions, who could help facilitate the process. Ram had no such 'source force' and Arya-Nepal I operated as an unregistered 'fabricator', and hence could not claim export-related public incentives such as MFA quotas (See Chapter 3). The registered factories, on the other hand, would charge fabricators, like Arya-Nepal I, fees for the use of their ration of MFA allotment, while also claiming export incentives given out by the Nepali government. Working under such testing conditions, Arya-Nepal I still managed to employ about 20 to 30 workers, and his older son, Sameer, helped him with production and merchandising. In the 1990s, after the Panchayati regime was ousted and Nepal liberalized its economy, Arya-Nepal I was formally registered with the government. The operation expanded in scale and scope by partnering with two other businessmen, also former fabricators and holders of business degrees, and Arya-Nepal II was created. Nevertheless, the partnership soured within a few years and Ram retired, transferring his share of the firm under the proprietorship to his son Sameer, who, by then had acquired his own college degree in business. After a few years, Sameer joined hands with one of the two partners of Arya-Nepal II, Navin Sharma (also a Bahun), to launch a much bigger garment venture, Arya-Nepal III, sponsored by an Indian investor. Arya-Nepal III continued to operate until 2004, finally shutting down when the garments industry died in Kathmandu as the MFA expired (see Chapter 5).

Arya-Nepal (I, II and III) manufactured low-end labels exclusively for the US market. During the entire decade it ran, it only ever manufactured six garment items – polo shirts, t-shirts, turtlenecks, halters, tank-tops, and jogging trousers – and almost all for only three labels: Walmart, Target, and GAP's Old Navy. At the heart of Arya-Nepal's business was the scale of manufacturing: almost all its purchase orders exceeded 50,000 pieces, and took a 'lead time' of 30 to 60 days to complete from start to finish, mobilizing some eight hundred regular employees. Purchase orders came with detailed size and design specifications with little room for improvization or originality. After all, one t-shirt would bring home only about 3 US dollars, which was expected to pay for all of its raw materials, labour, and overhead costs. The same t-shirt would sell at the retail price of 10 US Dollars in the United States, thereby dividing the value between the producer, shipper, and retailer at a third each. That these products were so simple, and that they were produced in such vast quantities, meant producers had to watch every penny when they laid out their production set-up.

Figure 4: Sample Designs at a Mass-manufacturing Factory

Every production order in Arya-Nepal III began with the preparation of fabrics. Buyers provided detailed specifications. Samples and prices were often agreed upon beforehand. Once the fabrics arrived, every roll was scanned for defects, both manually and also with scanning machines, before clearing it for the cutting masters. The two cutting masters in Arya-Nepal were among the highest paid employees, and understandably so, because of their ability to utilize every last inch of fabric, thus reducing wastage and reducing costs. Once cut, the patterns were then bundled and dispatched to the stitching plant. Upon arrival of the cut fabrics, Sameer, the production manager, led floor supervisors and technicians in the task of designing assembly lines and setting them up, while making sure that the machines were in the right order, manned by the right people, and that each person had just enough physical space to do their job (see Table 1). Then Sameer determined, in consultation with the floor supervisors and technicians, how much each worker in the chain should be paid. This depended on how long the job took, how skilled the workers had to be, and what types of machines were required. For example, stitching the neck into the main body piece (*palla*) was very time-consuming, and, hence, was one of the best-paid jobs in the entire chain; operating hemming and overlock machines required experienced – and hence expensive – workers; and although it was a painstaking task, cutting off the hanging threads, once the stitching was over, was an unskilled task and paid very little.

Table 1: 'Taylorist' Garment Assembly Line in Arya-Nepal

Work process	Machine type (No. of units required)	Time taken (in seconds)	Wages (Nepali Rupees)
1. Shoulder joint	Overlock (1)	21	0.40
2. Neck rib making - *tanki*	Single needle (1)	14	0.25
3. Thread cutting	scissors	salaried	salaried
4. Neck rib attaching	Overlock (2)	34	0.70
5. Quality check	n/a	salaried	salaried
6. Neck tape making	Overlock (1)	10	0.10
7. Neck tape attach (first piping)	Single needle (1)	56	0.70
8. Front neck cover stitch	Flatlock (1)	19	0.45
9. Back neck attach (*kachcha*, initial and *pakka*, final)	Single needle (2)	151	1.30
10. Sorting	n/a	salaried	salaried
11. Label making	Single needle (1)	14	0.20

Contd.

Work process	Machine type (No. of units required)	Time taken (in seconds)	Wages (Nepali Rupees)
12. Sleeve attaching	Overlock (1)	58	0.80
13. Checking, sorting	n/a	salaried	salaried
14. Armhole cover stitch	Flatlock (1)	41	0.60
15. Side seam overlock	Overlock (1)	52	0.80
16. Sorting	n/a	salaried	salaried
17. Bottom hemming	Flatlock (1)	48	0.75
18. Sleeve hemming	Flatlock (1)	49	0.90
19. Patch label *kachcha* (initial)	Single needle (1)	14	0.20
20. Patch label *pakka* (final)	Single needle (1)	14	0.30
21. Thread cutting	scissors	salaried	salaried
TOTAL (excluding salaried time and money)		**9.9 min**	**Rs. 7.45**

Once the rates were agreed upon and approved by higher management, notices were put up on the factory noticeboard, and the worker hiring process would begin. Factories like Arya-Nepal did not negotiate wages and work conditions with individual workers; these were publicly announced and workers had to take it or leave it as offered. Production was divided into such minute subtasks that, exemplifying the Taylorist production method at its height, a worker's withdrawal made no difference to factory productivity. Equally, workers knew that the assembly line would be dismantled in a few months once the production of the order was complete, and that they must be ready to seek work elsewhere, at least until the factory secured another order and a new assembly line was set up. Work in the garment industry always involved a massive turnover of workers.

Once production began, speed and rhythm were what determined Arya-Nepal's profits. It was not necessary for the mass manufacturers to know much about fabric handling or garment tailoring, but they were conversant with the practical techniques of dividing production into minute sub-tasks. These could be divided among a large number of people, so that even the unskilled or moderately skilled, could collectively deliver final products with the necessary quality and precision of time. What was important to keep this production line moving smoothly was to have the right kind of incentive schemes. All skilled workers, including the tailors who did the bulk of the work, were paid on 'piece-rates' that could vary enormously depending on the self-motivation they demonstrated in their jobs. Unskilled workers, including 'thread-removers' (who cut hanging threads after the stitching process was over), 'matchers' (who neatly paired up the right parts before the tailor ran them through the stitching machines), and, most interestingly, 'quality checkers', all received monthly salaries. The ratio between the skilled (piece-rate wage) and unskilled (salaried) workers was approximately four to one. The differentiation echoed the dichotomies between 'kamikazes' vs 'rentiers' in Zanabend's (1993) study of the workers in Chernobyl nuclear plant which explained varied appetites among the workers for risk and reward.

For Arya-Nepal, 'quality' meant accuracy of measurements and had very little to do with authenticity of inputs, innovation of designs, or creativity of process. Each purchase order came to Arya-Nepal with a sample piece and a measurement specification book (*naap khaata*) that detailed the required measurements of each piece. These specifications were the benchmarks against which quality was measured. The task of quality control was seen as punctuation in the otherwise uninterrupted flow of production. The quality checkers sat side by side with the tailors and checked measurements thrice: first, when the two main body parts, or *pallas*, were stitched together; again when the sleeves and necks were added to the *pallas;* and finally, upon completion of the stitching process. Although each checker relied initially on the specification chart – a simplified version of the *naap khaata* – which they kept prominently on their table, the rhythm of the process would mean that they would soon memorize the details so well that they would rely almost exclusively on their fingers and memories, rather than measuring tapes and charts.

Figure 5: Sewn Garments Being Piled Up for Thread-cutting at Arya-Nepal

After stitching, the garments would be passed on to the finishing department. But in between came the task of 'thread-cutting' which was undoubtedly the most feminized in the entire process of garment manufacturing. Women, almost always unskilled and thus least paid (but regularly salaried than on piece-rate wages), sat in the factory courtyard to go through every piece of stitched garment and cut out the loose thread hanging on the lines. Once this task was complete, the garment would then be sent back to the factory building, now to the finishing department. There they would first be washed to remove stains and dust, then machine-checked to see if any broken needles or other hazardous objects had got stuck in them, then any hanging threads would be removed, then they would be ironed, packed, and finally dispatched to the factory storage. These tasks flowed continuously, only punctuated by three to six rounds of additional quality inspections. Occasionally, petrol and chemical sprays would be applied to remove any stains present; otherwise, they would be sent for a required ordinary laundering in the newly-set-up facility within the factory. When the laundry capacity was inadequate or the machines malfunctioned, which happened every now and then, this task would be subcontracted to an external service provider.

The craftsmen and their ethnicities

In Nepal, 'craft' – at least the kind seen in the garment industry today – has as much to do with modernization and hybridity as it does with purity of material tradition. Modern design in Nepal does not necessarily adhere to traditional arts and crafts in a rigid way, nor does it follow a simplistic developmental teleology, marking an abrupt shift from craft to mass production. Rather, industrial modernization prompts a reworking of cultural icons into contemporary designs, drawing on historic, cultural, and social semiotics. In this, it resonates well with Michael Piore and Charles Sabel's (1984) proposition on flexible specialization; efficiency of production comes from adapting craft equipment to the task at hand, rather than what is seen in Keynesian systems, which leverage scale for efficiency.

In the phase of industrialization under state patronage, discussed in the preceding section, most Bahun-Chhetri businessmen took a classroom approach to garment manufacturing, whereby those with political connections formally registered their firms to reap export subsidies, and those without connections ran 'fabricating' operations. Many Janajatis – especially the Newars who were rooted in the elite culture of Kathmandu, and those of the Madheshis,

Marwaris, Rauniyars and others, who were rooted in the rich world of textile weaving in the northern Gangetic plains – avoided classroom knowledge of business, but still capitalized on the new patronages and markets that came with modernization. Not one person from the traditional tailor castes – the Damais and Sujikars from the hills, and the Darjees from the flat lands – owned a garment factory that exported to the West.[4] Notwithstanding the complexities of the cultural politics of garment manufacturing, some things can be clearly stated about the 'craft' production of garment: First, craft producers were always a minority; there were only nine such enterprises in Nepal in 2000, and from what my respondents told me, only seven in 1994, at a time when there were 1,087 'mass' manufacturers (Shakya, 2004). Second, almost all 'craft' factories produced ethnic-contemporary garments, as opposed to purely Western or purely traditional Nepali outfits. And third, incorporation of ethnic symbols into modern garment-making was only done by supposedly 'authentic' ethnic members of such semiotic practice. Below I discuss the work of one such craft producer which is a continuation of the discussion from Chapter 3 on fabric sourcing.

Figure 6: Chhote and Gayatri Rauniyar at Adam & Eve Boutique

Chhote and his wife Gayatri Rauniyar established their garment factory, A&E Boutique, in 1978. Their families used to be cloth merchants in Uttar Pradesh in India even though both families had settled in Birgunj town on the Nepal side of the border a long time ago. Chhote arrived in Kathmandu in the 1970s to study business at the local university and maintained a strong track record of extra-curricular activities throughout his youth. He was a trained boxer, spoke French, and also socialized with researchers, development practitioners, yoga enthusiasts, and other Western expatriates living in Kathmandu at the time. His personal efforts to gain exposure to western culture is possibly what helped Chhote break into lucrative craft market niche, while most of his relatives remained old-style cloth merchants selling to the locals.

When founded, A&E Boutique employed just one worker, from the so-called 'untouchable' caste of tailors, Shukra Pariyar, a Damai, and got him to stitch quilted garments using plain cotton fabrics weaved and dyed locally. The target clientele of this first step of the business was tourists visiting Kathmandu in the 1970s, who were looking for souvenirs to take home. These quilted garments often combined fabrics of four or five base colours, produced using simple techniques indigenously found in Kathmandu, and sewn into easy-to-wear, free-size garments. Under the Panchayat regime, trade was protected and high tariffs were imposed on imports including of the goods used to produce materials that would be exported later. Until the government withdrew import tariffs on garment inputs, Chhote worked exclusively with coarse cotton manufactured within Nepal. What made his garments attractive to customers were their quilted patterns and clever designs. For example, some of his jackets could be folded neatly to make children's handbags.

Figure 7: Two Early Adam & Eve Boutique Designs

Chhote recalled counting about 15 shops in Kathmandu which sold quilted garments at the time he started his shop. As the market for souvenir-garments grew, people from different walks of life, including those who had originally dealt in other handicrafts such as silver jewellery, gems, and masks, joined the garment trade. A few of them, Chhote remembered, initially worked through middlemen with contacts in the Japanese market, but eventually took on direct export orders themselves. Vetted by his Japanese buyers, some European and American buyers also came to offer Chhote purchase orders. Chhote found working for Westerners very different from working for Japanese buyers: while the Japanese gave him very detailed instructions about colour and cut, and still measured the finished garments to the last stitch upon arrival, Westerners accepted his suggested improvizations in style and size. This, Chhote said, was one of the main reasons why he switched to working with Westerners.

As Nepal liberalized its economy in the 1990s, especially after the government made provisions for import duties to be reimbursed once the final outputs were exported, Chhote began to expand his fabric range – an aspect central to the scaling-up of his garment business. In 2003, the stock of fabrics in A&E Boutique was, by far, the most impressive of all garment factories I visited in Nepal. Chhote said his new business was all about 'playing' with fabrics, like his father and grandfather did in Birgunj and Lucknow. In fact, Chhote never described his business as being about *luga* (clothes); it was always about *kapada* (cloth). He would talk about fabrics or *kapada* by the number and type of *tana* (warp) and *bana* (weft).[5] Yarn came in three variations: cambric (fine), sheeting (medium) and casement (thick).[6] Chhote's factory worked with all fabrics and added to these the regional crafts of bead work, mirror work, cut work, and embroidery in order to create a fusion that would have an 'ethnic-contemporary' look. The fabrics most frequently used were plant and animal-based such as chenille (often in sheeting), cotton (in casement), rayon (in cambric), linen (in cambric), silk, and wool, as well as soft leather; man-made fabrics, such as polyester, velvet, and brocade were also used. Most fabrics chosen were handloom woven, and very few of the selected fabrics were machine made.

Chhote and his designers often talked about fashion designing as a 'musical concert' where everyone had to play in harmony. Designing actually started with taking 'cues' from the buyer, he maintained. While the buyer spent weeks on end discussing a collection of fashion magazines he had obtained from the leading designers and fashion events in the US and Europe, the skill most valued in designers was that they should be able to see 'where their [the buyer's] eyes were going' when they were discussing designs. Chhote's designs were never replicas of the fabrics and designs from the catalogues that his buyers brought from the West, but their locally created designs always had creative affinities with the global designs consulted.

Figure 8: A Team of Fashion Designers at Adam & Eve Boutique

In true spirit of 'playing with fabrics', as Chhote described his business to be, the main fabric that was chosen for designing served as a blank canvas on which the remaining artwork was carried out. If plain fabric was chosen, it would be decorated with patch- or cut-work, following techniques such as *watchikan* of Kashmir or *applique* of Jaisalmer, both of which involve patching a different piece of cloth onto a main base to form large motifs of Hindu (with distinct shapes of animals, birds, flower and humans), Jain (even bigger motifs, mostly of larger animals such as cattle), or Muslim (with abstract floral, plant shapes, almonds, fruits, and the like) art. Often, less expensive fabrics would be used as the canvas on which more expensive fabrics, such as Benarasi *kinkhwab* (rich and kingly brocades woven with heavy use of *jari*s – gold and silver threads), *amrus* (brocade in pure silk), *asavalli* (with large motifs as in sari borders), and soft velvet leather, were used as patches. An important feature in this technique was that the traditional art forms were largely improvized in their applications. For example, Kashmiri motifs are traditionally very intricate, with delicate colours and finely stitched embroidery. This was not, however, what was mostly created in the factory. Instead, they worked with larger and coarser motifs, flamboyant colours, and bigger stitches. They also used machine stitching, turning to hand-work only when it was impossible to use machines. In this way, traditional crafts were adapted with a great deal of improvization.

While Chhote concentrated on designing garments, his wife Gayatri took charge of production. As in Arya-Nepal, production started with the cutting of the fabrics by two professionals called *masterji* who were among their highest paid staff members. After all, cutting involved the delicate handling of expensive fabrics, and required a great deal of patience in getting the curves right, especially when cutting small pieces for later application by patch-work and applique techniques. If the garment needed embroidery, then it would be cut into an individual base, without cutting the curves, so that these could first be sent off to the embroidery workshops at the other end of town, run by artisans who worked on contract. Once the *pallas* (cut parts to be stitched) were finalized, with embroidery if needed, they would then go to the tailors.

Figure 9: Sample Designs at Adam & Eve Boutique

Unlike the Taylorist mass manufacturing I discussed in the preceding subsection, Chhote's workers sat in three or four small rooms located on the ground floor, and worked as family units where wives assisted husbands, and younger men – but never young, unmarried women – apprenticed for the experienced kin and village men. Wages were paid on 'piece rates' as in mass manufacturing, but what counted as a 'piece' was a finished unit of garment and not the number of stitches. Quality testing meant a final check by Gayatri and her trusted assistants, who not only measured the *pallas*, but also commented on the 'touch' in the making of the piece. Once the tailoring was approved, the garment was then sent for 'finishing', which involved cutting and cleaning of thread, and any hand-stitching and beadwork needed. The garments were then returned to the 'quality' department for a last check. Finally, after everything was approved, the garments were packed and dispatched.

The semiotics in garment making: being versus doing

Both kinds of garment makers I describe above highlight the corporeality of garment making, either in the designing of the garments, as craft producers did, or in replicating Western designs, as the mass manufacturers did. But the 'making' of garments is not only about the materiality of work; it also has to do with the semiotics behind the design and the process. I intend to highlight this aspect in discussing my third case study, of Swakan-Chhemu, and its orientation towards medieval Tibet for seeking inspiration for designs that appealed to European customers. It is just one example among many, showcasing how cultural capital is embodied in the cultural and social identities of those practicing such vocations.

Swakan-Chhemu is a family business run by a Shakya family in Kathmandu. The Shakyas, along with the Tuladhar and Bajracharya sects of their ethnic group, are neither caste tailors nor cloth sellers, but Janajatis closely associated with Kathmandu Valley's medieval trade with Tibet. This centuries-old partnership triggered a process of mutual acculturation where each borrowed from the aesthetics and philosophies of the other.[7] China overran Tibet in 1949, and Tibetan refugees flooded Kathmandu, following the Dalai Lama's escape. These Tibetan refugees developed an everyday relationship with the Newars and, especially, the Shakyas, which later led to joint business ventures involving gem-cutting and jewellery, carving of Buddhist statues, as well as traditional mask making.[8]

From within the clan of Shakyas, Samyek Ratna emerged in the 1950s as a community activist in the political movement, which had developed a strategic alliance with democrats in India, against the Rana regime. It was during this time of national transition that the Gandhian principles of *Swadeshi* material culture seeped into the Kathmandu Valley. During the brief democratic stint in Nepal before the Panchayat regime was established, Samyek Ratna led co-operatives on cloth weaving and wood carving, and later even joined a controversial political outfit, *raksha mandal* (community defense circle), that would physically fight reactionary elements (*pratikriyavadi tatva*) threating the new democratic regime. *Raksha mandal* activists were later rewarded for their loyalty by the new regime, and, joining an emerging class of elites, Samyek Ratna went on to become the mayor of Kathmandu.

Samyek Ratna moved in elite circles but a major breakthrough came for him when he was introduced to Heinrich Harrer, an Austrian mountaineer and celebrity author of the acclaimed travelogue 'Seven Years in Tibet', who had developed a close relationship with the Dalai Lama during his long exile in Tibet. After China took over Tibet and sealed its borders, Harrer used Kathmandu as his base, developing a close circle of trusted friends committed to the Tibetan cause. It was through this network that Samyek Ratna got to know European Jewish-Buddhists looking to develop business ventures in Nepal that could help Tibet. Over time, Samyek Ratna entered into a formal agreement with one such entrepreneur based in London, and this eventually laid the foundation for Swakan-Chhemu.

Samyek Ratna had two younger brothers. The elder of the two, Ashok, was already active in the work of weaving Tibetan carpets in Nepal, a business made lucrative because of the Swiss government's business promotion intended to help Tibetan refugees living in Kathmandu. After completing his mayorship, Samyek Ratna took a job with the World Bank in Washington, DC, which then enabled him to invite his youngest brother, Vivek, to train at the prestigious Fashion Institute of Technology (FIT) in New York. Ashok remained in Kathmandu and switched to garment making after the business bubble of Tibetan carpet-weaving burst (O'Neill, 2005; Graner, 2002). Later, Vivek completed his degree at FIT and returned to Kathmandu to work with Ashok on garments, this time partnering with his London buyer's fashion designers. At this time, the person responsible for fashion-designing in Swakan-Chhemu was Claire, a young French designer, who did not really rely on Vivek for overall designing schemes but did so for 'orientalising' – a concept I elaborate on below.

Claire spent a considerable amount of time in Kathmandu looking for inspiration, but a typical designing cycle would start in Europe, where she would saturate herself in creative ideas by attending as many fashion shows as possible in European fashion capital cities. This could take a week, or even months. This was so she could make up her mind on a central theme on which to base her designs for the season. Once she was 'saturated' with ideas, she would go on a shopping spree, buying sample fabrics from established brands, such as Diesel, Fanlarina, M60, and Bench & Hooch, as well as almost anything which she liked in the Portobello and Camden Market street stalls in London.

These were just for inspiration, which when 'ripe,' would prompt her to sit down and sketch. Once the sketches were ready, and she was sure about her choice of fabrics, she would board a flight to Kathmandu.

Other than Vivek, from the owner's family, Claire's designing team in Swakan-Chhemu consisted of a young woman named Rubi, who handled Claire's communications with tailors, dyers, embroiderers, and accessorizers. To Rubi, Claire came across as rather eccentric, whereas Claire considered Kathmandu a difficult muse. She had to keep her artistic senses alive in order to find ways of translating Kathmandu into her design aesthetic. At times, she found inspiration in the complex melding of Hindu and Buddhist icons, or in an eclectic mix of modern and ancient practices, as she wandered aimlessly around Kathmandu in search of the right image, icon, and texture that might inspire her designs. Vivek was not necessarily a part of this wandering even if his presence was always sought when making final decisions on both designing and production. As the local and global designers forged co-designing within a producer-buyer hierarchy while negotiating friendship with business, the production of Swakan-Chhemu garments entailed effortlessly stepping in and out of the domains of sacred and profane just as it saw the worlds of the craftspeople in Kathmandu and cosmopolitan with consumers in Europe entangle inextricably.

Fashion aside, what Swakan-Chhemu did differently from all other garment businesses in Kathmandu was that it acculturated the factory premises. If Claire's designs were inspired by a medieval ethos in the chaos of modern Kathmandu, the organization of the Swakan-Chhemu factory space was essentially Newar. Despite being housed in a modern building, like most other garment factories in Kathmandu, the spatial organization of Swakan-Chhemu's factory hierarchy resonated with the Newar cultural practice, where upper floors stood for purity and were accessible only to insiders, whereas the lower floors were open to the public and, hence, considered socially inferior. Vivek and his older brother Ashok had their offices on the top (second) floor, within which they also allocated spaces for fashion designers as well as finance managers. These offices had fashionable wall-to-wall carpeting, requiring visitors to take off their shoes before entering. But this floor also had an 'outer' extension which could be accessed by walking through an outside balcony that did not require entering the main offices, and hence did not require taking off one's shoes. This extension housed a large and barren room for the 'finishing' department where women workers sat on a straw mat cutting out hanging threads after tailoring, after which the garments were then ironed and packed off.

The first floor too had two wings: the main wing was the fabric-cutting room which accommodated three separate units employing about twenty skilled workers. The cutting units were assigned, respectively, for knit fabric, woven fabric, and leather. The smaller extension to the main room was used for the storage of fabric. Almost all of the employees in these functions came from 'hill' ethnicities, although they varied in caste. A Guvaju girl (priestly caste) sat next to a Kapali man (barber caste, considered untouchable), both Newars from within the Kathmandu Valley. The Guvaju girl was adequately skilled and was recruited into the job after her father, a skilled cutting-master had an accident and became disabled. Next to them sat a team of Damai men (hill tailor caste, considered 'untouchabale'), some of whom had recently converted to Christianity. Caste or religion was not really an issue on this floor although everybody in Swakan-Chhemu would support the Damai cutting-master when a fight broke out between him and his Indian rival, Rana, from the Western Himalayas on the Indo-Nepal border.[9]

The ground floor was where most of the tailoring workers were based. Here, in stark contrast to the first and second floors, almost everyone was a Madheshi from the Tarai flat lands which is spread on both sides of the Nepal-India border. There were occasional instances where a Newar or Bahun-Chhetri tailor worked side by side with Madheshis from the Tarai. But such cases were rare, and non-Madheshis hardly ever joined the community of Madheshis. For example, Madheshi tailors organized themselves into working teams called *juwadi* (gambler groups), loyal to a *naike* (head man) who had fetched his village men from the Tarai to come out to Kathmandu. The *naike* sorted out job divisions and decided individual wages while making sure the workers had adequate arrangements for lodging and food (see Chapter 2). There were only two non-Madheshi workers, out of a total four hundred, in Swakan-Chhemu during my fieldwork; they never joined the Juwadi circle of the Madheshis but worked on their own.

The next year, Swakan-Chhemu added another floor, visibly makeshift in appearance, just like a *buigal* (attic) in Newar homes, which is used for storage and not living. This was perched on top of the main floor, where the owners and designers worked, to house the embroiderers who were also Madheshis. While the nature of their work was very different, as reflected in the wages they drew, the two Madheshi communities readily socialized with each other. The Muslims among them prayed together, while the Hindus invited each other to celebrate Chhath and Diwali. They all followed a common calendar of seasonal migration, even sharing factory transportation to go home and come back.

From culture to market

How are we to understand industrial modernity in terms of a global convergence of consumer tastes and production methods? On the one hand, it seems that traditional arts and crafts have not become obsolete but are rather making a comeback. On the other hand, ideas about material crafts being puritanically tradition-derived are contested by what actually goes on in shops and shop floors. Craft is not isolated but entwined with mass production. My ethnography of how Nepali garment entrepreneurs ventured into the global market illustrates a complex link between the two, where the dualities of 'traditional' and 'modern', as well as 'local' and 'global', give way to a multiplicity of patronages, alliances, and rivalries.

In the 1980s, Shah Safari was the originator of an exportable readymade garment industry in Nepal. What can we say about the clues it left behind as to what forms of cultural politics may emerge in Nepal in the decades following democratization and liberalization? A point to be noted of course is the overwhelming impact MFA had on Nepal, opening the floodgates of Taylorist production, which organized hordes of workers into neat (if anonymized) assembly lines, equipped with imported machines and scientifically measured spaces and systems. But is this the only way forward? In this chapter, I probe the possibility, raised by Piore and Sabel (1984) that flexible specialization might offer an industrial trajectory that is alternative to the multinational Keynesianism of giant assembly lines and neo-proletariat workers. Possibilities of such an alternative seemed rooted as much in Nepali culture as in its modernization, even if such an alternative is not considered by the twentieth century Nepali state. All of the policymakers I spoke to endorsed the teleology from craft to mass as the 'mainstream' solution. In their eyes, Nepal suffered from several drawbacks, ranging from a lack of natural resources, geographic isolation, weak infrastructure, and poor human resources. This perspective – jokingly referred to as the '*khattam kanchha*' (doomsday) theory among the hyper-optimists in Kathmandu – does not consider the nuances of mass and craft garment trade, nor does it acknowledge the characteristically different lives lived by the two communities inhabiting the garment world in Nepal. This perspective, that the Nepali garment industry would inevitably collapse once MFA expired, arrogantly dismissed the existence of a vibrant cultural subcluster within the mainstream garment ecosystem that was never dependent on MFA.

This denial of culture and craft offers a sharp contrast for my juxtaposition of shop floor ethnography against the policy forecast about the inevitability of post-MFA catastrophe – a thread I will pursue in detail in Chapter 5. While mass manufacturers saw doomsday approaching, the craft cluster was confident of their prospects well beyond the MFA expiry. A&E Boutique and Swakan-Chhemu, for example, had enthusiastic plans to expand and upgrade their productions, absorbing the spaces and machinery released by the mass sector after 2004. People have always known about the hope and promise of craft against the crisis in the mass. Chhote once said, 'to compete well in this world, we must offer something, to buy which, the buyer would not look at the price', or as Sameer from the mass sector put it, 'Westerners pay stacks of dollars to buy our kind of stuff, but only for something that is found only here, not what they can get everywhere else.' The Garment Association of Nepal had submitted multiple requests to government and foreign aid agencies asking for capacity building in fashion designing aiming to build a base for ethno-contemporary garments for which there seemed a niche for Nepal in the global market. It was a great irony that the hope of craft never really made it to policy discourse despite repeated attempts at multiple levels.

Several public conferences organized by the government, with assistance and guidance from the World Bank, the Asian Development Bank, UNDP, ILO, and several others, dwelled exclusively on mass manufacturing, seemingly with little awareness of its craft kin that existed side by side. Stories from Lesotho, Bangladesh and Mauritius were discussed in great detail but the craft sectors in the same countries were hardly ever mentioned. One European consultant, who had been flown into Nepal for a fortnight long 'mission', told me that his employer, the Asian Development Bank, had moved away from '1970s ideas like handicraft' because, 'we are all modern now', implying that qualifiers like 'craft' or 'mass' were redundant for the garment industry that seemed so ubiquitously modern to him. Modernity for him clearly meant anonymization and mechanization, and nothing else, even if most Nepali garment producers do not subscribe to such policy advice (see the last subsection in Chapter 3 on GAN). When I pointed this out, the aid agency consultant argued it was the 'government' that he worked for and took cues from, just as the state policymakers readily claimed they wanted what's best for the garment industry even if they routinely twisted the garment narrative so they did not contradict the prefabricated narratives of development preached by foreign aid advisors even before they begun their 'fact-finding' mission on the ground. In this, Celayne Heaton-Shrestha's (2006) argument about the nature of local-foreign engagement on development rings true. In the power-eclectic world of aid, disjunctures of perceptions and solutions are not resolved by designated intermediaries, but reproduced time and again to give rise to a 'bracketedness' where each party rigidly adheres to a self-centred assessment of the situation, thus justifying biased performative about collective development work.

By 2003, dangerously close to the MFA expiry which shook the garment industry globally, a different story spread through on the garment shop floors in Kathmandu. Mass manufacturers began asserting that the government was not taking up the Association's call for help in fashion-designing because the crafts people had conspired against it. Because crafts businessmen have been reluctant to let others learn their designing secrets, the increasingly anxious crowd of mass manufacturers insisted, that the crafts people were also sabotaging the Association's call to mobilize support for state policy help for incubating fashion designing. The self-inflicting syllogism at work here is as follows: policymakers stubbornly deny the existence of the craft subsector, so crafts people are hardly ever consulted for policy diagnoses; as mass manufacturing is coming to an end and the crafts are looking at a comfortable future, they were seen with suspicion of sabotaging the Association's attempts to persuade the government to help them with designing. As a consequence, foreign aid advisers, whose words and discourses are in any case too long-winded for the locals to follow, thus listed a bucket full of problem statements that covered everything and nothing – and furthermore the government did not react to the seemingly erroneous claims about designing sabotage because the industry was heading to a crisis anyway.

Global crises and local rumors aside, what is displayed in my ethnography are the closely guarded networks of trust and social affiliation as reflected in the successful businessmen's unwillingness to share their business secrets with less successful ones (Gambetta, 1993; Zucker, 1986). Friendships like Sameer's went only thus far; however much he and his friends appreciated each other's company, that did not get him into the crafts businessmen's studios. Equally their hang-out sessions did not die away just because 'business did not happen' between them. Similarly, CEO Navin migrated to California after the factory shut down, and his craft garment friends chuckled that he had been reduced to now working as a 'petrol boy' in America. He wasn't: He had taken over a local franchise of petrol pumps and was well into buying his second station when I met him, clearly a mark of prestige for a new immigrant. When he visited Kathmandu after a few years, his old garment friends, especially those in crafts business and still with money, gave him a jubilant party, complete with a cultural show by a famous *gazal* singer everybody loved, and everybody went back to being friends.

In its unwillingness to listen to the Association's proposition about the possibilities of leveraging crafts to hedge the mass sector from the looming MFA crisis, Nepali policymakers appeared indifferent to the reality that the narrow ambits of business trust would not widen their radius in the absence of policies and mechanisms that institutionalized trust (Moore, 1999; Fukuyama, 1995; Harriss, 2002 a; Harriss, 2002b). The result was that policymakers got away with a complete denial of the fact that a very vibrant and culturally-rooted method of garment-making existed and prospered side by side with mass manufacturing of anonymous designs. The anti-politics of development discourse on garment-making essentially pre-empted a valid question about cultural capital in industrial and social reproduction. Borrowing Bourdieu's (1984) notions of cultural capital, Nepal's garment industry was caught in an impasse because it is not always easy to convert economic capital into cultural capital because these require a gratuitous expenditure of time, attention, care, and concern. At the current juncture, this is possible in Nepal only through a complex web of kin, or kin-like, obligations, which has a limited range, especially during cultural and political transitions. Nepali policymakers seem dismissive of the industry's embeddedness into culture and politics. In the next chapter, I extend this discussion of trust and policy (mis)readings to cover the crisis within the garment industry, to make a compelling case for Nepali policymakers to consider culture and politics in comprehending industry and its trajectories.

Endnotes

1. See Surya (2005) for discussions on the first Indian blockade on Nepal following disputes on trade and transit agreements.
2. The economic blockade (*aarthik nakabandi*), started on March 23, 1989 amid speculations that King Birendra had lost India's confidence after he signed an arms deal with China. The blockade lasted until late April 1990, by when a popular uprising had forced the king to outlaw the pro-monarchy Panchayat regime, and declare Nepal a multi-party democracy, while agreeing to his own power being confined to the limits of constitutional monarchy. On the other side of the border, the National Front, led by V.P. Singh, defeated the incumbent Prime Minister Rajiv Gandhi's Indian National Congress (India), in a general election in India thereby easing the stand-off .between the two countries.

3. Singer (1972) observed a similar phenomenon among the Tamil Brahmins in India in the 1970s who abandoned earlier vocations of priesthood, intellectual pursuits, and bureaucratic jobs to launch their own business ventures.

4. The Damais from the hills (considered Dalit or 'untouchable') and the Darjees from the plains (also considered low-caste) mostly worked as basic tailors in mass manufacturing factories. The sujikars from within Kathmandu Valley (considered to belong to a relatively higher castes) however seemed to have the status of fashion designers in select few of the craft producers. In fact, even when they were carrying out the ordinary task of basic tailoring in these factories, they were treated by the factory owners as somewhat superior than those from the lower of the tailoring castes.

5. A standard fabric was referred to as 60x60, i.e., it had 60 yarn units of warp per inch and 30 yarn units of weft per half inch. Warp was always measured in inches because this was manually set and thus prone to some variation, whereas weft was mechanically (if not automatically) woven and so was measured in half inches.

6. In each, the yarn thickness ranged from 0 to 20 where 0 was the finest. A standard yarn was scaled at number 12.

7. Nepal's trade with Tibet dates as far back as Nepali legendary ruler Bhim Malla's signing of a business treaty with Tibet in the mid-seventeenth century that gave Nepalis unlimited rights to live and trade in Tibet including a monopoly over minting Tibetan coins.

8. See (Frechette, 2003) on the complexities involved in the way Nepali state and communities including Newars and Shakyas, handled the crisis in the lives of the Tibetans. She mentions three distinct waves of Tibetan migration and their naturalization as Nepali citizens, with active support from their Newar networks in Kathmandu, resulting in a vibrant Tibetan community in Nepal that is deeply immersed into the local ways of life.

9. I met Rana later in another factory, Arya-Nepal III, the next year, where he was perceived to be part of the hill Nepali team which occasionally took up issues against Indians from the flat lands. Although garment workers of varying caste and ethnicities worked amicably side by side during normal times, acrimonies did surface when riots broke out elsewhere. See Shakya (2015) for a critical analysis of how anti-India riots on Kathmandu streets, triggered by rumours involving a Bollywood star, seeped into the readymade-garment shop floors and how managers readily capitalized on the nationalistic animosity of workers to settle their own scores. During incidents such as these, people like Rana, with Indian citizenship with the hill origin, found it difficult to take sides between Nepalis and Indians (See Chapter 5 on how Rana fared in Arya-Nepal as opposed to Swakan-Chhemu).

5

The MFA Expiry
A Garment Tsunami

The expiry of the Multi-Fibre Arrangement (MFA) in 2004 was undeniably the end of an era. Under the MFA, Nepal had received the most benefits of all South Asian countries and Nepal suffered the most when it expired. Its impact was so intense that when a tsunami hit the shores of Aceh and Phuket just five days before the MFA expired, killing thousands of Asian locals and Western tourists, many saw it as a sign that doomsday prophecies were coming true. Watching television footage of killer waves swallowing cars, roads, and houses, and seeing hordes of both local and Western mourners hopelessly searching for their loved ones in the aftermath, one garment businessman described how the tsunami had torn apart the walls dividing 'us' from 'them', and was a warning of something even bigger. This was, after all, coming from a man whose business was heading towards collapse and his entire livelihood was at stake. 'Not even a mouse escapes a modern day jungle fire,' another garment businessman added before launching into a tirade about ours being *kali yuga*, the Age of Vice,[1] and hence destined for *pralaya* (catastrophe). It is easy to dismiss their doomsday thinking as a product of sour grapes, but it would be naïve to overlook the reality of how the MFA-expiry crisis fundamentally altered the Nepali garment community's views about the world and their place in it.

While the ocean tsunami struck Asian shores without warning, the Nepali garment industry's tsunami had been long in the making. The MFA was first signed in 1974, initially only for three years but was renewed easily until 1994, when the World Trade Organization (WTO) made the draconian announcement that it would be granted just 'one last chance' before being dismantled permanently on 31 December 2004. This came in response to reverberating calls from International Financial Institutions (IFIs) for a global free market. While the World Bank and the IMF made free trade one of the policy conditionalities under the Washington Consensus,[2] the WTO took it upon itself to push the United States to dismantle the MFA, in order to end US engineering of the global trade of garments. The MFA was indeed the United States' unilateral arrangement, through which it bestowed trade privileges on countries it chose, while erecting duty barriers for those that it didn't. The WTO seemed determined to dismantle such unilateral engineering in order to make way for global capitalism, something they considered beneficial for humanity (See Chapter 2).

It took a global confrontation to even get the United States to agree to dismantle the MFA (Hamilton 1990). Countries around the world undertook diagnostic studies to assess the potential impacts of the MFA expiry for their own industries. In Nepal, the government was assisted by major aid agencies including the World Bank, the Asian Development Bank, and United Nations Development Programme. Almost all of the reports echoed one another in claiming that the Nepali garment industry was not 'competitive enough', and a long list of 'constraints' were drawn up to explain why; the most 'binding' of them being that Nepali workers were more expensive than Bangladeshis and Chinese workers, and furthermore that it was difficult to fire workers in Nepal once hired.[3] Reports also highlighted several other issues, such as poor infrastructure and finance, lack of a domestic supply chain and international connectivity, and a poor governance structure. Based on this list of compromises on 'competitiveness', a localized understanding of American libertarian economics took root in Nepal, which national policymakers, as well as international donors, believed; Nepal did not deserve a garment industry in the first place and, hence, it must not grieve for its destined demise.

By 2003, policymakers seemed resigned to the view that the readymade garment industry in Nepal was beyond redemption, thus triggering a bureaucratic narrative that shifted blame onto others. The Secretary of the Ministry of Industry and Commerce was clear that the garment industry was not worth saving because it was not a 'real' industry, but rather a 'satellite' for Indian businessmen wanting to steal MFA benefits earmarked for Nepal; hence, the sooner Nepal got rid of such 'dowry' industries, the better. In a meeting with the Secretary, when I insisted that most garment factory owners and workers were Nepali, he insisted it was I who needed to revise my data, not him. After all, the designated garment industry researcher on the public payroll – who had not visited the actual factories, but had got the business association to supply him with necessary statistics for tabulation – had maintained that there was little 'value added' in this business, echoing the claims of aid agencies.

Most garment businessmen spoke of their industry as one that had 'a sword hanging over its head' (*taukomathi tarbaar jhundieko*). No factory owner considered a machinery upgrade or building expansion after 2003. Even when businesses received large purchase orders from prestigious buyers, that required physical expansion – as was the case with Arya-Nepal III's last order from GAP's Old Navy label demanding despatch of the merchandise by the year-end – they hesitated to invest in infrastructure that may go unused after 2004. Since GAP insisted that their production must not be '*chhyasmis*' (mixed) with other brands, Arya-Nepal III agreed to install a new shop floor, but calculations were done very carefully such that all costs of construction would be recovered by 2004. This meant that the walls of the new construction were thinner than usual, the machines were on loan, the furniture was kept to a bare minimum and was mostly second hand, and all of the workers were on piece-rate contracts. Everything had a makeshift feel to it. Yet, Sameer and Navin kept the cheery public relations rhetoric going till the last minute that, despite the end of the MFA, the business was 'doing well'. They were technically correct in pointing out that Arya-Nepal had more orders now than ever before, but that was because other factories had already shut down and some businesses needed a second party to pick up orders they could not complete. Arya-Nepal's staff called this momentary boom a '*nibhna lageko diyo*' (a lamp soon to die out), indicating that a lamp burns its brightest just before it goes out.

Death in the factory: *dasha*

The garment industry's misfortune took on a broad range of meanings, well beyond the economic, which interpreted its failure as divinely ordained. A particularly noteworthy instance of this is the way that the shop-floor imagination seized upon the tragic accidents that occurred around the time that the MFA expired, and appropriated them to narrativize the industry's ongoing struggle as an 'act of god'. For instance, a series of tragic accidents occurred in late 2003, related to Arya-Nepal-III. A fire broke out in September, as workers were applying petrol spray in the finishing room – a commonly used procedure to remove minor stains on garments. This severely injured five workers, causing the closure of the finishing unit; the factory was forced to subcontract this task to an outsider. Just a month later, a major bus accident killed one of its workers and seriously injured 26 others as they were being dropped off home in a factory-owned bus after a late night shift. Five months later, Navin, the CEO of Arya-Nepal, lost his elder brother, who had raised him after their parents died when he was still young. About a month after that, the 37-year-old brother-in-law of Sameer, the Production Manager, had a sudden heart attack and died. Such a series of sudden deaths left the owners and managers feeling as if the time was inauspicious. A lively and competitive business venture just a year ago, Arya-Nepal III began to lose momentum due to these unfortunate incidents, while more and more garment factories in the neighbourhood closed down, owing to deteriorating local and global conditions of production and trade.

Triggered by these occurrences, quite a few cosmological/astrological narratives spread on the shop floors. One that gained a considerable amount of traction concerned the idea of '*dasha*': an imbalance in one's cosmic relations, often leading to dissatisfaction, disappointments, disharmony, and other undesirable results. Although there are several *dashas*, such as when Rahu (the tenth planet in the solar system as per Indian astrology) entering one's horoscopic 'house', or Brihaspati (Jupiter) slides into the wrong astrological 'house', the most feared is Shanishchar (Saturn), especially when this planet transits through the first, second and twelfth houses from one's personal 'house', to the moon. Sameer and others in the garment business told me that Saturn takes two and half years to pass through each 'house', making the whole transit occupy over seven and half years (*sadhe saat*). They considered this the most ominous cosmic ill-luck there is, and they believed that the garment industry might be having its *Sadhe Saat* too.

Local newspapers speculated that King Gyanendra, who had recently dismissed parliament and taken constitutional powers in his own hand, had made such an ill-advised move under the evil spell of *Sadhe Saat*. There were suggestions that the ominousness of the royal massacre[4] just a few years ago had defiled the new king and his kingdom. Rumours soon spread that the Maoist rebel leader, Prachanda, had excellent planetary conditions (*kushal graha dasha*), and hence was likely to fare better in the ongoing national political struggle. This sat well with actual conditions on the ground. Not only had Maoists paralyzed the state in almost two thirds of the nation's rural territories, by 2003, Kathmandu was beginning to feel the heat of the Maoist People's War. A series of guerrilla attacks in the *mofussil* towns had disrupted the garment supply chain connecting Kathmandu with Nepal's closest sea access at the port of Kolkata, and things got worse as democratic parties launched their own protests in Kathmandu against King Gyanendra. Prolonged strikes (*hartals*) on shop floors delayed production, and, since the highways were also shut down from time to time due to political protests of *chakkajam* (locking of wheels), merchandise trucks were frequently delayed on the way. Owing to these, several garment businesses were forced to air-courier their consignments, which increased the costs fourfold in some cases, and entailed serious financial losses that threatened the sustainability of the entire enterprise. In despair, it seems, the garment industry people turned to spirituality as a last attempt for protecting their lives and work: it became increasingly common for factory owners to commission religious rituals on the shop floors, hoping they could ward off their *dasha*.

Nepali businessmen have long sought divine patronage for protection and prosperity. Even before the crisis loomed large on the horizon, garment factories routinely consecrated, on the shop floor, idols of the patron deities of traders: Laxmi (for ushering wealth), Ganesh (for auspiciousness), Bhimsen (for good business fortune), and Biswokarma (for protecting artisanship). Many employed priests (*pujari*) with monthly salaries to undertake daily worship rituals. The intensity of prayers increased, visibly so among the mass manufacturers, as the date for MFA expiry came closer. For example, when Arya-Nepal set out to build a new shop floor, to carry out what it considered its last purchase order from GAP, it organized an elaborate *yagya* (Hindu ritual of fire sacrifice) to ward off evil. A priest was flown in from its headquarters in Ludhiana just for this undertaking, and a whole team of priests from Nepal's holiest Hindu temple, Pashupatinath, was hired (See Chapter 6). Owing to local variations in meanings and rituals, the Indian and Nepali priests contested one another on almost all aspects of the procedure of this *Yagya*, even though they agreed on the fundamentals, thus invoking the paradox of how their gods are the same but their prayers differ (Shakya, 2007).

Figure 10: A Religious Ritual Being Performed at Arya-Nepal

Garment 'going air': management reform as the last hope

Though they lamented endlessly about *dasha*, and turned to religious rituals, this did not stop garment businessmen from seeking secular solutions. In the classic sense of the 'compartmentalization' that Milton Singer (1972) talked about, businessmen attempted to solve material problems, while at the same time, accepting the vagaries of destiny as a cosmological curse. Even if the *sadhe saat dasha* became a compartmentalizing device through which the broken and lost lives could be lamented, the businessmen did maintain rational efforts towards resolving everyday challenges to the best of their abilities, even as defeatism lurked on the periphery.

On average, it took about three weeks for a garment consignment to travel from Nepal to the United States, via land and sea, at the cost of 900 USD for a standard twenty-foot container. The expression 'going air', in the garment industry, basically meant that production lagged so far behind schedule that the consignment had to be sent by air to Kolkata port, and, at times, all the way to its final destination in the United States. The cost difference between sea and air freight was so high that factories could go bankrupt if their consignments went by air more than a couple of times a year. The garment industry terms of trade put the manufacturer alone at risk. Although the buyer would pay all of the costs, including transport, once the merchandise was loaded on the ship, it held rights to refuse the entire payment if the merchandise arrived late. Worse yet, since manufacturers were paid only on delivery of goods, manufacturers took bank loans to meet operating costs by using the Letter of Credit (L/C) as collateral, which meant that any refusal of payment drowned them in debt. Everybody in the garment business had seen at least one case where a business went bust because its merchandise had to 'go air'. Arya-Nepal II had shut down precisely for this reason; all three business partners had been financially blacklisted for the non-payment of their loans, and could not start another business until they paid off what they owed. Later, when Sameer and Navin founded Arya-Nepal III, in partnership with a Ludhiana-based firm, they had to be listed as employees rather than partners in the government records (see Chapter 4).

In the autumn of 2003, when two consecutive consignments had to be flown to Kolkata port, Arya-Nepal III saw the writing on the wall: the end was near. Emotionally weakened by the deaths of their own loved ones (mentioned earlier), Sameer and Navin still made one final attempt at reforming its shop floors. Their original idea had been to hire a top-notch

Indian business consultancy to help revamp operations, but they could not quite afford it. Instead, they recruited a local team of 'young and capable' business consultants from within Kathmandu to oversee changes in management. This team consisted of six young business graduates and fashion designers, with degrees from prestigious schools in Nepal and India. This team was expected to work under Nepali supervision in Arya-Nepal III in close coordination with its Indian managers. Their salaries, perks, and status were at par with that of the Production Manager, third in rank in the factory hierarchy.

The arrival of this new team sparked a great deal of interest in the factory. On the one hand, the factory workers saw these young people as potential saviours against the danger of redundancy hovering over their heads, and the team was given a warm welcome by both Nepalis and Indians. On the other hand, their distinctive attire and manners made the workers uneasy, and they remained outsiders to the garment community till the very end. The security guards at the main gate would salute them, not because they were functionally important, but because they came to the office every morning in their ties and scarves, looking important. Floor supervisors found it amusing that the new team would address them using the honorifics *tapain* and *ji*, as opposed to the familiar *timi*. The Nepalis were impressed that the team spoke with the Indian managers not in Hindi but in English. Others spoke positively of their habit of taking notes during discussions, and appreciated their knowledge of the latest computer software used for accounting, merchandising, and fashion-designing. Before long, the factory started organizing a series of daily and weekly meetings in the designated meeting room. This was in contrast to the earlier practice of standing in a loose circle in the middle of the stitching floor to discuss everything from machinery upgradation to factory downsizing; everybody from the CEO to the floor supervisor was free to walk in and offer his opinion.

However, frictions soon emerged between the old and new managers: some Indians, whose English was not as good as that of the young team, simply refused to speak the language, and, to the chagrin of the young team, meetings went back to being held in Hindi, a language in which they were not fluent. Although some measure of reform was put in place, some members of the young team faced an uphill task. On one occasion, a female merchandise expert on the new team was abruptly told by her Punjabi counterpart that she should tie her hair back at all times when she was in the factory, which sent shockwaves among the independent-minded team members. The youngsters were also not encouraged by the fact that the experienced floor supervisors and production managers estimated time and costs of production with quick mental calculations, while they themselves preferred to enter data systematically into the computer to make their forecasts. On one occasion, one of the new merchandising experts forgot to place an order for thread when placing an order for buttons. This was seen as a very basic mistake and became a popular joke among the old workers. What made the new team a laughing stock was their formal recommendation that the company should invest in expensive merchandise management software to prevent such mishaps in future.

Curiously enough, another piece of juicy gossip floating around the shop floor was that the leader of the new team was a Maoist party leader. With the Maoists spreading their influence over more than half of the national territory by this time, the public both sympathized with and were fearful of them. But they were still underground, and although members of Arya-Nepal III had met some of the Maoist labour cadre during bouts of strikes launched by the Maoists (see Chapter 6), many had never seen a 'real' Maoist leader. In the imaginations of the workers, the quiet and cautious leader of the management reform team, who usually kept his distance from others and stayed dedicated to his own tasks, was seen as a possible Maoist spy. He came from the mid-western region of Nepal which had long been a hotbed of Maoist guerrilla campaigns. This fact gave birth to rumours on the shop floor that, after holding a successful labour campaign a few years back, the Maoists were back in Arya-Nepal III, this time aiming to take over the factory management. A recent Maoist Convention had sanctioned the party strategy of 'Prachanda Path', named after their Supreme Commander Prachanda, which was to be a 'move to the Centre from the periphery.' At a time when the Maoists were still underground, speculation ran wild in Kathmandu media, and among ordinary people, on what exactly was meant by a 'move to the Centre.'

Rumours aside, the new team in Arya-Nepal III did not really find their stint in the garment factory to be very rewarding. They felt that garment manufacturing was a low status job and offered little career prospects. Two of them had joined the garment sector upon losing their previous employment in travel agencies, which had been desk jobs and thus had been seen as higher in status. One said that she would ultimately like to find something in the international development and aid industry. Another wanted to work for a boutique label where her skills would be more useful. Some favoured the idea of running their own business as opposed to working for a boss. Most of them frequently referred to older kin or friends with careers in more glamorous professions – such as hotel management, the aid industry or the media – as their role models. One said that, out of shame, he had not told his girlfriend that he worked in the garment industry. Many confessed that their families and friends expected them to move on to better jobs after an initial stint in garments. Their common assessment of the garment job was that it was more about *charko bolnu* (speaking loudly) and *chappal khiyaunu* ('wearing out shoes'; signifying a lot of legwork) than more prestigious *dimagko kam* (intellectual work). It did not help that the garment industry hit a major stumbling block with the MFA expiry a year later. By March 2004, all six in the management reform team had resigned.

After this unsuccessful attempt, and following two other consignments 'going air', Arya-Nepal-III finally invited the Indian consultancy group it had originally wanted to call. This group of consultants drew up a detailed business plan for a supply-chain upgrade through better sourcing, packaging, merchandising, and accounting systems. It was suggested that the business petition the government for a bail-out but this plan never materialized. Instead, in February 2004, Arya-Nepal III decided to downsize and sell one of its two production units. There was open disagreement between Nepali and Indian parties within Arya-Nepal III as to which of the two units should be kept. The Nepalis wanted to keep the larger building, whereas the Indians wanted to retain the smaller. Later, the same trusted priest of the Indian investor, who had commissioned the *yagyas* before to cast dasha off factory premises, was flown into Kathmandu to undertake a detailed astrological study to decide which of the two buildings were more ominous. He reported that it was the larger building and hence should be discarded, but the Nepali camp disagreed. Bowing to pressure from the Nepali side, Arya-Nepal kept the main factory building and let go of its smaller plant in Balaju, a neighbourhood a few kilometres away from the main location at Sitapaila (See Illustration on 2). The closure of the building was a strong signal to the workers that the problems of the business were becoming insurmountable and that it was at the end of its tether.

'It's the unions who shut down the factory'

The closure of the Balaju plant triggered a long chain of reactions in Arya-Nepal III. Convinced that their days were numbered, the more seasoned workers left to look for other jobs, while the younger and angrier lot decided that it was time to 'do something' (*kehi garnai parne bela ho yo*). They discussed the matter with the existing trade union registered in the factory – the Nepali

Congress' Nepal Trade Union Congress (NTUC) – and came back dissatisfied with the solutions offered. Their efforts to reach out to the Maoists were in vain because they were underground at this time, waging war in the rural areas. It then emerged that the centre-left trade union General Federation of Nepal Trade Unions (GEFONT) had an especially militant, if renegade, wing, which had helped workers in other factories that were closing. Hearing of this wing, four of the shop floor supervisors came together to mobilize workers, in to have sufficient membership for registering a GEFONT trade union in Arya-Nepal. In doing so, they were not only signalling a pre-emptive move against the business owners, but were also boldly 'crossing the floor' between Unions (see Chapter 6).

The Nepali CEO, and the Production Manager, as well as their Indian counterparts, obviously advised the workers against this, but they stayed adamant; they were sure the factory was heading toward a bigger layoff, and that only the Union could ensure fair compensation. In a one-on-one meeting that was collegial but tough, Sameer, the Production Manager, pointed out to the would-be chairman of the new Union – a junior employee who supervised workers in one of its twelve assembly lines – that he (Ajay) was a novice teenager, and that he had had no prior experience when he had come looking for work in the factory. Sameer reminded him that the company had not only promoted him to the job of line supervisor, but had also employed his mother, wife, and sister. He was told in no uncertain terms that Arya-Nepal III was the sole *annadata* (giver of food) for his entire family. He was asked to be loyal to the company, especially in a time of crisis like this one. He was told by Sameer that while his mother was the one who gave birth [to him], the factory was the one which gave him a career in a fatherly way. The worker did not contest any of this. His only response, towards the end of this long chastisement, was that he wanted to make sure that the 'elderly women on the workforce would not lose their jobs', and also that the Trade Union would support the Nepali owners against their Indian counterparts, in their struggle to keep the factory afloat. He left the factory promising he would think it over once more before the workers finalized their decision as to whether or not to register the new Union.

Sameer tried to visit Ajay at his home the same night for a follow-up conversation. However, Ajay had been warned about this by his fellow workers, so he did not go home that night, even though Sameer waited there until midnight. It made a powerful impression on the workers that the Production Manager, who ordered them around on the shop floor, had visited and waited at a worker's humble home till late at night. But this only heightened their fear that the circumstances were indeed dire; they feared that the management might try to sabotage their unionizing efforts. No further conversations took place. A week later, everybody learned that the new Trade Union had indeed been registered. They began to mobilize workers for a showdown but, in an unexpected preemptive move, the owners filed for bankruptcy and padlocked the main gate before the workers could organize their protest.

Did the Union really pose so acute a threat that the factory had to shut down overnight? While factories had in the past faced militant labour protests, the common understanding among factory owners was that the Union, by escalating demands on severance packages, would make it especially hard for businessmen to negotiate a closure. Experiences abounded of businessmen suspending shop floor operations, but being unable to close their books because of legal cases filed by the Union, that dragged on for years, or even physical threats, making negotiations particularly acrimonious. Fearing similar problems, the owners of Arya-Nepal III finalized a deal with its Indian investor, Mr. Jain, that, in return for closing down the factory overnight, they would be relocated to Mr. Jain's office in the United States. Navin and his family emigrated immediately. After working in that office for about a year, Navin started his own business in California – the petrol pump franchise I mentioned at the very beginning of this book. Meanwhile, the Indian employees moved back to their Ludhiana headquarters immediately.

Sameer remained in Kathmandu to complete the necessary paperwork, while keeping his distance from the unhappy workers. He had been particularly dismayed when the new Union chief Ajay had told him that labour protests were meant to ensure the safety of everybody's jobs, including that of managers and owners, and to ensure that the Nepalis in Arya-Nepal III would not succumb to pressure from their Indian financiers. Sameer remarked upon the irony of this: 'How was it possible that my "welfare" was being looked after without my own knowledge, and by the very people who acted against my wishes?' The workers felt that the Union was their last hope, as the factory looked set to shut down; the owners remained adamant that they had to shut the factory 'clean cut' before Unions meddled in their affairs. The 'whole-timers' in the GEFONT Union, who had been assisting workers, maintained their position throughout: Arya-Nepal III 'needn't' have shut down, because a factory that had run for years could have easily run for a little longer, and that by shutting the factory overnight and blaming it on the Union, they were simply making an infant Union its scapegoat (*baliko boko*).

Ethnicity and craft in the time of crisis

The mood among the craft garment producers could not have been more different than their mass counterpart in and around 2004 as the MFA was expiring. Many had ambitious plans for expanding their operations by buying machines from mass manufacturers as they went bust. The prices of sewing machines clearly plummeted as the mass sector hit rock bottom, allowing those in the craft sector to upgrade from the old Indian *tullu* machines with add-on motors that they were still using (see Chapter 2). It was ironic indeed that the craft sector, which produced superior designs, had lagged behind in technology and office management. Some crafts businesses poached people from the closing mass factories: accountants who could assist their own trusted *khajanchis* (who had the traditional job of keeping finance ledgers) to introduce computerized book-keeping systems, cutting masters who were used to modern cutting machines, and operators of finishing machines which could mechanically detect any needles or metal parts stuck in sewn garments. But this upbeat mood among craft producers lasted only for a few years before they too became victims of militant labour uprisings and had to shut down (see Chapter 6)

In this hour of crisis, identity raised its head in curious ways as workers were reshuffled between craft and mass subsectors. I have discussed the rift between the Indian and Nepali camps in Arya-Nepal III as it headed for the fall. Most belonged to one camp or the other, but some were caught in between. Take Rana, for example, a labour supervisor from the Himalayan foothills of Kumaon, in India, who had been working in Kathmandu garment factories since the 1980s. Despite his passport, he was considered Nepali in Arya-Nepal III because of his 'hill' background, and he was particularly appreciative of this, because his former employers, in Swakan-Chhemu, had considered him Indian. I discussed in Chapter 4 how the Swakan-Chhemu owners favoured a hill Nepali over Rana who they categorized as 'Indian'. Sadly, as tensions grew in Arya-Nepal III, he found himself being increasingly isolated, as both the Nepali and Indian camps saw him an outsider. Finally, when operations shut down, and the Indians went back home, while the Nepalis joined militant unions, Rana was left stranded. He retired from garment work and returned to Kumaon.

Ethnicity manifested itself differently elsewhere. It was only in the 2003 election of the Garment Association of Nepal (GAN), that one or two craft producers who were Janajati by ethnicity were elected to the Executive Committee, which had earlier been controlled exclusively by mass manufacturers from the ranks of Bahun-Chhetris or Marwaris. This was a remarkable achievement for the Janajatis, who were often stereotyped as being incapable of holding public posts. The Janajatis themselves had earlier accepted their marginalization in GAN as a sacrifice for the 'collective good.' The idea of 'collective good' was that GAN should have influential people in key positions so that the industry could have easy access to high level policy makers and politicians. People readily invoked the example of the Carpet Association of Nepal, led by the Janajatis, which could not bring the state on board in time to pre-empt its disastrous collapse in the 1990s because their association executives did not have the right contacts in the government. But as the garment community seemed headed towards its own demise, and as more and more of the mass manufacturers holding key positions had to shut their factories down, GAN began to warm up to the Janajatis and the craft producers, which explained the election of a few Janajati craft producers to its Executive Committee in 2003.

Weathering the storms of capitalism

What are we to think of the MFA crisis and the human tragedies it triggered in the garment industry? A wart on the nose of neoliberal free trade as David Harvey (2007) would have it? The wrath of the 'invisible hand' as Alfred Chandler would have put it? A lesson for those who could not keep up with the tide? Or a crisis of national capitalism for a country caught in violent political transition? It might be all of these. But it also has implications for probably the most questionable premise of the neoliberal era which we are part of, one anchored in the present-day politics of international development discussed at the very beginning of this book. A botched narrative about development which is reproduced endlessly in public media as in dinner talks: the supremacy of market forces over state regulation, and the legitimacy of the hegemony of productivity and competitiveness over concerns about social justice. That the neoliberal conception, of competitiveness and free market receives so much attention, is a slap in the face of displaced garment workers whose plight went unreported in Nepali media, even though the media, after its 'democratization' after 1990 and then 'revolutionization' in 2006, claimed that it now gave voice to the subaltern. Other than the periodic listing of garment statistics in their 'business and industry' pages at the very end, the story of tens of thousands of garment workers, who lost both livelihood and hope, never made it to Nepali newspapers. What are we to think of this media apathy to an acute social crisis unfolding right under its nose?

Media apathy within Nepal needs to be contextualized in the global media discourse on the garment tragedy, which did not account for the singularities in garment trajectories across countries, but also overlooked MFA as the common root of origin for garment industries in many third world countries. The fact that the Nepali garment industry has always been different from its contemporary counterparts in South Asia has hardly been recognized, even among scholars who take a keen interest in this specific industry. While the Nepalese garment crisis fell victim to the double jeopardy of subaltern voicelessness and elite policy denial, its nemesis from the MFA fiasco received much attention. Bangladesh was widely touted, by the World Bank and IMF among others, as the ultimate success story of neoliberal times – a small David of a developing nation, who bested the Goliath of China, in vying for the American market for cheap garments. Less than a decade later, however, when the Bangladesh success story was eclipsed by multiple tragedies of fire and building collapse costing hundreds of lives, one saw a lapse of memory on the part the international media, which simply dismissed these incidents as examples of the shoddy industrialization of the Third World.

When, on April 24, 2013, Rana Plaza which housed one of the biggest garment factories of Bangladesh collapsed, it captured the attention of the international media for several weeks. The benevolent bureaucracy of labour audits – entirely paid for and maintained by global buyers to keep its well-meaning, if naïve, consumers happy – had completely overlooked the widening cracks on the Rana Plaza building, which housed thousands of workers toiling away for fashionable multinational labels like Benetton and GAP. Emboldened by the complacency of the buyers toward safety standards, the owners of the factory had ordered their workers to remain at work on that fateful day, even though other offices in the same building had already moved their staff elsewhere (Saxena, 2014). Workers had no access to a Union *of their own* to voice their protest because unions were deemed a threat to industry competitiveness, and the Bangladeshi government had come down heavily in support of profit-hungry corporations, insisting that buyer-driven labour audits alone would be enough to ensure the safety of the workers. They hadn't. The building collapsed in broad daylight killing 1,100 workers in just one afternoon, and there had been no sign of collective protest from the garment workers, despite being made to work in an unsafe building, even after it had been abandoned by workers from other industries.

What was hard to ignore was the orientalist tone of the reporting in international media when the crisis hit Bangladesh garments. 'Another preventable tragedy in Bangladesh', reported the New York Times about the Savar factory collapse – a statement echoed by the BBC, Globe and Mail, and others, who refused to see this crisis as anything but yet another Third World disaster with the typical actors: greedy businessmen, corrupt politicians, incompetent bureaucrats, and a large mass of poor people with no other options but to put themselves in the line of death. The orientalist perspective was also defeatist; it told policymakers that the contemporary state of the garment factory was justified because it still offered a step up the ladder for the billions of impoverished people around the world.

In proposing a future course of action in Bangladesh and elsewhere, the rationalist line only called for technical solutions such as tightening factory inspection laws and penalizing the factory owner. Even if the media later implicated global businessmen, along with local ones, it still did not acknowledge the political aspect of this tragedy. 'Depoliticising' indeed is a tried and tested tool through which entities and institutions responsible for development tend to shield themselves from scandals (Harriss, Stokke and Tornquist, 2004; Ferguson, 1990). Aid agencies continued to refrain from dealing with actors and issues considered political, even when some of these agencies, especially those who work with the government as their main counterpart, routinely require developing countries to put in place policies that drive industry politics in the first place. A case in point is the World Bank's indicators on 'Doing Business', which had earlier preached flexibility in labor recruitment and dismissal as a precondition for industrial competitiveness – a condition that could be ensured only by incapacitating labour unions.

Eventually, as questions were raised following the soaring death tolls in Savar and elsewhere, the legitimacy of the rhetoric of international aid agencies about the free market, and their preaching of the deregulation of labour, came under some scrutiny.[5] Even so, despite repeated calls from local activists, the role of the MFA in the making of this series crises in the garment industry remained unacknowledged (Shakya, 2013a). To take just one small example of important information that went unreported about the Rana Plaza disaster: investigations had confirmed that bureaucratic and technical procedures for safety clearance of buildings had been compromised in Bangladesh, as in Nepal and elsewhere, because of the pressure built by the MFA 'gold rush' of the 1980s. Since the MFA was initially planned only for three years, but had been followed by a series of short-term extensions, buildings were built as temporary shelters. Eventually, when the MFA expired in 2004, and a horde of buyers descended on Dhaka, abandoning earlier deals elsewhere in

Asia and Africa, a second wave of quick construction followed, which again compromised safety while aiming to meet the quick delivery targets imposed by buyers on manufacturers. But nothing was said in the global media about the direct bearings of the MFA on compromising human safety in Bangladesh. Liberal media reporting conveniently turned a blind eye on the politics of international trade, and gave an 'auditing' spin to a crisis that was essentially a product of politics of race, class, and nation (Shakya, 2013a).

Endnotes

1. Kali Yug or the Age of Vice is the last of the four stages the world goes through as part of the cycle of yugas described in the Sanskrit scriptures. The preceding ages are the Satya Yuga or the Age of Truth, Treta Yuga or the Age of three Avatars of Vishnu, and Dvapara Yuga or the Third Age.
2. John Williamson, World Bank's Chief Economist for South Asia region, coined the term 'Washington Consensus' in 1989, to refer to ten specific tenets of economic liberalization prescribed by Washington DC for countries undertaking Structural Adjustment.
3. The Asian Development Bank reported in a public conference held in Kathmandu in 2005 that the high wages paid were the key constraint in the Nepali garment industry lacking in competitiveness. When this was challenged by some of the participants, ADB's Country Representative for Nepal, immediately switched to suggesting that high electricity tariff might instead have deeper impacts on the Nepali garment competitiveness than wages. The results were altered as swiftly as they had been drawn earlier, thus exposing the shaky ground on which draconian claims such as these stood.
4. On June 1, 2001, the drug-induced shooting spree, allegedly carried out by the crown prince Dipendra Shah, killed 10 members of the royal family, including King Birendra and Queen Aishwarya. See Hutt (2017) for discussions on public meanings of the royal massacre as a call for a republic in Nepal evolved and materialized during the next decade and a half.
5. See Lakshman (2013) for a newspaper summary of the criticisms of the methodology used for producing 'Doing Business' Indicators. See Shakya (2011) for an analysis of the tension between 'Doing Business' Indicators and the overall premise of the Structural Adjustment programs.

6

Workers and Unions
Ethnicity and Class

In the preceding two chapters, I discussed how ideas about garment workers largely embodied the situations of factory owners within the market economy, during both normalcy and crisis. This chapter depicts the world of workers in the context of the union movement, originating at a time of rupture and culminating during the phases of repair and reconfiguration, when the garment people were asking what development and democracy might mean for them. What cannot be denied about Nepal is that the garment workers were mired in controversies around class and cultural identity. Even when the industry was in full swing, generating as much as a quarter of Nepal's total exports, many called it a 'dowry' from India, because of the horde of Indians pouring through the open border. But the controversies about this industry's origins and roots became darker with the collapse of the industry itself, which essentially shifted the earth beneath the feet of those who drew their livelihoods and identities from garment.

At one level, the exodus became a marker of identity for garment workers from Nepal post-MFA, in that everybody who could get out of the industry and the country did so. Perhaps it is expected that poor workers in a poor country cannot afford to hang around factory shop floors after the collapse of their industry and the loss of their jobs. Jane Guyer (2004) talks about postcolonial economic domains being situated in a transcultural space between home and abroad. Even more relevant is Charles Piot's (2010) ethnography of the lotto visa applicants of Togo, among whom the enterprise of exodus ceased to become a rational necessity but has taken on a life of its own and produced its own excesses. Like the Togolese normalising their escape from joblessness and poverty through trans-Atlantic migration, the majority of former garment workers from Nepal now find themselves morphing into a new precariat labour force in geographies unknown to them, devoid of everyday citizenship and national belonging, as they are forced into toiling away in menial jobs in 'emerging' economic powers such as the Gulf or East Asia, if not in Europe and America. India alone is said to have absorbed over a million Nepalis, under a bilateral agreement which allows for an open border and easy work permits, a remnant of a controversial 1950 treaty that is both applauded and loathed in the region.[1]

The workers who remained in the country no longer work on garments today, but are spread thinly across the retail sector, from small pawn shops at bus stations and makeshift stalls in flea markets, to registered shops in and around Kathmandu, not to mention those working as house servants and security guards, office messengers, hotel and restaurant workers, and yet others employed in the making of consumer goods. My garment industry friends proudly told me that one of the biggest movie actresses of Nepal, who later went on to emerge as a leader of the post-revolutionary party Naya Shakti or New Force, used to work with them in garments. They also recounted dozens of names of people who had moved on to start their own shops and small businesses. Those not as lucky had to make do with jobs as waitresses and bar dancers in Kathmandu, Delhi, and Mumbai among other places; there were also rumours that many women from the garment industry had resorted to prostituting themselves in the red light districts. Several others were absorbed as seamstresses in the workshops in Thamel that made everyday clothes for tourists visiting Nepal.

For the men from the garment industry, Qatar became a sought-after destination for earning money and proving their monetary masculinity, echoing old narratives about cross-Himalayan journeys to Tibet where men went to earn gold.[2] Most former garment workers moved on to other jobs and careers, though a very few – those working in the crafts sector – were still able to survive in the garment industry. Even so, despite the death of the industry, there remained a strong solidarity among the erstwhile workers; they still came together whenever the Unions called for sit-downs (*dharna*) and rallies (*juloos*). Resistance, if not rebellion, became an undeniable marker of the solidarity among garment workers. An instance that stirred the nation occurred around the time when twelve Nepalis had been publicly beheaded by Islamic fundamentalists in Iraq on August 31, 2004, and, to the horror of the civilized world, the gruesome video had been publicly uploaded to the Internet. No significant action was taken by the Nepali state, even though there were riots in the streets of Kathmandu demanding punishment for the concerned manpower agencies who had taken those Nepalis to Iraq in the first place (Bajracharya, 2015). In this charged context, a former garment worker telephoned the country's Union leader from Iraq where he had been smuggled to, despite his agent signing him up for a job in Qatar. Many considered it exceptional that, following this one telephone call, the Union leader in Kathmandu mobilized the garment industry to put pressure on the government to track down the group of workers and negotiate a safe passage for them to Qatar, where they had originally been promised jobs.

Beyond this isolated incident though, how are we to make sense of this powerful constituency of workers who remain in solidarity based on their past experiences even if they no longer have a common platform? Sherry Ortner (1999) talks about the emergence of identity through a joint process of allusion and illusion. This might be useful in understanding the 'mimesis' through which garment workers negotiated their identity in a staunchly neoliberal world, especially after the industry collapsed, thus raising doubts about their primary past as garment workers. The perceptions of the workers, about their own identities and situations as well as their collective sense about destiny, changed remarkably, as the death of the industry so abruptly altered their lives and its meanings. In this sense, garment workers are the quintessential '*bhuktabhogi*' (sufferers) of neoliberalism, whose turbulent journey into the loss of livelihood transformed them into fiery comrades in a movement that sought to fundamentally reconfigure the state of Nepal. A synthesizing trajectory of labour resistance, that shows how the 'political' avatar of working class struggle raised its head to contest 'civil' ideas about employer-driven worker identities, leads me to engage with discourses of subalternism and post-subalternism (Chatterjee, 2004, 2008). To arrive at this point about the politics of union militancy, this chapter begins by recalling the way garment workers redefined class, nation, democracy, and development, in a manner which provoked responses and counter-responses from the elite who controlled a state-in-transition.

Elite ideas about garment workers

Before beginning my fieldwork in 2002, I spent several weeks reading newspaper articles on the garment industry and interviewing people reputed to be knowledgeable about the field, including government policy makers and analysts, aid-funded industry specialists, academics, journalists, and activists. Almost everybody advised me, an anthropologist who sprinkled the word 'culture' every now and then in her discourse, to drop the garment industry in favour of other fields which were more 'real' and 'Nepali', and thus 'culturally' better justified. The alternatives suggested were varied: craftsmen of all kinds, traditional singers and dancers, herbalists and other agribusiness communities. More scientifically-minded people suggested that I should focus on 'up and coming' industries, dealing with medicine and other chemical products, as well as those relating to Information and Communication Technology (ICT). It was even suggested that, if I had to concern myself with clothes, I should focus on either the 'better rooted' textile industry or the 'more cultural' enterprises of ethnic tailoring, beading, and embroidery, which are in demand not only on traditional occasions like weddings and festivals, but also attract the attention of expatriates and tourists, though they seldom make it to the export market.

When pressed to explain why it was that the readymade garment industry, a big part of the Kathmandu industrial landscape, was not considered 'real' or 'Nepali', a government official in the Ministry of Finance gave this answer.

> You will have to know more about the industry to know what it is: First of all, these garment factories you see around here are all fake. None of these were here ten years ago and none will remain ten years from now. They are hanging around here just because of America. The day America tells them to leave, they will pack their bags and go. The hordes of workers you see milling around in Baneswor and Ring Road – Indians from head to toe – will all go back to India. And second, while they are here, what is it they are actually doing? There is no 'value added' in this industry. They work for pennies – everything is brought here from elsewhere; the only thing they do here is stitch things together and, pronto! It becomes 'Made in Nepal'.

While statements like these have been made about the Nepali garment industry all too frequently, my ethnography threw up two issues for closer inspection. The first is that the entire industry in Nepal is considered 'fake' or non-existent. A blatant claim like this only points to the elitism of Kathmandu's intellectuals who did not seem to have taken the trouble to visit a running garment factory, even if they were located just blocks away from the posh quarters where they lived. A few who took paid jobs to analyse the garment industry seemed to have relied exclusively on secondary data and discourse analysis. In this scenario, the narrative about the Nepali garment industry being 'Indian' simply made it easier for them to deny existence of something they did not know much about. But it was the position taken by another echelon of influential Nepalis – the development donors and national policymakers who did meet people from the garment factories regularly, although only in their cosy offices and not on the messy shop floors – that did more damage. At one level, the macroeconomists among them preached that 'growth' should come from a teleology of competitiveness, where countries may begin with simpler and lesser-valued industries that may be 'informal', but eventually would go on to encompass more capital-intensive and higher-yielding industries, considered more 'formal' and hence more 'real.' At another level, industry specialists remained stuck with earlier definitions of legally registered businesses as 'real' and the others as fake. The vernacular term for an unregistered business was, as I have mentioned before, 'fabricator', whose stratificatory roots date back to Nepal's protectionist era of the 1980s when the government allowed only so many businesses to be officially registered, and people with no political connections or 'source force' had to operate illegally as fabricators. I discussed in Chapter 4 how the politics of garment factory ownership changed after the new (and democratic) Industrial Policy of 1992 simplified procedures for business registration, making it open to all.

A decade after this, as the garment industry seemed destined to hit rock-bottom, following the WTO's decision to dismantle the MFA structure in 2004, a calculated rhetoric emerged among international diplomats and policymakers. Partly emboldened by local understandings about the 'inauthenticity' of the fabricators of the past, and partly strategized to pre-empt the brewing grievance against the state for its inaction in preparing Nepali factories to anticipate and prepare to face the catastrophic dismantling of the MFA, the perspective that gained currency was that Nepali claims to have had a genuine garment industry were fraudulent. Nancy Powell, the United States ambassador to Nepal at the time, suggested publicly that Nepal's garment exports might have merely been Chinese goods passing via Nepal, where the only value added to the garments by the Nepali exporters was to attach the label 'Made in Nepal'.[3] The Nepali government turned a blind eye to sweeping statements like these without ever issuing a single statement to correct the factual errors in such claims made by foreign dignitaries, thereby sealing the fate of some 90,000 workers who were directly employed in garment manufacturing, and many more who earned their livelihoods within the garment industry supply chain.

The roots of such public apathy in a supposedly democratic state perhaps lay within the flawed inner psyche about Nepal's place vis-à-vis India. A young bureaucrat at the Ministry of Industry and Commerce once put an cartographic spin on this idea of cross-border shift of a garment industry in this way: 'Just look at this map; it shows the best lit cities on earth.' There was a clear border visible between Nepal and India, with the Indian side much better lit than the Nepali side of the border. 'Now imagine if each instance of an Indian entering Nepal, especially the garment businessmen entering in the 1980s, was a lighted dot. Our side of the border would be the best lit patch on earth if we could show each Indian garment businessman who crossed the border to shift factories to Nepal.' During this leisurely conversation (*basibiyalo*), which went on for about an hour, everyone in the room happily agreed to a sweeping claim about the garment business reshuffling in South Asia after the MFA was put in place, that 'the Hindu businessmen from India had come to Nepal and the Muslims had gone to Bangladesh'. They seemed to believe that no amount of policy regulation would have put a stop to Indians snatching all budding business opportunities in Nepal. By this logic, then, Nepal need not have any policy response for the reversal of industrial labour relocation from Nepal, back to India.

The second issue here, especially if we pay attention to the excerpt in the earlier quote about 'Indian workers going back to India', involves the perception that garment workers were 'not Nepali' and hence their presence in the industry was not 'real' or sufficiently authentic. As much in the early days of the garment industry, in the 1980s, as during its demise two decades later, policymakers continued to assert that garment was an industrial 'dowry', or benevolent gift, from India (see Chapter 2 and 4). Because many Indians crossed the border to grab much of the Nepali share of the MFA quota in the late 1970s and early 1980s, the Nepali garment industry could indeed have been called 'Indian' at that point of time. But a lot happened in the two decades following the so-called 'flight,' which remained completely unacknowledged in the policy rhetoric in Kathmandu. See Chapter 2 for a discussion on how the garment industry has been 'Nepalized' in capital and labour, while diversifying the sourcing of its raw materials, and accomplishing an impressive technology upgrade in the 1990s (Shakya, 2004).

If we consider the labour employed in the garment sector, the 'old' garment workers – with over a decade's experience on the garment shop floors – had earlier worked in big cities in India, such as Delhi and Ludhiana. Ethnically, many were Madheshis from the Tarai flat lands spread across both sides of the Nepal-India border. The genealogies of the Madheshi garment workers were densely spread across both sides of the Nepal-India border, which was imagined and administered as 'open' for the citizens of the two countries to travel and migrate back and forth.[4] Although the popular Madheshi uprising of 2008 forced the Nepali state to consider borderland Madheshis as equal to other Nepalis (Sijapati, 2013; Gautam, 2008), one has to remember that the hill and valley people had been openly biased against Madheshis just few years prior to that uprising (Shakya, 2016). The biases were not going to go away so soon. The elite class, who held influential policy positions, were certainly not free from an anti-Madheshi bias, especially in a situation when the bias seemed to offer them an easy way out of a looming crisis that they were partly responsible for creating.

Despite the denial of this by policymakers, it has to be underscored that the 'new' garment workers, who joined the industry in the 1990s, came as much from within Kathmandu and the surrounding hills as from the plains of the Tarai. In stratificatory terms, garment work certainly attracted 'caste tailors': the 'untouchable' (or Dalit) caste of Damais from the hills, as well as the Muslim Darjees from the Tarai. As the industry expanded in scale, and the number of hill workers overtook those of Madheshis, the workforce also diversified in terms of caste, ethnicity, and region. It remained true, however, that there were fewer women working in the garment industry in Nepal than in Bangladesh or Sri Lanka. Less than fifteen percent of tailors were women in Nepal, compared to about 80 percent in Bangladesh and even more in Sri Lanka.[5] Gender aside, I will now further substantiate my claim that hill workers have been populating the garment workforce, along with their Madheshi counterparts, for at least a decade and half before the industry collapsed.

Labour ethnography of the garment shop floor

The 'old' Madheshi workers and 'new' hill workers had been assimilated seamlessly into the garment shop floors by the 1990s, as the industry underwent fundamental changes in factory set-ups and machinery. *Karigars*, originally artisans working under the patronage of a *thekedar*, or *naike*, and, later, individual workers operating as assembly line tailors, are at the heart of garment-making in all factories. I discussed in Chapter 4 that they need to be differentiated from the remaining blue collar workers (often referred to as 'staff', as opposed to the middle-level managers, who are called supervisors, technicians, store-keepers, etc.) on two counts. First, *karigars* were skilled in operating tailoring machines and were better paid, whereas 'staff' were unskilled, handling only simple tools such as measuring tapes and scissors, and hence lesser paid. Labour comprises about half of a factory's total costs,[6] of which the lion's share went to *karigars*. But there are other implications. While *karigars* were employed on job contracts that pay wages based on 'piece rates', the staff were regular employees on monthly salaries. The economic hierarchy between the two is obvious; a hard-working *karigar* would take home a whopping ten thousand rupees or so – three times more than what a non-gazetted government employee earns in Nepal – whereas most staff salaries were fixed at the government's minimum wage of three thousand rupees or so per month. Some 'staff' became *karigars* over time but not everybody chose to take that path because, as the saying goes among the garment people, to be a *karigar* was to become a *'byavasayi'* (entrepreneur): not only must s/he be prepared to work longer hours to earn more money, but s/he also must keep wide networks to find out about market wages and factory reputations, the bases on which to make deals with factories. To a certain extent, this explains why *karigars*, both among the Madheshis and the hill workers, remained overwhelmingly male in Nepal even when the industry became multi-ethnic and multi-regional over time.

Before the garment restructuring of the late 1980s, during the time when Madheshis dominated the garment labour force, each group or 'ring' of (ten to thirty) *karigars* swore loyalty to a contractor (*thekedar*) who negotiated a lump sum amount with factory owners and then determined individual work and pay within the ring.[7] These rings almost always drew on community and kinship ties, in that everybody was a Madheshi and most came from the *thekedar*'s village or kinship circle. The group travelled together to and from Kathmandu, and shared food and lodging while at work, including collectively looking after the young apprentices (*bakaras* or 'goats') within the group. They called their work system *'jugad'* (thrift, in Hindi), which was later modified by Nepali workers and businessmen to *'juwadi'* (gamblers) because their operating method involved setting up work in a circle, as if to play cards or to gamble, with workers systematically passing semi-finished cut pieces of fabrics around the circle for everybody's inputs. One of the defining features of a *juwadi* ring was that they owned their own machines, called *'tullu'* for the motors added on to what had originally been built as pedal-operated machines.[8] The *juwadi* system, an immediate precursor of the Taylorist assembly lines, dominated the Nepali garment industry until the late 1980s.

Nepal opened up its market in the early 1990s, and within half a decade or so, the garment industry had upgraded in both scale and sophistication (see Chapter 2 and 4). Most importantly, factories now invested money to buy their own tailoring machines, initially the Indian *'tullu'* machines, and later the Japanese, German and Taiwanese machines, which cost ten times more than the Indian machines but were more efficient. Such wholesale buying of sewing machines by factories was what virtually uprooted the old *juwadi* system, and dismantled the patronage of the *thekedar*s or *naike*s, while diversifying the ethnic composition of the industry. From being artisans owning their own tools, the *karigar*s now became the proletariat who sold their labour for wages. Further, the idea of 'skill' got redefined as the factories later came to adopt a 'scientific' assembly line system; jobs were anonymized to such an extent that a single tailor would add no more than a single straight stitch before it got passed to the next worker. The idea of skill was also transformed on three other counts. First, it was now the factory which decided how each machine and worker should be stationed on the shop floor; not communally as a group of workers, but rather by following 'scientific' methods of spatial organization, reinforced by indicators prescribed under global standards of practice. Second, the maintenance of machines now became the responsibility of technicians on a factory salary, and not the artisans. Third, it was no longer their 'own' *thekedar*, or one they considered *apna aadmi* (in Hindi, one with personal connections), who oversaw the quality and speed of their work but also arranged for their food and lodging while they are away from home during their seasonal stints in the garment factories. Now, they were directed by supervisors on factory salaries who went home after the shift, leaving the tailors to fend for themselves.

The sweeping changes that the worker-employer relationship underwent, on the garment shop floors in Nepal in the late 1980s and early 1990s, is almost reminiscent of what Marx had described about the Manchester factories in the late eighteenth century. The anonymization of work, which began with centralized labour recruitment *en masse* that put an end to the Madheshi dominance in the garment workforce, essentially disembedded workers from their social and political spheres and turned them into the proletariat. Earlier, the negotiations of businesses with *juwadi thekedar*s would take into account relationship and reputation in addition to price because a *thekedar* had to deal with expectations from 'his' ring of *juwadi*s. New recruitment for assembly line workers was in 'piece rate' wages only. As long as one was able bodied, and had a basic knowledge of tailoring, he or she could be employed. Piece-rate contracts were such that both the factory and worker were free to back out at any time. Factories fired workers the day their purchase orders were complete, and workers quit the day they found better wages somewhere else. In fact, labour turnover in the garment industry assembly lines was one of the highest in the country because of the seasonality of production, which meant that *karigar*s had to always be ready for a change of job, either to avoid unemployment or to secure higher wages.[9]

Labour anonymization also forced the industry into a fierce competitive spiral, where the fittest survived and the rest didn't. An average garment factory used to have three hundred or so tailoring machines before labour anonymization; but within a few years, they had doubled or tripled in size. Momento Apparels, the largest garment factory in Kathmandu, with well over a thousand machines (and tailors), was owned by a hill Bahun-Chhetri, Chandi Raj Dhakal, who went on to head both the Garment Association of Nepal and the Federation of the National Chamber of Commerce before being mired in corruption scandals. Another large factory with just under one thousand machines (and workers), Cotton Comforts, was also owned by hill Bahun-Chhetris, and they went on to win the 'best performer' award for several years in a row. Outside Kathmandu, Surya Garments, on the border with India and also owned by hill Bahun-Chhetris, ran fifteen hundred machines. Tens of thousands of hill workers had joined the garment industry by the late 1990s, and the number of Madheshis had declined so much that they had to be defended by their hill co-workers when xenophobic riots engulfed the streets of Kathmandu in 2001 over statements allegedly made by a Bollywood film star, which hurt the feelings of the Nepali hill people (Shakya, 2013b).

Surrounding the core of *karigar*s were the unskilled staff, and almost all of them were from the hills and valleys. Once the *'pallas'* (pieces of fabrics) were cut out from the large sheets of textile, a large 'sorting' team – almost all women and from the hills – tied up set-pieces neatly into marked bundles, and assigned them to the correct *karigar*s in the assembly lines. Line supervisors – all male and mostly from the hills – were responsible for planning the number of 'tasks' and the 'jobbers' required for each. If necessary, tailored pieces were then sent for embroidery or screen-printing. Then came the largest unit – all females again from the hills – which sat together to patiently and painstakingly cut the loose threads from the tailored pieces. When complete, these pieces were then sent to the 'finishing' department again manned by hill workers where they would be cleaned (through petrol spray or dry cleaning if required), labelled for size, pressed, and then packed into specified cardboard boxes. It is safe to say that the elites' racist and ultranationalist dismissal of the garment workforce as 'Indian' had no evidence on the actual shop floors.

Three phases of a Union movement

The misplaced policy rhetoric on the ethnic and national rooting of Nepal's garment industry seemed to have little regard for voices from shop floors and their social and political contexts. In discussions about what was needed for the steady development of the garment industry in Nepal, it soon became common practice among policy makers and aid donors to make Unionism the culprit of the garment disaster (see Chapter 5). Clearly, this narrative of blaming the Unions suited businessmen and policymakers alike because it offered simple answers to complex problems. I discuss below a charged public debate staged upon the closure of what many would say was the last standing garment factory of Nepal.

Surya Nepal Garments was officially shut down on August 16, 2011, after surviving seven years beyond MFA expiry, which had already caused several other factories to shut down much earlier. Prominently reporting this on its front page, a national daily, *The Republica*, squarely blamed Maoist Trade Union leader Tej Lal Karna, whose men had allegedly locked up some of the managers in Surya Nepal, and according to national media, threatened to physically harm them.[10] This unruly behaviour of the Union activists, the newspaper claimed, had not only cost 3,000 workers their jobs but had also cost the business one billion rupees in lost turnover. It was considered even more unfortunate that the Unions were attacking the last remaining garment factory, one that had managed to capture the emerging South Asia market after the United States shut its doors to Nepali garments. This news report was backed by a strong editorial the next day,[11] which wrote, 'We ... demand in the strongest terms that the political parties promptly de-politicize the trade union movement. We believe this is crucial for restoring investor confidence at a time when the country is in dire need of investments for generating employment and keeping the economy afloat.'

A week later came an opinion piece penned by Rameshwor Khanal, who was in the public eye at the time for having tendered his resignation from the post of Secretary of Finance, the most senior position in the public bureaucracy managing the nation's economy. His resignation had been especially acrimonious because it came a few months after the Nepali Maoists joined the coalition cabinet following a general election. The Maoists had garnered a large number of seats, but no single party could muster enough votes to elect a Prime Minister. That the former guerrilla rebels had been 'mainstreamed' into democratic politics was a watershed moment in Nepali history. With this came a growing polarization between the liberals and the left, with speculation as to which way the moderate Communist Party of Nepal, United Marxist Leninist (UML hereafter) would tilt. Tensions grew as Jhala Nath Khanal – known to be more sympathetic to the Maoists than his predecessor, Madhav Kumar Nepal from the same party – took over.[12] There were rumours that the new Left cabinet sought to side-line pro-liberalization Secretary Rameshwor Khanal during the preparation of the national budget.[13] So, when Secretary Khanal finally tendered his resignation, just two months after the new Prime Minister took oath, the liberal camp quickly portrayed him as a great democratic legend. A comparison was swiftly made with a similar resignation: Devendra Raj Panday had quit as the Secretary of Finance soon after the 1980-81 referendum, as a mark of opposition against the Panchayat system, and had later joined the Nepali Congress, to eventually become the Minister of Finance under the caretaker government when Nepal ousted the Panchayat regime and became democratic in 1990. Almost paralleling the moves of his predecessor, but disappointing many who expected him to join liberal politics, Secretary Khanal later briefly took affiliations with a new party, Naya Shakti, founded by his former arch enemy, the former Prime Minister Baburam Bhattarai, the key ideologue of the Maoist People's War in Nepal (see Chapter 7).

Considering that Rameshwor Khanal later joined the left-leaning Naya Shakti, it was remarkable, at the time, that he took up the issue of Unionism immediately after his high profile resignation in August 2011. In a well-publicized opinion piece that might have been his first public statement since his resignation,[14] he regretted the Union attack on a factory that had chosen to locate itself in the economically backward town of Biratnagar to help regional and national development. After those making 'hefty profits' on the back of MFA privilege had left the field, Khanal wrote, it was 'Surya Nepal [that] wanted to be a phoenix and prove that nothing is invincible …. Seven years later, they learned that they were wrong!' Khanal blamed the closure of Surya Nepal on a splinter faction of the Maoist trade Union that had called a strike 'for no fault of the factory.' His argument seemed to be that the Unions should have celebrated the fact that at least one factory was doing well and some of their fellow workers still had their jobs at a time when the rest of the industry was already dead. In that piece, Khanal mocked the Union leaders who had supposedly turned up riding motorbikes and waving cell phones fancier than what the businessmen they were protesting against could afford. Khanal's opinion piece ended on an emotional note, '… my tears on the closure of Surya Nepal Garments!'

The Unions disagreed. One factory-level Union leader said, 'The *sahu* (employer) wants us workers to be what he is, self-centred and cunning *shyal* (foxes). That is how they have been ruling us till this date. But we who live on our toil (*pasina bagaayera khaneharu*) are not like them; our blood is different. They want us to look away when our brothers are thrown away jobless and are crying out for help. That cannot be done. For us, money is not everything, *nyaya* (justice) is, and they better know this. Workers will fight for justice and to protect their rights (*adhikaar ko rakshako laagi ladnechhan*).' A full-time Union activist Datta, whom I met much later, in the centre-left Union federation, had a more mature perspective that recalled his varied experience with businessmen of different temperaments and styles. An American buyer who was impressed by Datta's personal charisma had once even offered to take him to the United States because he thought he could persuade 'the blacks and the Latins' in his factory to work harder. A Nepali businessman once broke down in public when Datta tried to tell him not to fight the workers too hard since he had no sons to inherit his wealth. Another, a Nepali businesswoman, who had been sabotaging his moves in her factory, was so impressed upon finally meeting him in person that she publicly gave him a hug and promised to be co-operative, though little of that finally materialized in deed. The gist of what Datta wanted to say was that all these men and women in different situations and with different temperaments were members of the same 'capital class', who supported one another, and that workers needed to do the same: when 'brothers' in one factory lost their jobs, others needed to strike in solidarity. As the entire industry was shutting down, businessmen running few 'islands of success' should not think that their workers would not take up the cause of those who had sunk in the 'ocean of despair.' 'No one has forgotten', he said, 'that an entire cohort of garment factories had chewed up the workers and then spit them out while the state remained a passive bystander.' Who could they trust but their own class?

Early activism: a Union *for* workers

The garment industry had become one of the largest employers in Nepal by the early 1990s, yet it was not for another two decades that a Union movement emerged on the garment shop floors. It is true that the first ever Union strike was held in Biratnagar Jute Mills in 1975, under the leadership of Nepali Congress stalwart Girija Prasad Koirala. This strike had virtually no labour-specific demands, and was essentially one front of the broader political movement aiming for a national regime change. A few decades later, the left-leaning parties, still underground during the one-party Panchayat regime, founded a General Federation of Nepali Trade Unions (GEFONT hereafter). After successfully ousting the Panchayat regime in 1990, the Nepali Congress founded its own Nepal Trade Union Congress (NTUC hereafter) in 1992, under the new democratic law allowing Union formation. A decade and half later, Maoist guerrillas launched their own popular resistance on the shop floors in addition to fighting a violent People's War in the countryside. They eventually founded a new Union body in 2006, All Nepal Trade Union Front (ANTUF hereafter).

Democratic rule legalized and strengthened the Union movement in the 1990s, but early unionization, at least in the garment industry, was more enterprise-driven than worker-driven. For example, in the early 1990s, when the new labour laws[15] made it mandatory for firms with more than ten workers to have a Union, almost all of the garment factory owners quickly signed up with NTUC. The reason, the factory owners told me, was that NTUC's Nepali Congress was, after all, the party that had brought democracy to Nepal. It also served them well that the relatively posh neighbourhood of New Baneswor in the heart of Kathmandu, where most of the garment factories were situated at the time, was considered a stronghold of the Nepali Congress.[16] Workers conceded that the justification for the factory owners embracing the Nepali Congress was valid, emphasizing that the Nepali Congress had good people who had suffered prolonged imprisonment and torture to fight for democracy (*jail-nail bhogeka*). However, when probed further about workers' democratic rights and justice for the downtrodden, the workers dismissed this as 'politics' and that whey might as well let the owners handle such issues, since they themselves were on the shop floors to 'shed the toil' after all – a statement I unpack below while recounting Union trajectories on the garment shop floor.

The first step towards Unionization came from the owners. It was they, not the workers, who registered the first Unions in their factories, after Nepal democratized. One owner went to the extent of nominating himself as the President of the Union in his factory. He did not face any resistance from workers, who merely voted as he asked. The Unions did not quite know how to handle this; the newly written Labour Act of 1992, issued by the Ministry of Labour, had directed that only junior employees with operative and administrative jobs could join Unions, while the Trade Union Act of 1992, issued by the Ministry of Trade and Commerce, kept it open for managerial staff to join the union ranks. This ambiguity provided the ground for a pro-capital NTUC affiliated with Nepali Congress to accept one owner's nomination as Union head. The rhetoric he maintained was that, since the factory was a family, especially in its practice of producing craft invoking cultural tradition, he, as the patriarch, should lead the workers in both work and the Union.

In mass factories where owners did not take up Union positions, they still engineered its functions. One such factory, located in Sitapaila in northwestern Kathmandu, entered into an alliance with NTUC, and ensured that the Union head worked more for the factory owners than the workers. This was demonstrated when the factory faced hostility from both local gangsters, whose local quarters had been taken over by the factory, as well as local householders, whose agrarian idyll was disturbed by the factory's presence. To resolve this, the factory summoned NTUC's man in the neighbourhood – the 'chairman' as people addressed him – who was also a muscular black-belt in martial arts. The Chairman started his 'mission' of taming the gangsters and winning local hearts by expediting and expanding the outreach of philanthropic activities the factory had already initiated. For example, a local sewer system was constructed and existing electricity distribution lines were extended to reach nearby villages, which earned significant goodwill for the factory from the locals. A (Hindu) temple was consecrated on the factory premises with complete provision for daily prayers (See Chapter 5). Subsequently, the Chairman recruited a number of his loyalists into the factory workforce, who acted as unofficial security guards to keep a close eye on local gangsters. During times when tensions built, these men would be ready to fight off gangsters who tried to disrupt factory operations.

During all of these assignments, the Chairman's 'point person' in the factory was the Production Manager, whose office became the Chairman's *adda* (base) during his factory visits, with an endless supply of tea and biscuits. From what I could see, his interaction with the workers, save those who he recruited to the system, was limited to a polite nod of *namaste*. No public events had ever been organized for workers and no collective bargaining had ever taken place on issues concerning wages and conditions of work. On the rare occasions when there were accidents involving workers and compensation was due from the owners, the Chairman mediated between the two parties to negotiate a settlement, but almost always upon the request of factory owners, not the workers.

Keeping the Unions at an arm's length was a practice that the workers I spoke to during my earliest fieldwork (2002–2003) said was 'good' for everybody because, after all, 'we [they] are a new industry and we are here to work to take home money, not to do politics; Unions are not for us.' Many said that a garment worker was not a member of the proletariat but a free entrepreneur (*byavasayi*) because of the 'piece-rate' practice. Even if the 'freedom' associated with his idea of 'enterprise' was just that his employers did not pay him pension and other benefits, garment *karigars* considered themselves superior to their salaried counterparts who earned much less. While the factories hired and fired workers at will, workers were not at a loss as long as the industry ran smoothly, in that some factory was always recruiting when another factory paused operations.

We cannot ignore two important aspects that contributed to this disinterest of the workers towards the Unions. The first was a neoliberal spirit, of individual freedom and merit-based progress, which piggybacked on the rhetoric of democracy in Nepal. That factory workers and owners had marched together during pro-democracy protests sowed the seeds for a kind of utopian illusion where the reasonably better-paid *karigars* agreed with the views of factory owners; equating democracy with a set of individual (economic) freedoms, such as the freedom to consume as one wished, and take up jobs in one's chosen field. The second, with deeper implications for workers, was the inability of the Unions to engage with new forms of labour. Unions took a one-track approach: collective bargaining was all about raising wages and making 'temporary' workers 'permanent'. It hardly considered the majority view, at least within the garment industry and especially as the MFA deadline came closer, that workers wanted more clarity on the future of the industry where their contracts were situated and they also sought Union support seeking protection in times of turbulence.

The dialogues between Unions and workers concerning the garment industry were, hence, mutually frustrating. GEFONT was hesitant to give even general membership to 'piece-rate' workers, let alone any space in its full-time positions. It did not help the garment workers that GEFONT had put in place a complex apparatus of Union hierarchy and by-laws that tied its own hands with regard to which workers they could have as members. The few garment workers who did take up membership with GEFONT were then made to sit, at Union meetings, next to a bigger pool of salaried textile workers, a sector one-twentieth of the size of the garment sector, and listen to ideas of how collective bargaining could get them salaried contracts. The Union was silent on the question of wage rates; and salaries could not compare with the going piece-rate wages because the garment industry 'piece-rates' were much higher than the regular salaries in other industries. This left the garment workers with little incentive to join the Union. On the one hand, *karigars* had always looked down upon their salaried counterparts because they did dull tasks and were tied to one factory and one owner through their contracts. On the other hand, *karigar*s considered their higher income to be a result of their individual hard work and enterprise (*gari khayeko*) and scorned the 'labour mentality' of working in one place (*basi basi khanu*) and 'cooking salaries' (*talab pakaunu*). The idea that GEFONT was going to turn them into salaried staff in the name of Union justice was not something they found too appealing. Most 'piece-rate' garment workers left GEFONT after few meetings.

There was one more reason why garment workers kept their distance from the Unions, and *vice versa*. NTUC and GEFONT were both dominated by Bahun-Chhetris from the hills who also wore the same tinted lens through which policymakers viewed the garment industry: that it was 'Indian' because the majority of *karigar*s in the garment industry were Madheshis. A new party, Nepal Sadbhavana Party, had sprung up in the 1990s to represent the Madheshi constituency, but its ideology remained insulated from class consciousness. It was only in 2008 that the Madheshi movement gained new heights and a new party, Madheshi Janadhikar Forum (Forum hereafter), began to flex its muscles in the arena of national politics; but even then, it kept its distance from issues related to class.

An anecdote I heard from one of the GEFONT leaders about a Union meeting held in 2014 speaks volumes about the (absence of) the politics of labour within the Madheshi parties. An aid donor convened a trade Union meeting to discuss labour policy in Nepal. GEFONT and NTUC had respectable representation in that meeting. The Prachanda faction of the Maoist trade Union ANTUF was represented by Shalikram Jammarkattel, who initially led a team of Union 'Young Turks' but later went on to preside over the Maoist party's central Union. The Baidya faction of ANTUF was not represented, nor was the Federal Socialist Party, which was newly formed to represent the interests of hill Janajatis. There was a spectrum of Unions with links to various Madheshi parties. The Forum, by then the fourth largest party in Nepal, had its Union represented by a virtual non-entity – someone who had never worked with Unions and with no labour credentials other than having worked as a barber himself, and that he used to be a lowly cadre member of the Nepali Congress before joining the Forum. Two other factions of Madheshi parties that attended the meeting were worse; they sent people with no associations with labour movements, and who, according to GEFONT leaders, simply made a laughing stock of themselves. Mainstream parties commented that Madheshis had brought back the Panchayati politics of 'tokenism', whereby the feudal lords had their wives and mistresses head women's associations, while their loyal servants headed workers' fora. In 2007,

GEFONT launched a joint trade Union coordination centre intending to avoid exactly this kind of situation, arguing that Unions should have a joint representative body rather than be divided along party lines[17].

An interlude of Maoist politics

The rise of Maoists in Union politics at the turn of the century deserves a closer look. The Maoist movement's second national convention, in 2001, marked a major breakthrough when it ratified the 'Prachanda Path', Nepal's own version of The Great Leap Forward, which called on its cadre to expand its base from rural to urban areas (Hutt, 2004). The practice of *chanda sankalan* (collection of donations) became the Maoist way of mobilizing urban factories to contribute to the People's War they were waging in the remote hills. While other parties had also collected *chanda*, none were quite so aggressive as the Maoists. For one, Maoists did not simply come and beg for money as other parties did, but turned the act of charity collection into their core political strategy for finance collection. A typical garment factory owner, for example, would receive proselytizing communications on Maoist letterheads about the *sarvahara* (proletarian) revolution; this would be duly followed up by telephone calls, requesting a secret meeting to discuss their contributions to it. At the meeting, the businessman would learn that it was not a request for voluntary donation, but a demand for a carefully calculated figure to be paid as a levy. This figure could be anywhere between a few thousand and several lakh Nepali rupees, even after negotiation. It shocked the businessmen that Maoists had access to their 'real' account books (as opposed to the 'official' books submitted for formal auditing). What also intrigued them was that Maoists had ethnicized their coercive politics of funding (*chanda atanka*). There were claims that the Maoists were lenient on the Janajati entrepreneurs while the so-called 'feudals' (Bahun-Chhetris) and 'imperialists' (Marwaris, Madheshis and Indians) were treated harshly (See Chapter 5).

Ceasefires offered the Maoists breathing space from rural guerilla warfare, and also allowed them time and energy to mobilize urban shop floors for peaceful, if militant, resistance. The first government-rebel ceasefire was brokered in July 2001 under a Nepali Congress cabinet, during which the Maoists openly organized mass meetings in Kathmandu. Their cadres canvassed factories calling on owners to send their workers to attend Maoist mass meetings. While most factory owners felt it wise to comply with the request, some did not, and had their factories vandalized in retaliation. Star Fashion Garments of Hattiban, for example, only had a few window glasses broken by stone pelting, whereas Roli Garments of Balaju incurred bigger losses after a 'pressure cooker bomb' was planted in its premises. The businesses had hoped that their earlier ally, NTUC, would come to their help, but it remained a passive bystander. It also came as a surprise to the factory owners that their trusted workers, who they had believed would come back to work after attending the Maoist meetings, chose to remain and participate in sloganeering against class exploitation. Within a few months of proselytization and mobilization, the shop floors had clearly turned red.

As the owners put it, workers became *chhunai nasakine* (uncontrollable) and the work had stalled on the shop floors. Those who saw themselves as the best paid 'workers-cum-entrepreneurs' (*karigars*) until a few weeks ago, now demanded 'proper' contracts with 'proper' salary and benefits. The same workers who had earlier dismissed GEFONT's call for an end to casual work in factories, now walked shoulder-to-shoulder with the Maoists, calling for the several hundred subcontracted workers to be made permanent factory employees. To the relief of the factory owners, the government-Maoist ceasefire collapsed in November 2001 and the government took a firmer stance against the rebels. Some owners were quick to call the police into the factories. The Maoist activists had already gone underground by the time the police came; the police could only arrest factory workers whom the owners identified as fervent Maoist supporters. The long held belief about the factory being 'one big family of owners and workers' was in tatters as the workers picked up the pieces of their broken spirit and resumed work after this brutal crackdown.

The Maoists resurfaced in January 2003, following a second ceasefire called by royalist Prime Minister Lokendra Bahadur Chand.[18] This time, most businesses quickly secured a negotiated settlement with the Maoists by paying necessary 'donations'. A deal was brokered through mediation of the stalwarts of a civil society movement who had wanted the Maoists to join hands with other political parties in overturning the royalist take of power.[19] While most garment factory owners backed this dialogue, some stayed out. The entrepreneurs who had received more lenient treatment from the Maoists, mostly the Janajatis, chose to deal with the Maoists individually (see Chapter 5). The hardliners, royalists, and Indians wanted a royal military protection of factory premises against Maoists. Amid the chaos and confusion, the Maoists announced an end to the ceasefire in August of the same year, and went back underground; garment factories returned to business as usual.

Collapse of the industry and the Union *of* workers

The Maoists' return to war more or less coincided with the MFA expiry that caused the collapse of the bulk of the garment industry, even if a few managed to keep afloat for up to half a decade more. The fact that tens of thousands of people were losing jobs at a time when the nation was ringing with calls to revolution led to a seismic shift in the consciousness of: the working class. A particularly intriguing aspect is the manner in which both Maoists and democrats seized upon this new public imagination and appropriated the Union movement for their own transformative strategies. While the Maoists argued for a complete overhaul of the labour Union mechanism and the wholesale rejection of the state's take on labour, the democrats called for an end to labour anarchy so that potential entrepreneurs, interested in the garment sector, might be encouraged to conceptualize new businesses that could potentially bring employment for the jobless workers and prosperity for all.

Nothing had prepared the workers for a collapse on the scale that we saw in the garment industry, between 2003-2006, though some of the owners might have had an inkling of the oncoming catastrophe. Factories fell like dominoes, one after another, day after day, until there remained just six or seven factories in 2006, from over two hundred factories in 2002, and where there had been over a thousand in 1995. All attempts to revive the industry failed, including seeking aid from international donors, and lobbying for leniency on tariff in the US and European parliaments. The livelihood of garment workers was destroyed, triggering an exodus to India, Asia, Africa, and the West that I described earlier. Those who chose to remain either quietly found other jobs, or decided to reach out to the Unions.

'We just want an answer; we just want to understand,' was the voice emerging unanimously (*ek mukhle bhannu*) among the workers. After all, there had never been an acknowledgement of the suffering of the garment workers, let alone a formal policy response or even some informal support from the state. Factory after factory padlocked its gates, with almost no prior notice to workers and almost no explanation, even as the tragedy befell; no one knew what, if anything, could have saved them from closure. The workers suffered because they had no sources of information about the industry, except the rumour grapevine, and this remained the case even as the crisis hit. It is true that garment workers had seen extreme seasonality: factories routinely went on recess between purchase orders, and some would even shut down if orders got cancelled or consignments derailed. But it had never been the case that so many factories shut down together, leaving workers nowhere to find jobs. What was worse was that owners and managers stayed out of reach to protect themselves from the angry workers. Many of the owners and managers emigrated abroad permanently, like Navin from Arya-Nepal did. Workers could not get past the padlocks on the factory gates, to speak to anyone, who would at least hear them out, even if he or she could not provide material support. 'What we see is darkness all around us; what we hear is silence that deafens us,' one worker told me, as he stared at the big padlock hanging on the main gate of the factory that still held his wages for the past few weeks of labour.

Eventually, disgruntled workers knocked on the doors of the Unions. They could not reach the Maoists who were underground at this time, and NTUC and GEFONT were not very responsive. The impasse gave way, however, as it emerged that a small group of vanguard Union cadre from GEFONT were prepared to back the garment workers, going against the Union rank and file. Workers soon crowded the office of this GEFONT Union splinter group that was clearly going rogue. Soon rumours began to make the rounds that there were Maoists within GEFONT, and that its garment faction was actually no longer just GEFONT. Even so, no direct connections were made at this time between GEFONT's garment faction and the Maoists' formal Union, founded as early as 1996, All Nepal Free Trade Union (ANFTU). Maoists hardly raised the Union banner even when they took workers to mass meetings during the 2001 and 2003 ceasefires. The same remained the case as this GEFONT faction led by Salik Ram Jammarkattel among others backed a rag-tag group of garment workers, calling for a revolution that would right the wrongs in how the resources and opportunities had allocated historically, not only across class but also caste and ethnicity. A significant turning point came only when the Maoists signed the 12-point agreement with the democratic Seven Party Alliance (SPA) in November 2006, which secured a long-term peace deal and gave the Maoists space within mainstream politics. Soon afterwards, ANFTU merged with another faction affiliated with the communist party, Ekata Kendra (Unity Centre), and named itself All Nepal Trade Union Federation (ANTUF). As the Maoists went on to join the parliament in January 2007, they sent clear signals that ANTUF, along with other grassroots level organizations, would be their new battleground.

Almost the entire rank and file of ANTUF's executive committee came from GEFONT's rebellious garment worker wing that I talked about earlier. Within days of formally crossing the floor, this dissident faction went on to label GEFONT the 'old establishment', and hence a class enemy, which needed to be uprooted for a revolution to really take hold. They openly declared that GEFONT's comprehensive by-laws about a contractual requirement for Union membership was obsolete because a Union should not need a piece of paper from the capitalist establishment to prove he (or she) is a worker; it should be his or her fellow comrades who should be able to vouch for his class identity.' With this, and with the simmering anger at the failed garment industry hitting an all-time high, ANTUF became the new Union prince among garment workers. Within a few years of its founding, it overtook other Unions by a large margin, eventually boasting of a million members – more than double the combined membership of all three existing Unions. The ANTUF workers, with a large majority belonging to the garment sector, indeed became the mass who marched in all Maoist protests, not only on issues of labour but on everything involving transformation of the nation.

As the vanguard of the Union movement descended upon the streets of Kathmandu, the capitalist hypotheses about Unions led to a (misplaced) optimism about the garment industry. While most of the garment mass manufacturers had shut down by this time, the craft producers were doing business as usual (see Chapter 4). If anything, they had ambitious plans to take over the abandoned infrastructure and machines of the mass manufacturers to modernize their own systems. One such business, A&E Boutique, had just completed the construction of its new factory which cost over a hundred million rupees, a very handsome sum of money by Nepali standards. Other craft manufacturers had similar plans, and they seemed to genuinely believe that workers uprooted from mass manufacturing would come to them to beg for work, and that the high-priced tailoring machines lying unused would soon be available dirt-cheap. But these expectations were proven wrong, and the plans for upgrade had to be shelved because their workers too turned against them as Unionism gained ground elsewhere within the industry.

Craft producers were convinced that their workers faced no imminent threat of losing their jobs, and so they felt they should consider themselves lucky. Workers attributed such reasoning to a capitalist psyche (*punjivadi sochai*), unsuitable for a 'new' Nepal intent on reversing neoliberal trends. For one, workers had their own grudges about payment and treatment. For another, after the ongoing mayhem in the mass sector, a new discourse was gaining ground among the working class, that only a regulated workforce could ensure protection to workers when disaster struck, and that workers could not afford to isolate themselves from Unions at any point in time. What complicated the matter further was the violent rivalry between Unions, initially between

GEFONT and ANTUF, but eventually between the two factions within ANTUF, after it split following the split of the Maoist party in 2012, which only added to labour militancy. The bickering among the Unions split workers who had earlier been part of a unified front. As rival Unions took increasingly radical positions on issues relating to wages and working conditions, labour militancy escalated further. Most of the remaining garment factories especially those belonging to the craft sector shut shop during this last wave of militancy.

Class, culture, union

Among the few vicinities within Kathmandu where garment factories still continued their operations, however minimally, was a neighbourhood in the southeastern end, Gwarko. The local politics in this corner of the valley was strikingly different from elsewhere, and one that brought back culture and ethnicity into Union organization. In the early 1990s, when new labour laws made Unions mandatory and almost all factories registered themselves with the pro-capital NTUC, factories located in Gwarko had remained left-leaning. Reflecting on this, Varun, who owned a factory in Gwarko, had told me in 2002 that he was also a 'Congressi' at heart and would vote so in the election, but that he considered it only fair to let the workers go with GEFONT because, 'that corner of the Valley (or *tole*) is red and to let Congressis cross their threshold would be an act of betrayal of class.' A few years later, when the ultra-red Maoists began to flex their muscles against moderate-left GEFONT, Varun refused to let his workers attend Maoist programmes or even pay Maoist levies; he renewed his allegiance with GEFONT against the Maoist ANTUF. His name was later seen near the top of the 'black list' of the most watched capitalists that the Maoists circulated, but no physical harm was done to this factory. 'It is the *tole* that protected me,' Varun mulled, claiming that he was the 'Gwarko man' which inplied that he shared ethnic and cultural ties with the community in his *tole*, who would not let harm come his way. Eventually the Maoists lost interest as he proved a hard nut to crack.

Over the following years, as Unionism rocked the ailing garment industry, Varun's factory also had labour uprisings on the shop floors, with workers demanding higher wages, better employment conditions, and social welfare. Varun downsized his operations substantially after having raised workers' wages by 40 percent as business and labour associations had agreed. When I met him around the time when Surya Nepal was shutting down, Varun's factory was running at one-tenth of its original capacity. When I asked how was it that labour relations in his factory were not inflamed amid the heightened drama that was being acted out elsewhere in the industry, he emphasized his 'rootedness' to the *tole* community. Varun's *tole* underwent several political changes during the following years. On the one hand, several young people from Gwarko had, by then, ditched UML and joined the Maoists, while the older generation stayed with the moderate left. On the other hand, there was a renewed sense of ethnic and communal solidarity, as social inclusion and ethnicity-based federalization became new rhetoric on national transformation. It appeared that the cultural bodies, whose scope had been earlier limited to *guthis* (communal trusts), *jatras* (festivals), and *pujas* (religious rituals), were now beginning to flex their muscles in grassroots politics of autonomy, inclusion, and local wellbeing.

The *tole sudhar samiti* (locality development committee) of Gwarko, a modern body of local politics but with representation of the elite and activist families from the community, was instrumental in ensuring that partisan politics did not compromise local welfare and communal harmony. It spoke the language of local patronage; that shops, factories, temples, and charities belonging to the *tole* should be looked after (*swaya ma*) by people of the *tole*. At times, *tole* activists came forward to mediate Varun's negotiations with ANTUF on labour-related issues. In fact, this transitory phase of new local politics seemed to suggest that local elites and activists of the *tole sudhar samiti* were among the very few who could wade through the charged politics of labour militancy and reactionary crackdown. How long and how well such anomalous alliances between the classes will persist is something that can only be seen with time. It may take years, if not decades, before anything could be said definitively about how various social movements may cross paths in the nooks and crannies of Kathmandu. The new patronage of culture, which upheld class interests while protecting *projet capitalisme*, seems to both complement and contest conventional class politics that dismissed 'culture' as either obsolete or feudal in character.

Can we read the Gwarko story thorugh a lens of subalterneity, while situating it within the broader garment Unionism? Partha Chatterjee (1986, 2004) proposed that democracy alone may incorporate the 'political' elements of class and culture into a modern, secular civil society, but warned that the modernization of the 1990s may have unleashed a new subalternization process in South Asia. While Nepal's democratization echoed predatory modernization, Unionism's response to it, at the turn of the century, came at a time which Michael Burawoy called 'the third wave of marketization',[20] one which disembedded markets from society even more. Ironically, the 'making' of a new class of workers, facing extreme disenfranchization in the face of MFA expiry in the garment sector, almost resonates with Breman's (2004) account of the 'unmaking' of an industrial working class of textile workers in Ahmedabad, India in the face of privatization in the 1970s and 1980s. Speaking about the new wave of neoliberal state politics few decades later, Amita Baviskar and Nandini Sundar (2008) have suggested a double-edged outcome of the paradox of democracy and corporate neoliberalism: state withdrawal from concerns of social justice, on the one hand, and policies for protection of corporate interests, on the other. The resulting social and political movements may give rise to a new subaltern, hit doubly by the double-edged sword, and possibly committed to resisting both, triggering a Polanyian 'double movement'.

At the heart of the disembedding phenomenon in Nepal's garment industry lay the state's and popular media's apathy to labour grievances in the face of the double jeopardy of neoliberal hegemony and social oppression. Ironically enough, a new proletariat movement was gaining momentum in Nepal just as the third wave of marketization hit the globe. As workers became disillusioned after losing their jobs, and receiving no support from the state, they went on to build a collective movement almost from scratch. While the mainstream Unions remained indifferent to concerns of the new proletariat, the state media that gave echoed the voice of the elites adopted a heavy-handed approach, either dismissing labour grievances as the sour grapes of incompetence, or delegitimizing garment workers as 'un-Nepali'. The Ministry's blunt response to the demise of the garment industry – that 'it fell because it was not competitive enough' – almost echoed its global buyers' disembedded mercantilism, that buyers are like 'fleas' who abandon dogs when they fall sick. This vacuum was eventually filled by a new labour militancy that took up the Maoist banner and challenged the 'old regime' (*purano satta*) as a whole, thus connecting labour concerns with a wide range of social-political demands, including a secular republic that would acknowledge the cultures of the non-ruling ethnic communities, as in the case of Gwarko.

Why were existing Unions indifferent to the calls of the new proletariat? Comparing Nepal with South Africa, which also democratized during the 1990s and faced a new wave of Union militancy at the turn of the century, Buhlungu (2001) called this a 'paradox of victory', a reflection of the way that the old notions of sacrifice had been replaced by a new individualist ethic of material gain. Leaders of the mainstream Unions seemed to have taken up opportunities offered by neoliberal democracy to consolidate their own power within the Union movement. A case in point is Bishnu Rimal, the founder Secretary General of GEFONT, with degrees in business management and engineering science, who dominated GEFONT for fifteen years, through most of Nepal's democratic era. Rimal was the hand that helped GEFONT through its modest beginnings as an underground rebel outfit to becoming a 'giant Confederation' after democracy. His role during the turbulent Unionism within the garment industry was solicitous: the rigid bureaucracy he had constructed for GEFONT kept the agitating garment workers out of Union reach, but Rimal kept his cool as his own activists ditched him to found a revolutionary ANTUF under the Maoist banner. He was candid, '... we built the formal Union without which we cannot fight Union battles, but reflecting on it, it might be true that this mechanism did not address the concerns of those who lay at the peripheries of the industrial core.' Later, as the ANTUF movement waned and it too sought to institutionalize its cadre, especially after its own split along that of the Maoist party, its leaders came to Rimal to seek advice and support.

What do we make of the new Unions, especially in the garment industry, voicing the grievances of those victimized by new marketization? It can be said that they took the 'broadening' road under the Maoist banner, a trajectory bearing an uncanny resemblance to the unionization of South Africa – a country with a parallel calendar of democratization and labour militancy – in the 1980s, which spoke of a broader culture or rights (Beckman et al, 2006). In South Africa and Nepal, and indeed elsewhere in the Third World, the new Unionism seemed to originate from the fissures in old Unions, linked to issues of complacency and rigid bureaucracy, but above all to the individualistic ethic of material gain promoted by neoliberal capitalism. Any substantial effort to comprehend what is happening to labour in Third World geographies would have to acknowledge a global paradigm shift at the turn of the century, when neoliberalism co-opted democracy and questioned its credibility for the groups left behind. Yet most of the explanations given by labour sociologists and anthropologists are based on the assumption that there is a clear-cut dichotomy between 'full-time' and 'shop floor' Unionism, or between political and civil societies (Hensman, 2011).

Neoliberalism has blurred the lines between political and civil societies, a reflection of what had happened in Nepal just a few decades ago as a unified Union-Party struggle ousted the Panchayat regime in 1990. A decade and a half later, as labour militancy splintered existing Unions, a synthesizing trajectory seemed to emerge again. A vanguard ANTUF inserted itself into the Union scene by challenging GEFONT as the gatekeeper of the old regime (*purano satta*) that chose to ignore the striking workers. Fifty or so violent clashes erupted between the two Unions, as the new Union tested its reach, especially experimenting with alliances with new local mobilizers in old cultural *toles* which now hosted new industrial life such as garment factories. Eventually, however, the two Unions became collaborative partners in the Joint Trade Union Coordination Committee (JTUCC), which had been originally founded by GEFONT as an anti-ANTUF alliance with its lesser rival NTUC of Nepali Congress. The new Union movement of the new century gained counter-legitimacy by targeting mainstream Unions and by forging broader alliances that went beyond immediate calls of collective bargaining. In doing so the meanings of 'political' and 'civil', and the lines between 'class' and 'cultural', were continually redefined, while the boundaries of factories and *toles* were blurred time and again. This ethnography may offer a useful point of departure for a critical anthropology on new social-political movements of the twenty-first century and the role of workers within them.

Endnotes

1. Article 7 of the 1950 treaty allows nationals of both countries the same privileges in the matter of residence, ownership of property, participation in trade and commerce on a reciprocal basis. The political legitimacy of this treaty is questioned in Nepal because it was signed by Mohan Shamsher Rana just three months before his regime was ousted through a popular uprising in Nepal. The regional context of the treaty was that it came immediately after the Chinese takeover of Tibet in 1949, and a few years after India's independence in 1947. Through Article 5 of the treaty, India gives Nepal freedom to import arms from or through India, thereby implying that it should not import arms from elsewhere. Indeed India did seal its border with Nepal in 1989, to register its disapproval of the fact that King Birendra had imported some ammunition from China.

2. I have discussed in Chapter 2 how a near-legendary minister Bhim Malla had secured, in the 17th century, a special treaty with Tibet allowing Nepalis the monopoly on trade with Tibet, including exclusive rights to mint all Tibetan coins. The treaty also gave Nepalis privileges to reside in Tibetan territories. This was the beginning of the trend of Nepalis going to Tibet to trade and earn money.

3. Remarks made by Ambassador Nancy Powell at a formal talk programme organized at the Nepali embassy in Washington DC in December 2004.

4. See earlier discussion on the 1950 treaty between Nepal and India, and its mutual provisioning of the privileges of residence and trade for each other's citizens in their own territories.

5. Inspired by regional stories about feminization, some factories did make concerted efforts to hire women. Lovely Fashion, within Kathmandu Valley, and Surya Nepal Garments, on the eastern border towns, had launched on-the-job training for women but both these ventures failed in the long run for reasons other than gender.

6. See Shakya (2011) for cost calculations, which also estimates 20 per cent of the costs as overhead and 10 per cent on utilities for a factory making an average 10 per cent profit.

7. See de Neve (2014) for a discussion on how the labour contractors in the South Indian garment industry tended to be part entrepreneur and part rent-seeker in the way they controlled and managed their own time and resources while still working under the roof of a factory owned by a bigger capitalist.

8. See Mollona (2009) for a discussion on labour consciousness among the steel workers of Sheffield, differentiated between 'hot' and 'cold' based on their ownership of the tools that they used for their job.

9. Workers compared notes in various places. The hill workers gossiped in the tea stalls or temples in and around the rental squats in the peripheries of Kathmandu where they lived. The Tarai workers, most of them Muslims, met up during the Friday mosque prayers. These Friday meetings would be followed by such large labour turnover on the garment shop floors that, supervisors commented, the Muslim workers were even called the '*Shukrabares*' or the 'Friday people'. Women were just a small part of the garment labour force, and did not seem to have a network system of their own; instead, they had access information from men through real or fictive kinship.

10. See The Republica front page article published on 17 August, 2011, 'Labour unrest fall out: Surya Nepal shuts down major garment unit.'

11. See The Republica editorial published on 18 August, 2011, 'Surya Garment closure.' (p. 6)

12. Jhala Nath Khanal ruled only seven months, and when he tendered his resignation on August 29, 2011 largely owing to criticisms from within his own party, Maoist ideologue Dr Baburam Bhattarai took over as the Prime Minister and Nepal shifted decisively to the left.

13. There were further speculations that the new Finance Minister and Deputy Prime Minister Bharat Mohan Adhikari (who was said to have had regular consultations with the Maoist supremo Prachanda) had serious differences with the Secretary of Finance, Rameshwor Khanal, over national policies on VAT, fiscal discipline and energy development. Ironically, officials of the Custom Office and Customs Duty observed a pen-down to protest government treatment of its fellow official, and the Chairman of the Civil Servants Union went as far as to issue a press statement saying that Secretary Khanal's resignation was the result of political pressure.

14. Published on the front page of The Republica under the section 'expert opinion' on 22 August, 2011. See a rejoinder by Mallika Shakya published on 25 August, 2011 in the same newspaper under the section 'counterview' with title 'Garment Rise and Fall: Islands of Success and Oceans of Despair' (p. 6).

15. Some of the key labour laws enacted by the democratically elected government, after Nepal became a multi-party democracy, include Labour Act, Child Labour Act, Trade Union Act, Transport and Vehicle Management Act, Child Labour Promotion and Protection Act – all enacted in the early 1990s.

16. In fact, New Baneswor was seen so Congress-friendly that the party President Krishna Prasad Bhatterai contested general elections from that constituency. To everybody's shock, however, he lost the election. Political commentators attributed his loss to speculations that the elite Baneswor people did not bother going out to vote because everybody was absolutely certain Bhatterai would win anyway. He became the butt of political jokes, as he had also lost the 1951 election despite being one of the most popular leaders during the anti-Rana movement.

17. The Comprehensive Peace Accord that formed the basis for JTUCC was signed on 21 November 2006 between GEFONT, NTUC, DECONT and ANTUF. The JTUCC was founded on December 1, 2007.

18. The so-called 'clean' (for his corruption-free track record) royalist Prime Minister Lokendra Bahadur Chand called for an all-party consultation to prepare for a government-Maoist talk which the parties rejected. Three rounds of talks were held between the two parties, where the Maoists submitted a 35-point agenda and the government removed the terrorist tag and Interpol Red Corner notices on the Maoist leaders. The Maoists went on to open a public relations office in Kathmandu. But eventually, the talks failed and the Maoists announced the end of the ceasefire in August 2003.

19. Daman Nath Dhungana and Padma Ratna Tuladhar attended some of the meetings between Maoists and the garment businessmen, but the person who was most invested in this task was Narayan Man Manandhar who had the job of managing industrial relations at the Federation of the Nepali Chamber of Commerce and Industry (FNCCI).

20. By 'the third wave of marketization', Michael Borawoy (2010) meant evasive social disembedding of markets, succeeding two earlier waves that had given rise to proletarianization of labour in the eighteenth century and the rise of national capitalism in the former colonial peripheries two centuries later.

7

Reconstituting the Garment Afterlife

We witness in the garment ecosystem in Nepal, a long and messy process in which ethnicity, class, and competitiveness morphed together to constitute a macro-social assemblage that steered normality and was deeply affected by the crisis of MFA. It has been my position throughout this book that the way the garment industry is situated, both within Nepal and the international scene, is neither purely economic nor purely cultural but rather an amalgamation of these and more. Politics raised its head at every turn, ranging from the ruling (or economic) elites' access to policy incentives and the cultural elite's access to niche markets, to developmental contestations that ended the MFA, and a class uprising that called for a regime change in Nepal. The metaphor of an 'industrial ecosystem', central to my narrative about the garment life cycle in Nepal, necessitates that each incumbent individual and institution is seen as part of a macro-sociality of ethnicity, class, and power. My ethnography shows how identity overshadowed the trajectories of class solidarity and business competitiveness. In this sense, the rhetoric of an anonymous supply-demand equilibrium directing industrialization trajectories is inadequate. What is necessary is to look at industries as part of a *dispositif* that drives the trajectories of national capitalism, on the one hand, and the People's War, on the other. In this chapter, I bring this argument up into the present time. I begin with the question of work in the context of the garment industry and then shift to discussions on life first, then rule, and conclude with a note on development.

Work and life

'Work' encompasses a wide range of productive arrangements an individual has with others, and in turn, individual and collective identities are deeply rooted in what one does for living. This is clearly a broad statement and can be stretched to mean a myriad of things. Work is a constituent of class status, but a proposition in this book is that it is also an identity marker that shapes the materiality of everyday lives, while situating individual beings within the twinned schemas of cultural hierarchy and political order. Applying this understanding to the work of garment-making means deconstructing stereotypes about those who worked in the readymade garment industry; they were seen either as neoliberal agents of international trade or as proletariat labour – lumpen or otherwise – and nothing else.

Let's look at the proletariat labour stereotype. The irony about Nepal's scholarship on 'work as labour' is that it is almost non-existent, even with a strong tradition of Marxist activism and discourse (Bhusal, 2007; Mishra, 2014). In a seminal book published in 1979, Seddon, Blaikie and Cameron subscribe to the proto-definition of labourers as those who take a wage, but differentiate the way the labourers in Nepal seem to approach their employment, from the general conditions of the proletariat working class in that they retain strong links with agriculture, so much so that they claim that a labour-centred political ecology may not evolve in Nepal too soon. In the preface to this book's 2002 edition, David Seddon reflects that surprisingly few studies have looked into the question of an urban labour force, in the thirty years spanning the two editions of the book, even as this era saw a Maoist People's War which fundamentally changed the nation. While the effect on everyday lives in remote villages, which later became Maoist strongholds, have been reported in a large number of ethnographies, much less has been said about the Maoist mobilization of urban trade Unions. The few studies that do look into the labour trends in Nepal concern themselves with either the developmental implications (Shrestha, 2013), or with ethnographic and activist reporting (Kattel, 2013). In order to theorize the state while analyzing class formation and labour uprising in Nepal, I considered it necessary to listen to other experiences where labour militancy in this century has its roots, in the dark legacies of the undemocratic past of the 1970s, as well as the unfortunate coincidence of democracy with the most extreme wave of marketization in the 1990s (Shakya, 2016).

Viewing 'work' as a marker of identity has generated its own discourse within anthropology, perhaps dating back to Alan Macfarlane (1976), who showed how the cosmopolitan experiences of the Gurungs as mercenaries in the British and Indian army were rooted in the localized politics in Nepal. Messerschmidt (1976a, 1976b) extended the work on the Gurungs, discussing their communal strategies towards occupational specialization and ecological adaptation. Various other caste and ethnic groups in Nepal have been studied, and studied extensively, using frameworks of stratification by Dumont and Srinivasan. Even so, the problem here is that – as was discussed at length during a conference in Delhi in 2017 that sought to generate a conversation between Nepal and the rest of South Asia on this topic – efforts to unsolipsize the scholarship, on the conjoining of cultural and occupational identities, have been delayed in Nepal. An exception, here, is Ortner's seminal book on the 'life and death' of the Sherpas, which offered a poignant imagination about the 'deorientalization' of ethnographies on Nepal, in as early as 1999.

In this book, I have reflected on the complexities of knowing to emphasize the limitations of 'acquired' (*padhera janne*) skills against the pervasive powers of 'embodied' (*parera janne*) cultural capital, to discuss the social reproduction of work in Nepal. Reproduction in this sense is necessarily a complex collective act with a long gestation period, not singular and certainly not individual. In the early chapters, I discussed Nepal's location at the crossroads of modernization. In the 1850s, Nepal was a crypto-colonial country ruled by the Rana 'Shogunate', under a European-style penal code that drew on the ancient doctrines of manusmriti although it also launched mercantile industries for the ruling castes (Kshyatriyas) in partnership with the Marwari trader castes (or Vaishyas) under the British guidance. After the Ranas were thrown out in 1950, naive assumptions were made about democracy, that a constitutional annulment of caste alone would uproot the caste-based norms for life and work. Eventually, King Mahendra usurped power within a decade, and instituted a Hindu 'Panchayati' state that privileged the Bahun-Chhetris over others. Three decades of Panchayat rule ensured that discourses on development and culture were conveniently bifurcated, so that the primordiality of the cultural equations of power remained veiled under the modern polemics of a 'soil-suited' democracy (Panday, 2011). My ethnography presents how political and cultural elites exercised new patronages by assuming gate-keeping roles that allowed them to influence policies on development and cosmopolitanism. Garment shop floors and business associations remained culturally regulated, even as developmental rhetoric on competitiveness dismissed culture as backward, and politics as counter-productive. The second innings of democracy, in 1990, was clearly a missed opportunity in that it again failed to implement a fundamental state restructuring, or to 'politicize democracy' – to borrow John Harriss' (2004) words – in a way that would have meaningfully removed the state's cultural biases in democracy and development.

The latter chapters detail the crisis and its aftermath, documenting the public appetite for a wholesale reconfiguration of cultural politics. It took policymakers and garment businessmen by surprise that the labour uprising under the Maoist banner would not settle for only wage bargaining, but would call for a cultural reconfiguration of the state *dispositif*. The anthropology of the People's War in Nepal has not looked into the labour question, possibly because of its rural focus, while methodological nationalism has prevented a multi-sited ethnography that would stretch its field beyond the borders of Nepal. My book is a lonely journey that took anthropology to mean universal humanism, along the lines of what Kant pursued towards achieving new orders of morality that may allow us new and better ways of living together (Hart, 2015). In this sense, my use of the framework of 'embeddedness' anticipates a social movement that may reverse the state's neoliberal turn, or in Polanyi's words, 'a double movement' that may punctuate the utopian disembedding of markets from social regulations (Stiglitz, 2001).

The aim of this chapter is to raise the question of embeddedness for consideration by the new regime, to inform decisions about the new constitution. and to examine its implications for the fresh round of elections for the local and national bodies of rule. But before that, I would like to take a detour to catch up on the lives of the garment people a decade after the collapse of the industry. It is important to be specific about the transformations they underwent, and about the meanings of those transformations, when commenting on the history of (industrial) development and also reflecting on the methodologies that prompted those comments. The next section presents an ontological reflection on the study of the event and its afterlife, while providing an update on the lives of my respondents beyond the garment industry, not so much of those who left Nepal, like Navin who I mentioned at the very beginning to explain why I wrote this book, but of others like Chhote and Sameer who remained in Nepal, and with whom I ended up doing research.

Life beyond work

A reflection on my original entry into the garment world makes me think about the contrasts I experienced when I returned to the field to study the aftermath of the collapse. My first write up on garment manufacturing was in 1997, for an MPhil course I was pursuing in Economic Planning. I was clearly transitioning into anthropology from development economics when I extended this study for a PhD programme that began in 2001. A reflection on this personal transition now makes it clear that my approach then was to study the shop floor cultures rather than an industrial ecosystem, let alone consider questions of the larger *dispositifs* of culture, market, and nation. It certainly made it convenient that everybody on the garment shop floors seemed to spend almost all of their waking hours in the factory. Factory owners arrived at office during breakfast hours and stayed until dinner time, and then went out regularly for late night drinks with their garment industry buddies. Workers, especially the *karigar*s on piece-rate wages, took multiple 'shifts' thus staying at work till late evening. It appeared to the novice anthropologist that the garment shop floor constituted a schema of its own, and belonging to the garment community meant spending all of my waking hours on the shop floor too. The garment industry had its own rhythms of work and leisure. In between purchase orders – and this downtime happened in all of the garment factories even when the MFA was in place – workers often took jobs in other factories with running operations, while the owners were running around (*daud-dhoop*) to secure new orders. During times when the Unions called a strike, workers took part in the protest, while owners looked for ways to either sabotage the strike or negotiate their way out so that work could resume. Only the men in the middle ranks could afford to take time off from the garment work to sit back and socialize, allowing the researcher rather rare occasions to hang out with them outside of the factory environs. However, what was rather striking about our out-of-factory socializing was that our conversations, and even jokes, ended up being mostly about garments.

'Garment' as a point of reference began to shift only very slowly – almost grudgingly – in pace with the slow demise of the industry. The owner of A&E Boutique, for example, underwent an intense and prolonged transition period before he fully retired from the industry and came to terms with it. My notes of the 'post-garment' conversations with him, during my visits to Kathmandu between 2004 and 2010, reminded me of how slow the process of exiting can be for those whose entire working life revolved around garments. Chhote had maintained that he did not fear MFA expiry since the garment items he exported were not quota-based. If anything, he expected to emerge a 'winner' and had designs to upgrade his production by taking advantage of the distress sale of machinery in factories that went bust. Though an unexpected wave of worker revolt brought his production to a standstill (see Chapter 6), he kept hoping that his workers would 'come to their senses' once they realized how lucky they were to still have their jobs at a time when those in the mass manufacturing sub-sector had been retrenched. His logic did not make sense to the workers. They considered it a betrayal to back out of the strikes until the 'class' question was fully resolved and justice was done for their entire brethern. Chhote felt his workers were being carried away by misplaced loyalty; the workers probably felt that it was Chhote who was being emotional in the way he dealt with workers and Unions. One Union full-timer later recalled how Chote was totally offended when someone suggested that he should be more lenient on workers because he only had two daughters and no sons, implying that his assets would eventually pass out of his family's hands anyway. The standoff lasted for almost a year. Ironically, Chhote was finally persuaded to put the garment world behind him after he wedded one of his daughters in the UK, and he needed to leave Kathmandu to help her settle into her new life.

Retirement seeped into Chhote's life only very gradually. He and his wife had stopped going to the factory some time in 2009, and I began to visit their home just a block away from the factory. One evening, as we sat in his sitting room catching up on life, he told me how hard it was for him to accept this major disruption: 'One part of my heart is very angry to the extent of being vengeful... I can send my family away, I can stay back on my own, and do something about these people who leave you hanging such that you cannot live and you cannot die,' were his words. Just a month or so ago, Chhote had apparently been on a prolonged mountain trek, something he had never done in his life, 'to listen to the quietness,' he said. The following year, the factory was legally and materially shut down. Later that year, Chhote began to make the rounds of the stock exchange office to learn the ropes of capital investment. His beautifully designed sitting room, where he used to host friends and businesspeople, now lay buried under stacks of fabric rolls brought over from the factory and piled up everywhere. Through word of mouth, people who learned of the fabrics would come by and purchase a few bundles. Over the years, the piles thinned out, and by 2013 or so, Chhote had found a reasonable foothold in the local stock trading business.

As the NEPSE index soared to all time high in the following two years, Chhote began see that investing in stocks was far more suitable work for him than 'scraping his bones' (*haddi ghotnu*) on the garment shop floors. He was even invited to appear on a local television talk show to comment on the developmental potentials of the Nepalese stock exchange. Two years later, when the stock market dipped to its lowest point, he kept calm and continued to enjoy life with family and friends. Over the time, he gained much public respect for his knowledge on stock investment, and more so, his willingness to share this knowledge with those who asked.

While Chhote settled down to a different occupation, covering just a small distance from Kalimati where his factory was earlier located to the Singha Durbar Plaza where the Nepal Stock Exchange office is located, others travelled further afield. This was especially true for members of the Marwari community, with whom Chhote maintained a cordial relationship even though he himself was not a Marwari, though some perceived him to be so. A particularly popular migratory route among the ex-garment members of the Marwari community was a road connecting Kathmandu to the border town of Birgunj, some hundred and fifty kilometres south, and on to Kolkata much further south and east. I visited many former garment businessmen in the Kolkata main market (Boro Bazar) where I ended up discovering yet another layer of the paradox of ethnicity that I described earlier. Probably triggered by the awkwardness of meeting an old acquaintance in a new place and changed circumstances, I tried to talk to an old friend, Ankur Kabra, about our common friend Chhote, whom I referred to as a 'fellow Marwari', and he casually responded, 'Oh … Chhote is a Marwari only in Nepal, not in Kolkata.' Hearing this, I burst into laughter, because exactly the opposite would often happen in Kathmandu a decade ago: when I would suggest that Chhote was a Rauniyar and not a Marwari, the garment businessmen would say that it did not matter, because everybody with north Indian roots doing business in Nepal was called a Marwari in Nepal. Continuing in the same vein of self-mockery, Ankur added, 'You see, this Madheshi baggage, can also be left behind in Nepal when crossing the border. Chhote ['the Uttar Pradesh man'] would do the same if he was to move to Kolkata,' recalling, with irony, our past conversations: I reminded him that Marwaris used to differentiate themselves from the Madheshis earlier, and that it had all changed after the Madheshi movement gained momentum in 2008. I admitted that I would be political about where any of my multiple identities would be highlighted: a Newar when joining lavish Newar New Year celebrations in London and Washington DC; a Nepali when joining embassy events or protesting fascism back home; a West-educated intellectual when conducting fieldwork among the 'natives'; a South Asian when with a multinational company; a Buddhist; an intellectual; and so on. We both shook our heads about identities being location- and situation-specific.

Conversations about Marwari-ness led on to a long chat about how only the 'authentic' Marwaris, with ancestral mansions (*hawelis*) and individual affiliations with the Rani Sati temple in the Marwar region of Rajasthan, have a social support system in Kolkata if they turn up there after being uprooted elsewhere. As I spent more time among the Marwaris in the Boro Bazar of Kolkata, I listened to accounts that emphasized how it was the '*vaisya dharma*' (merchant duty) of the well-to-do Marwaris in Kolkata to host their kin and relatives turning up at their doors from the 'faraway hills'. 'When things are right, we Marwaris move up to the hills, not only in Nepal but Northeast India, Myanmar and beyond; when things go wrong, we return to our base,' I was told, alluding to the fact that the history of migration is a circular one. The MFA expiry, which I had earlier taken to be so unique in setting off waves of social and industrial uprooting, turned out, after all, to be just one of many such upheavals the Marwaris had encountered over the generations. A quick look at the social history of Marwaris in Nepal reminds us that they had been invited to the border towns of Nepal in the 1850s by the Rana rulers on British advice. When a major earthquake hit in 1934, Marwaris helped the Ranas rebuild Kathmandu and, in return, were granted special rights of trade. This first echelon of elite Marwari merchants then facilitated the movement of others to follow the trail they had created, capitalizing on cultural institutions like *pati* and *sattal* (lodgings for, respectively, travellers and pilgrims), that were open to all, and *basaha* (places of work and lodging for business apprentices), available only to Marwaris. This extension of fieldwork among the garment businessmen, in their 'post-garment' life, reminded me that the 'culture' of the spatial shop floors is necessarily embedded within larger schemas of (multi-)national culture and (multi-)national capitalism, and that the nature of embeddedness often adapts to changes in broader circumstances (Shakya, 2013).

Three decades after Granovetter's (1984) oft-cited essay on the dichotomy of 'under-' and 'over-socialized' embeddedness, and a counter-discourse that emerged around Beckert's (2009) idea of macro-sociality, it seems timely to remind ourselves of the epistemological traps of looking for a 'industry culture', even when its dwellers give the impression that industry is a mesocosm of society. Looking at my own trajectory of research on the garment industry, I see that, just as the Union voice was muffled under the clamour of 'competitiveness' and 'productivity', until the industry went bust and a labour uprising took over, it was difficult to imagine the voice of the 'post-garment' life until I encountered those narratives, some of which took me by surprise, like the one I related about 'Marwariness'. An entrenched ontological position about 'garment' seemed to solipsize 'culture' into work behaviour; to signify not only businessmen's pursuit of profit and the idea of cultural capital, but also workers' solidarity for the collective and the idea of class formation. This solipsism also imagines industrial ecosystems as existing in isolation from societies, nations, and civilizations. A decisive reversal of the mainstream theorizing of 'culture' for a larger appetite for problematizing the complexity and flux of being human, might be necessary for economic anthropology to study culture in the traditions set by Weber and Simmel.

Rule

The collapse of the readymade garment industry coincided with a transition that saw the birth of a 'new Nepal', which sought to redefine nationhood. A few years after the expiry of the MFA in 2004, just as the garment people found their feet after the collapse of the industry, the state of Nepal also finally negotiated its way out of a decade-long civil war that killed over ten thousand Nepalis. The country was abuzz with the idea of a 'new Nepal', when an alliance of the seven largest democratic parties (known as the SPA) joined hands with the still-armed Maoists to sign a pact that would, simultaneously, end the People's War, and ensured the end of monarchy. From this pact stemmed an unarmed, but militant, public uprising that forced the government to reinstate the parliament that had been suspended under emergency rule. This parliamentary reinstatement in 2006 led to the dethroning of the king, and the promulgation of a new interim constitution, with promises of a fundamental state-restructuring, that would realize the rhetoric of 'multi-ethnic, multi-lingual, multi-religious, multi-cultural and diverse regional characteristics', while also materializing its preamble that Nepal would be an 'egalitarian society founded on the proportional inclusive and participatory principles' (Government of Nepal, 2006).

The call for 'economic equality, prosperity and social justice', as stated prominently in the interim constitution, was a contrast from the spirit of the 1990 constitution that had defined democracy to mean individual freedom, a notion that had been quickly hijacked by the global neoliberal yardstick of 'economic liberalization' which simplified freedom of choice to mean consumerism. I have argued that the regimes forged in the 1990s leapfrogged into what Burawoy (2010) called the 'third' wave of market liberalization, skipping two earlier waves that had given rise to labour proletarianization in the eighteenth century and the rise of national capitalism in the 1960s (Shakya, 2017; Bond, 2005). One could argue that there has been some form of alternative thinking about industrialization and development along the way. Nepal has, after all, been known more for its craft products than mass manufacturing, although the two have been entwined at times (Shakya, 2011a). Even so, the paradox of Nepali policymakers embracing the mass manufacturing model against the possibilities of what Piore and Sabel (1984) called 'flexible specialization' was never really accounted for, especially during the 1990s when Nepal sought to integrate with global markets riding the waves of marketization and globalization. It is logical to hope that the 2006 regime change was a genuine moment of reflection that probed the meanings of democracy beyond consumer freedom. But what remained in place for the next eight years was murky policy and political stagnation. It was only after the devastating earthquake that hit Kathmandu in 2015, killing 9,000 people, that a breakthrough could be made towards ending the transition and promulgating a new constitution. What followed thereafter was a kind of political regeneration that saw a disintegration of established political parties thus allowing the growth of a new political equation from the centre-left. I end this book by situating the mesocosm of industrial ecosystem that I presented earlier into the imaginations of a euphoric 'Naya Nepal' and its residues beyond 2006. A fleeting look into the making of several 'new' political forces, registered a decade after its revolutionary regime change, may help us consider the contours of development in Naya Nepal.

It is probably fair to say that the idea of a new politics captured the imagination of the people of Kathmandu after the Aam Admi Party took Delhi by storm in the 2013 local elections. That political parties may be instituted from social (and developmental) movements, as opposed to being rooted in deliberative politics, emboldened a whole range of actors to join politics in Nepal. First was a group of youth entrepreneurs who called themselves Bibeksheel Nepali (Rational Nepalis) and had been campaigning for 'post-ideological' (to mean clean as in corruption-free) development through 'pragmatic reforms' that would free the country from the clutches of old politicians. They gained strength so quickly that their party's candidate garnered the third-highest number of votes in the contest for the position of mayor of Kathmandu during the 2017 elections. The second was the Sajha Party, registered just months before the elections, and led by a veteran journalist and philanthropist, which spearheaded a popular movement against corruption. These two soon merged into one party, naming itself the Bibeksheel Sajha Party, to prepare for the national elections held in December 2017. It is the last of these new political forces – and in my opinion the one most closely rooted in the country's civil war and its peaceful resolution – within which I contextualize my narrative of post-garment industrial development in Nepal. This third party, Naya Shakti

(New Force), was founded by the former Prime Minister Baburam Bhattarai, the chief ideologue of the Maoist civil war that spearheaded the 2008 regime change in Nepal. First, let us take a quick look at the rapid round of political events that triggered this party's formation.

In the late evening of 20 September 2016, that saw Nepal finally promulgate its new Constitution – after nine years and two Constituent Assemblies – it was clear that a political '*nikas*' (way out) was possible only by leaning on the national grief about the devastating earthquake of 2015. Invoking sentiments around the national loss, Baburam Bhattarai, who headed the constitution drafting committee, pleaded with all political forces to settle their differences and come on board for a national consensus for stability and development. A Special Committee, formed by the Bhattarai-led Constitutional Political' Dialogue and Consensus Committee, held a round of marathon meetings thereafter, bringing on board most stakeholders to resolve key issues of the constitution, including demarcation of the boundaries of the federal provinces and modalities of provincial representations in the central parliament. While a political breakthrough was heralded by the major political parties on August 10, the nation remained divided over whether to embrace the new constitution or protest it, because the document did not adequately address the ongoing movement on identity and inclusion. The Tarai/Madhesh region, where Nepal shares an open border with India, remained defiant in its opposition to the post-earthquake political alliance, even though the few Madheshi members in the Constituent Assembly, representing Nepali Congress and various Left parties, put their signatures in the constitution being finalized. It seemed that the Centre sought to win over at least the Tharus within the Madheshi alliance; this might have morally weakened the Madheshi protests in that the Tharus are considered the indigenous inhabitants of the Tarai/Madhesh region. Most Tharu representatives in the Constituent Assembly did come on board as signatories but not all, and there were doubts till the very last hour about whether the last of the Tharu leaders from the Madhesh movement, Bijay Kumar Gachchadar would put his signature on the document; he didn't. There were speculations about Baburam Bhattarai's abrupt departure from the Constituent Assembly after having signed the document. As the ceremony headed to its conclusion, it became clear that Nepali politics would now undergo yet another reshuffling of power.

Less than a week after the promulgation of the Constitution, Baburam Bhattarai, the chair of the second Constituent Assembly's all-powerful Constitutional Committee, resigned from Parliament, as well as from his own party's general membership, and declared himself an independent citizen calling for a 'progressive nationalism' that would push out the 'fake nationalism' which he claimed was in place. He said he was unhappy with the way the aspirations of Madheshis and Janajatis had been thwarted in the new state of Nepal, and that he was particularly unhappy with the final federal model that was agreed upon amongst the major political parties. The discourse on Naya Shakti, or New Force, which emerged in Bhattarai's affiliation in the coming months, revolved around a central slogan: *'abako nikas, aarthik vikas'* (economic development is the new way out). Bhattarai also explained that his new organization would abandon all tactics of armed struggle and Maoist ideology to claim the centre-left space to work towards national capitalism and inclusive development[1]. His party went ahead full-thrust with chanting slogans of 'developing national capitalism' and 'moving away from resistance-oriented politics to a development-oriented politics.' While Baburam Bhattarai dillydallied about explaining whether or not he had ditched his communist ideology, and whether or not would he publicly criticize the Maoist armed rebellion he had engineered in the past, his party spokesman Khimlal Devkota explained the logic of Naya Shakti in this way:

> We service-people (*sewak*) are straightforward people; we are not those who dwell in banal logic and philosophy (*kora tarka ra siddhanta*). Our country needed to travel through one phase of fundamental restructuring (*aamool parivartan*). It was not possible to shake the old regime (*purano satta*) without the resolve of blood and toil (*ragat ra pasina sahitko athot*).... but please, you tell me what happens when a [public service] bus drives through its route and finally reaches its destination? It must now go back to its original point to resume – to repeat – the same journey. All passengers must get off the bus once the final destination is reached. They must get on in a different bus to further their journey. This is exactly how it works in our politics of development. We wish to see our country self-governing, prosperous and inclusive (*swaadheen, samriddha ra savaaveshi*). For this, we had no choice but to leave the Maoist platform and embrace this new journey with an honestly open mind.[2]

This reminded me of the disappointment I saw in the face of a Maoist cadre and former guerrilla commander, when he learned of Baburam Bhattarai's separation from the party. Recalling how the Party, during the armed rebellion, had questioned the loyalty of the commanders inclined towards Bhattarai's emphasizing of the 'two-line struggle' which called for diversity of intellectual positions thus seeing the party as a 'unity of opposites', this commander felt that

Bhattarai's decision to ultimately divorce the Party only showed he probably never was loyal to it anyway.

> He called on the nation to come together to feel the pain of the earthquake, but now look at him. Does he look like the kind of person who can feel any emotion of pain (*peeda ko anubhav*)? He says he is doing this for the country, that the country now needs new politics. Is the Party a contractor's job, that it should be ditched once its utility is over? We risked our lives in that Party, with an oath to live and die together; this was how that party was built. And now he tells us, so easily, that the old phase is over and now we ought to embrace a new name. How? ...[3]

When Naya Shakti announced its interim central committee in January 2016, it had brought on board a diverse team including, among others, former Secretary of Finance Rameswor Khanal known for having tendered his resignation to mark protest against a Left government (see Chapter 6), former AIG Ganesh Rai, and well known film artisists. Noted businessmen of the country marked their presence at the event. This stirred a debate on whether this is Bhattarai's UML-ization or AAP-ization.[4] However, disappointing many who had placed their hope on the Left delivering on a political startup that can reconfigure imaginations of development, Naya Shakti did not do well in the subsequent elections. With it, Bhattarai's political stature began to steadily decline.

In October 2017 came an announcement that shocked most Nepalis, who were busy celebrating their national festival Dashain, that the three most significant Left parties – the mainstream Maoist party led by Prachanda, CPN/UML led by KP Oli, and Baburam Bhattarai's Naya Shakti – had announced a new Left alliance for the upcoming two-phase provincial and federal elections. Not just that, the three parties had committed to formally merge following the elections, abiding by the requirements of the election by-laws. Speculations made rounds that this recent deal with Oli and Prachanda brings Bhattarai back to the centre of Nepali politics, and, by extension, intellectual and policy debates on development.[5] Within ten days, however, came the news that Bhattarai had quit the alliance over disagreements on distribution of election constituencies. He later announced his own candidacy in his core constituency of Gorkha, against the Alliance candidate Narayankaji Shrestha, facing backlash from his political counterparts but also disappointing the Left-inclined intellectuals who went on to issue a public appeal against voting for Bhattarai questioning his Marxist credentials.[6] Amidst the charged politics of allegations and counter-allegations, Baburam Bhattari won the election with a clear margin which ensures a role for him in the next legislative body under the new constitution, which was written under his leadership.

Even so, while it is too early to say anything definitive about the way deliberative politics is converging with development, let alone comment on the emerging power dynamics involved with the collective of new parties and political establishment, the situation certainly offers fertile ground for research for those interested in Nepal's transition out of both developmental failure and a People's War. This is the macro-social and macro-political landscape against which I read my fieldwork on the garment ecosystem that consists of the ethnographies of craft and mass sectors as well as the analyses of class and corporate consciousness. My proposition is that a meaningful departure from neoliberal policymaking will not come by replacing one individual policymaker with another or piecemeal restructuring of select few policy institutions but that this can only come when a new national imagination takes roots under a new state and national leadership.

Synthesizing development with politics and culture

Heather Hindman (2014) recently hinted at the emergence of a 'post-political' call in post-conflict Nepal that combined elements of anarchy and libertarianism (see also Peck and Tickell, 2002). She argued, as Kul Chandra Gautam (2015) also seemed to infer that Nepali millennials have lived with political instability throughout their lives, so much so that youth from privileged backgrounds have come to dismiss politico-bureaucratic structures as a hindrance to achieving their individual goals, much like their denial of the cultural structures that scaffold their being. My data on industrial ecosystems, covering two decades of neoliberal democracy in Nepal, offers a clear example of the transitions of social reproduction, but also of the adaptations and even small breakthroughs that the transitions gave way to. Recall the array of new cultural, industrial and political practices that have been discussed in the previous chapters: the way in which the garment ecosystem denoted a new industrial culture that was much more entrenched in neoliberalism than aspects of the national capitalism of the 1980s; the cosmopolitan waves of ethnic clustering and alliance-building especially in times of industrial crises; the new class uprisings that imagined a new Nepal more pluralistic and just; and the denouement of the People's War into a political regeneration that saw several small political parties arraying themselves against the mainstream few.

What does it mean for a post-transition New Nepal that the former left and the right are contesting one another's developmental imaginations to capture the new middle ground of deliberative democracy? What does it mean, especially, for possible new ways of theorizing industry, development, and nationhood? And how would that theorization reconcile the rooted views of Dor Bahadur Bista (1992) and Devendra Raj Panday (1999)? Dor Bahadur Bista (1992) controversially claimed that development in Nepal suffers from a fatalistic public psyche, while Devendra Raj Panday (1999) declared that its democracy failed to deliver on development just as its Panchayati predecessor. How is one to engage with such opinions about 'failure' when thinking about industries like readymade garments, which have clearly failed as material foundations of development, even if the more profound of the developmental questions about fundamental state-restructuring emerged from the movements created from the heart of its failure? I emphasize that both Bista's and Panday's works were concerned with exactly these profound questions of the macrosociality of development which seemed to get muffled by the clamour of self-styled development experts who dissect development into depoliticized, piecemeal projects such as growth, competitiveness, wage and working conditions, etc. Do we call this a paradox of failure or success, that elements of 'success' emerging from a failing developmental landscape have metamorphosed into entirely different spheres of life?

The garment people have now become other people, many of them living their lives somewhere away from Nepal, but does that necessarily mean we can ignore them for conceptual or methodological convenience? I remain intrigued by the emerging work of theorizing the collapse and its afterlife, and am looking for ways to study the macro-sociality of industrial and political life cycles especially in the way crises are depicted in neoliberal ways of thinking (Arif, 2011; Beckert, 2009). I read the mainstream policy discourse, often sponsored by the aid industry, as symptomatic of a very real crisis about freeing development from its neoliberal capturing. Further, I want to remain open to new possibilities that are emerging out of the recent transition that sees a politico-genesis as part of deliberative development. How can the cultural and political synthesizing of development be problematized in studying New Nepal? That is the question I leave open for anyone who wants to dig into the economic anthropology of Nepal, beyond the graveyard of the readymade garment industry of the past century.

Endnotes

1. See commentary by Biswas Baral in Republica Daily on 30 January 2016, 'Of Naya Shakti and "halal" revolutions' for detailed reporting on a joint platform held by Baburam Bhattarai with leaders of other political parties where he claimed that most mainstream parties including Nepali Congress and CPN/UML waged arms against the state in the past but later were absorbed well into parliamentary politics.
2. based on an informal conversation with the author during a rally on Naya Shakti campaign, December 2015
3. based on an informal conversation with the on September 29, 2015
4. See Dr. Saroj Dhital's op-ed 'Naya Shaktiharu' [New Forces] in Nagarik Daily published on 11 December, 2015.
5. See Biswas Baral's op-ed in The Wire dated 5 October 2017, 'Eleven Years in the Making, Left Alliance Could Herald New Era of Political Stability in Nepal,' where he speculates that a task that had proved impossible even during the euphoria of the Maoist Party's entry into democratic politics in 2008 might have now fructified through handholding by the , possibly meant to counter the Congress-Maoist coalition earlier backed by India. Further, Baral speculates that Oli and Prachanda might have calculated that Bhattari's inclusion into this alliance – despite Naya Shakti's declining political stature – was necessary to ease India's concerns. See Amit Dhakal's op-ed on Setopati.com, dated 4 October, 2017, 'EMale-Maobadiko Dashain Surprise' [UML-Maoists' Dashain Surprise] for detailed negotiations on the modalities of election campaigns as well as steps towards a future merger.
6. See Baburam Bishwakarma's op-ed *'Bukhyacha Jasta Buddhijivi'* [Intellectuals Who Act Like Scarecrows] in *Kantipur Daily* published on 28 November, 2017 which criticizes the press statement issued the day before by eleven eminent Left-leaning intellectuals denouncing Bhattarai and exhorting the public to vote for his election rival Narayan Kaji Shrestha in his home constituency.

Bibliography

Adhikari, Jagannath. 2008. *Changing Livelihoods: Essays on Nepal's Development since 1990*. Kathmandu: Martin Chautari.

Arif, Yasmeen. 2011. 'Aid, Affect and Afterlife: Reconstituting Life After Catastrophe.' University of Delhi, Department of Sociology, Occasional Paper Series.

Asian Development Bank. 2016. *Bangladesh: Consolidating Export-Led Growth*. Manila: ADB Reports.

Baca, George. 2004. 'Legends of Fordism: Between Myth, History, and Foregone Conclusions.' *Social Analysis* 48 (3): 169-178.

Bajracharya, Sepideh. 2015. 'Measures of Violence: Rumor Publics and Politics in the Kathmandu Valley.' *Journal of Material Culture* 20 (4): 361-378.

Banaji, Jairus. 2003. 'The Fictions of Free Labour: Contract, Coercion, and So-Called Unfree Labour.' *Historical Materialism* 11 (3): 69-95.

Banerjee, Abhijit and Kavita Munshi. 2004. 'How Efficiently is Capital Allocated? Evidence from the Knitted Garment Industry in Tirupur.' *The Review of Economic Studies* 71 (1): 19-42.

Barrientos, S., K. Mathur, and A. Sood. 2010. 'Decent Work in Global Production Networks.' In *Labour in Global Production Networks in India*, edited by A. Posthuma and D. Nathan, 127-45. New Delhi: Oxford University Press.

Barth, Fredrik. ed. 1969. *Ethnic Groups and Boundaries: The Social Organization of Cultural Difference*. Oslo: Universitetsforlaget.

Baviskar, Amita and Nandini Sundar. 2008. 'Democracy versus Economic Transformation?' *Economic and Political Weekly* 43 (46): 87-9.

Beckert, Jens. 2009. 'The Great Transformation of Embeddedness: Karl Polanyi and the New Economic Sociology.' In *Market and Society: The Great Transformation Today*, edited by Chris Hann and Keith Hart, 38-55. Cambridge: Cambridge University Press.

Beckman, Bjorn. 2004. 'Trade Unions, Institutional Reform and Democracy: Nigerian Experiences with South African and Ugandan Comparisons.' In *Politicising Democracy: The New Local Politics of Democratisation*, edited by J. Harriss, K. Stokke, and O. Tornquist, 171-200. London: Palgrave Macmillan.

Beckman, Bjorn, Sakela Buhlungu, and Lloyd Sachikonye, eds. 2006. *Trade Unions and Party Politics: Labour Movements in Africa*. Pretoria: HSRC Press.

Bernal, Victoria. 1994. 'Peasants, Capitalism, and (Ir)Rationality.' *American Ethnologist* 21 (4): 792-810.

Bezuidenhout, Andries and Sakela Buhlungu. 2008. 'Union Solidarity under Stress: The Case of the National Union of Mineworkers in South Africa.' *Labour Studies* 33 (3): 262-87.

Bhagawati, Jagadish. 2008. 'The Critiques of Free Trade.' Talk given at a World Bank seminar series on Export Competitiveness, Washington, D.C., 12 October 2008.

Bhusal, Ghanashyam. 2007. *Aajako Marxvaad ra Nepali Kranti [Today's Marxism and the Revolution in Nepal]*. Kathmandu: Nepal Adhyayan Kendra.

Birnbaum, David. 2000. *Birnbaum's Global Guide to Winning the Great Garment War*. Hong Kong: Third Horizon Press Ltd.

Bista, Dor Bahadur. 1980. 'Nepalis in Tibet.' *Contributions to Nepalese Studies* 8 (10): 2–19.

_____. 1991. *Fatalism and Development: Nepal's Struggle for Modernization*. Delhi: Sangam Books.

Blakie, P.M., John Cameron, and David Seddon. 2001. *Nepal in Crisis: Growth and Stagnation at the Periphery*. Revised and Enlarged Edition. Delhi: Adroit Publishers.

Blokker, N. 1989. *International Regulation of World Trade in Textiles: Lessons for Practice, A Contribution to Theory*. Leiden: Brill Publications.

Blyth, Mark. 2003. *Great Transformations: Economic Ideas and Institutional Change in the Twentieth Century*. Cambridge: Cambridge University Press.

Bond, Patrick. 2005. *Elite Transition: From Apartheid to Neoliberalism in South Africa*. London: Pluto Press.

Bourdieu, Pierre. 1977a. 'Symbolic Power.' In *Identity and Structure*, edited by D. Gleeson, 112-19. Driffield: Nafferton Books.

_____. 1977b. *Outline of A Theory of Practice*. Cambridge: Cambridge University Press.

_____. 1984. *Distinction: A Social Critique of the Judgement of Taste*. Cambridge: Harvard University Press.

_____. 1986. 'The Forms of Capital.' In *Handbook of Theory and Research for the Sociology of Education*, edited by J.G. Richardson, 241-58. New York: Greenwood Press.

Boyer, R. and Jean-Pierre Durand. 1997. *After Fordism*. Translated by Sybil Hyacinth Mair. London: Macmillan Press.

Breman, Jan. 1996. *Footloose Labour: Working in India's Informal Economy*. New York: Cambridge University Press.

_____. 2004. *The Making and Unmaking of an Industrial Working Class: Sliding Down the Labour Hierarchy in Ahmedabad, India*. Amsterdam: Amsterdam University Press.

Brooks, Ethel. 2007. *Unravelling the Garment Industry: Transnational Organizing and Women's Work*. Minneapolis, London: University of Minnesota Press.

Brubaker, Roger. 2010. 'Ethnicity Without Groups.' In *The Ethnicity Reader*, edited by Montserrat Guibernou and John Rex. Cambridge: Polity.

Buhlungu. Sakela. 2001. 'The Paradox of Victory: South Africa's Union Movement in Crisis.' *New Labour Forum* 8 (Spring-Summer): 66-76.

Burawoy, Michael. 2010. 'From Polanyi to Pollyanna: The False Optimism of Global Labour Studies.' *Global Labour Journal* 1 (2): 301-13.

Burghart, Richard. 1984. 'The formation of the concept of nation-state in Nepal.' *Journal of Asian Studies* 44 (1): 101-25.

Cadène, P. and Holmstrom, M. eds. 1998, *Decentralized Production in India: Industrial Districts, Flexible Specialisation and Employment*. New Delhi/London: Sage Publications.

Carswell, Grace and Geert De Neve. 2013. 'Labouring for Global Markets: Conceptualising Labour Agency in Global Production Networks.' *Geoforum* 44 (1): 62-70.

Chandavarkar, Rajnarayan. 1994. *The Origins of Industrial Capitalism in India: Business Strategies and the Working Classes in Bombay, 1900–1940*. Cambridge: Cambridge University Press.

Chandler, Alfred. 1977. *The Visible Hand: The Managerial Revolution in American Business*. Massachusetts: Belknap Press.

Chari, Sharad. 2004. *Fraternal Capital: Peasant-Workers, Self-Made Men and Globalization in Provincial India*. California: Stanford University Press.

Chatterjee, Partha. 1986. *Nationalist Thought and the Colonial World: A Derivative Discourse?* London: Zed Books.

————. 2004. *Politics of the Governed*. New York: Columbia University Press.

————. 2008. 'Democracy and Economic Transformations in India.' *Economic and Political Weekly* 43 (16): 53-62.

Clarence-Smith, W.G. 1995. 'Cocoa Plantations in the Third World, 1870s-1914: The Political Economy of Inefficiency.' In *The New Institutional Economics and Third World Development*, edited by John Harriss, Janet Hunter, and Colin M. Lewis, 157-172. London: Routledge.

Clegg, S.R. et al (eds). 1990. *Capitalism in Contrasting Cultures*. Berlin: Walter de Gruyter.

Coase, R.H. 1937. 'The Nature of the Firm.' *Economica* 4 (16): 386-405.

————. 1960. 'The Problem of Social Cost.' *Journal of Law and Economics* 3: 1-44.

Collier, Paul and John Page. 2009. *Industrial Development Report 2009. Breaking In and Moving Up: New Industrial Challenges for the Bottom Billion and the Middle-Income Countries*. Geneva: United Nations Industrial Development Organization.

Comaroff, John and Jean Comaroff. 2009. *Ethnicity, Inc.* Chicago: University of Chicago Press.

Cornia, Giovanni Andrea, Richard Jolly, and Frances Stewart. 1988. *Adjustment with a Human Face: Protecting the Vulnerable and Promoting Growth*. London: Clarendon Press.

Dale, Gareth. 2010. *Karl Polanyi: The Limits of the Market*. Cambridge: Polity.

Dasgupta, Partha and Ismail Serageldin. 1999. *Social Capital: A Multifaceted Perspective*. Washington, D.C.: World Bank.

De Neve, Geert. 1999. 'Tamil Warps and Wefts: An Anthropological Study of Urban Weaving in South India.' PhD thesis, University of London.

_____. 2009. 'Power, Inequality and Corporate Social Responsibility: The Politics of Ethical Compliance in the South Indian Garment Industry.' *Economic and Political Weekly* 44 (22): 63-71.

_____. 2014. 'Entrapped entrepreneurship: labour contractors in the South Indian garment industry.' *Modern Asian Studies* 48 (5): 1302-33.

Dickerson, Kitty. 1999. *Textiles and Apparel in the Global Economy, Upper Saddle River.* New Jersey: Merill, Prentice-Hall.

Dickson, Marsha A., Suzanne Loker, and Molly Eckman. 2009. *Social Responsibility in the Global Apparel Industry.* London: Fairchild Books.

Dixit, Kanak Mani. 2001. 'Bahuns and the Nepali State.' *Nepali Times*, 19 October.

Dowlah, C. A. F. 1999. 'The Future of the Readymade Clothing Industry of Bangladesh in the Post-Uruguay Round World.' *The World Economy* 22 (7): 933-53.

Drucker, Peter F. 1972. *The Concept of the Corporation.* New York: John Day Co.

Ebers, M. 1997. *The Formation of Inter-Organisational Networks.* New York: Oxford University Press.

Ferguson, James. 1990. *The Anti-Politics Machine: Development, Depoliticization, and Bureaucratic Power in Lesotho.* Cambridge: Cambridge University Press.

_____. 2005. 'Decomposing Modernity: History and Hierarchy after Development.' In *Postcolonial Studies and Beyond*, edited by Ania Loomba, Suvir Kaul, Matti Bunzl, Antoinette Burton and Jed Esty, 166-81. North Carolina: Duke University Press.

Fernandez-Stark, Karina, Stacey Frederick, and Gary Gerefi. 2011. *The Apparel Global Value Chain.* North Carolina: Duke University Centre on Globalization, Governance and Competitiveness.

Fine, Ben. 2001. *Social Capital versus Social Theory: Political Economy and Social Science at the Turn of the Millennium.* London and New York: Routledge.

Frechette, A. 2003. *Tibetans in Nepal: The Dynamics of International Assistance Among a Community in Exile.* New York and Oxford: Berghahn Books.

Fujikura, Tatsuro. 2013. *Discourses of Awareness: Development, Social Movements, and the Practices of Freedom in Nepal.* Kathmandu: Martin Chautari.

Fukuyama. Francis. 1992. *The End of History and the Last Standing Man.* Los Angeles: Avon Books.

_____. 1995. *Trust: The Social Virtues and the Creation of Prosperity.* London: Hamish Hamilton.

Furubotn, Eirik G. and Rudolf Richter. 2005. *Institutions and Economic Theory: The Contribution of the New Institutional Economics.* 2nd ed. Ann Arbor: University of Michigan Press.

Gaige, Frederick. H. 1975. *Regionalism and National Unity in Nepal.* Berkeley: University of California Press.

Gambetta, Diego. 1993. *The Sicilian Mafia: The Business of Private Protection.* London: Harvard University Press.

Gautam, Bhaskar. ed. 2008. *Madhes Bidrohako Nalibeli [Contours of Madhesi Revolt].* Kathmandu: Martin Chautari.

Gautam, Kul Chandra. 2015. *Lost in Transition: Rebuilding Nepal from the Maoist Mayhem and Mega Earthquake*. Kathmandu: Nepalaya.

Geertz, Clifford. 1963. *Old Societies and New States*. London: The Free Press.

————. 1980. *Negara: The Theatre State in Nineteenth-Century Bali*. New Jersey: Princeton University Press.

Gellner, David. 2003. *Resistance and the State: Nepalese Experiences*. Oxford: Berghahn Books.

Gellner, David and Declan Quigley. 1995. *Contested Hierarchies: A Collaborative Ethnography of Caste among the Newars of the Kathmandu Valley, Nepal*. Oxford: Clarendon Press.

Gereffi, Gary. 1999. 'International Trade and Industrial Upgrading in the Apparel Commodity Chain.' *Journal of International Economics* 48 (1999): 37-70.

Gereffi, Gary. 2002. 'Prospects for Industrial Upgrading by Developing Countries in the Global Apparel Commodity Chain.' *International Journal of Business and Society* 3 (January 2002): 27-60.

Gereffi, Gary and Miguel Korzeniewicz, eds. 1994. *Commodity Chains and Global Capitalism*. Westport, Connecticut: Praeger.

Gershenkron, Alexander. 1962. *Economic Backwardness in Historical Perspective*. Cambridge, Massachusetts: Harvard University Press.

Goodall, M. 1978. 'Bureaucracy and Bureaucrats: A Few Themes Drawn from the Nepal Experience.' In *Himalayan Anthropology: The Indo-Tibetan Interface*, edited by James Fisher, 227-32. The Hague: Mountain Publishers.

Government of Nepal. 2006. *Nepal Interim Constitution*. Kathmandu: Constitution Assembly Secretariat.

Graner, Elvira. 2002. 'Labour migrants in the Kathmandu Valley: A Demographic Analysis of Carpet Workers.' *Population and Development in Nepal* 10: 97-108.

Granovetter, Mark. 1984. 'Economic Action and Social Structure: The Problem of Embeddedness.' *American Journal of Sociology* 91 (3): 481-510.

Green, Nancy. 1997. *Ready-To-Wear, Ready-To-Work: A Century of Industry and Immigrants in New York*. Durham, North Carolina: Duke University Press.

Guyer, Jane. 2004. *Marginal Gains: Monetary Transactions in Atlantic Africa*. Chicago: Chicago University Press.

Ha-Joon Chang. 2002. *Kicking Away the Ladder: Development Strategy in Historical Perspective*. London: Anthem Press.

Halperin, R.H. 1975. 'Polanyi and Marx.' Paper presented at the Annual Meeting of the American Anthropological Association, San Francisco.

————. 1984. 'Polanyi, Marx, and the Institutional Paradigm in Economic Anthropology.' *Research in Economic Anthropology* 6: 245–72.

Hamilton, Carl B. 1990. *Textiles Trade and the Developing Countries: Eliminating the Multi-Fibre Arrangement in the 1990s*. Washington, D.C.: World Bank.

Hamilton, G. G. and N. W. Biggart. 1988. 'Market, Culture, and Authority: A Comparative Analysis of Management and Organization in the Far East.' *American Journal of Sociology* 94 (supplement): 52-94.

Hann, Chris. 2017. 'Hayek versus Polanyi in Montreal: Global Society as Markets, All the Way Across? *FocaalBlog*, 11 July. Accessed on 16 August 2017. Available at www.focaalblog.com/2017/07/11/chris-hann-hayek-versus-polanyi-in-montreal-global-society-as-markets-all-the-way-across/.

Hann, Chris and Keith Hart. 2011. *Economic Anthropology: History, Ethnography, Critique*. Cambridge: Polity.

Hardgrove, Anne. 2004. *Community and Public Culture: The Marwaris in Calcutta*. Oxford: Oxford University Press.

Harriss-White, Barbara. 1996. 'Maps and Landscapes of Grain Markets in South Asia.' In *The New Institutional Economics and Third World Development* edited by John Harriss, Janet Hunter and Colin M. Lewis, 87-108. London: Routledge.

_____. 2003. *India Working: Essays on Society and Economy*. Cambridge: Cambridge University Press.

Harriss, John. 2002a. *Institutions, Politics, and Culture: A Case for 'Old' Institutionalism in the Study of Historical Change*. London: Development Studies Institute, London School of Economics.

_____. 2002b. *Depoliticising Development: The World Bank and Social Capital*. London: Anthem Press.

_____. 2006. *Power Matters: Essays on Institutions, Politics, and Society in India*. New Delhi: Oxford University Press.

Harriss, J., Janet Hunter, and Colin M. Lewis. eds. 1995. *The New Institutional Economics and Third World Development*. London: Routledge.

Harriss, John, Kristian Stokke, and Olle Tornquist. 2004. *Politicising Democracy: The New Local Politics of Democratisation*. London: Palgrave.

Hart, Keith. 2015. *Gandhi as a Global Thinker: Anthropological Legacies of the Anti-Colonial Revolution*, New Delhi: SAU Contributions to Con-temporary Knowledge Lecture Series.

Hart, Keith, Jean Louis Laville, and Antonio D. Cattani. 2010. *The Human Economy: A Citizens' Guide*. Cambridge: Polity.

Harvey, David. 2003. *The New Imperialism*. Oxford: Oxford University Press.

_____. 2007. *A Brief History of Neoliberalism*. Oxford: Oxford University Press.

Hawamanne, Sandya. 2008. *Stitching Identities in a Free Trade Zones: Gender and Politics in Sri Lanka*. Philadelphia: University of Pennsylvania Press.

Heaton-Shrestha, Celayne. 2006. '"They Can't Mix Like We Can": Bracketing Differences and the Professionalization of NGOs in Nepal.' In *Development Brokers and Translators: The Ethnography of Aid and Agencies*, edited by David Mosse and David Lewis, 195-216. Connecticut: Kumarian Press.

Hensman, Rohini. 2011. *Workers, Unions and Global Capitalism: Lessons from India*. New York: Columbia University Press.

Herskovits, M. (1940) 1952. *Economic Anthropology: The Economic Life of Primitive Peoples*. Reprint, New York: Norton.

Hertz, E. 1998. *The Trading Crowd: An Ethnography of the Shanghai Stock Market*. Cambridge: Cambridge University Press.

Herrigel, G. 1994. 'Industry as a Form of Order: A Comparison of the Historical Development of the Machine Tool Industry in the United States and Germany.' In *Governing Capitalist Economies: Performance and Control of Economic Sectors*, edited by R. Hollingsworth, Philippe C. Schmitter, and Wolfgang Streeck, 97-128. Oxford: Oxford University Press.

Herzfeld, Michael. 2002. 'The Absent Present: Discourses of Cryptocolonialism.' *South Atlantic Quarterly* 101 (4):899-926.

Hindman, Heather. 2014. 'Post-political in the Post-conflict: DIY Capitalism, Anarcho-neoliberalism and Nepal's Ungovernable Mountains.' *Cultural Anthropology* (website), 24 March. Accessed on 29 March 2014. https://culanth.org/fieldsights/507-post-political-in-the-post-conflict-diy-capitalism-anarcho-neoliberalism-and-nepal-s-ungovernable-mountains

Hoffmann, Michael. 2014. 'Red Salute at Work: Brick Factory Work in Post-Conflict Kailali, Western Nepal.' *Focaal* 70 (2014): 67-80.

Hollingsworth, J.R. 1997. *Comparing Capitalisms: The Embeddedness of Institutions.* Cambridge: Cambridge University Press.

Hutt, Michael, ed. 2004. *Himalayan People's War: Nepal's Maoist Rebellion.* Bloomington: Indiana University Press.

Hutt, Michael and Pratyoush Onta. 2017. *Political Change and Public Culture in Post-1990 Nepal.* New Delhi: Cambridge University Press.

Isaac, Barry. 2005. 'Karl Polanyi.' In *A Handbook of Economic Anthropology*, edited by James G. Carrier,14-25. Cheltenham, UK and Northampton, US: Edward Elgar.

Islam, Mohammad Tarikul and Mohammad Bakhtiar Rana. 2012. 'Dynamic Capability Helps Upgrading Bangladeshi Apparel Firms in the Global Value Chain: Knowledge Spillover Perspective.' Paper presented at the Aarbourg International Conference, July 2012.

Jeffrey, Craig. 2014. *Timepass: Youth, Class and the Politics of Waiting in India.* California: Stanford University Press.

Jones, Richard M. 2008. *The Apparel Industry.* London: Blackwell Publishing.

Kabeer, Naila. 1991. 'Cultural Dopes or Rational Fools? Women and Labour Supply in the Bangladesh Garments Industry.' *European Journal of Development Research* 3 (1): 133-60.

_____. 2000. *The Power to Choose: Bangladeshi Women and Labour Market Decisions in London and Dhaka.* London and New York: Verso Books.

_____. 2004. 'Globalization, Labor Standards, and Women's Rights: Dilemmas of Collective (in)action in an Interdependent World.' *Feminist Economics* 10 (1): 3–35.

Kattel, Mukunda. 2013. 'Identity and Violence: The Illusion of Destiny.' In *Debating Transformation*, edited by M. Kattel. Kathmandu: GEFONT.

Klein, Naomi. 1999. *No Logo: Taking Aim at the Brand Bullies.* Canada: Knopf Canada and Picador.

Knorringa, Peter. 1996. *Economics of Collaboration: Indian Shoemakers between Market and Hierarchy.* New Delhi: Sage Publications.

Knorringa, Peter and Khaled Nadvi. 2016. 'Rising Power Clusters and the Challenges of Local and Global Standards.' *Journal of Business Ethics* 133 (1): 55-721.

Komiya, Ryutari; Okuno, Masahiro and Kotaro Suzumura. eds. 1988. *Industrial Policy of Japan.* San Diego, California: Academic.

Kopytoff, Ivor. 1986. 'The Cultural Biography of Things: Commoditization as a Process.' In *The Social Life of Things: Commodities in Cultural Perspectives,* edited by Arjun Appadurai, 64-91. Cambridge: Cambridge University Press.

Kosak, Hadassa. 2000. *Cultures of Opposition: Jewish Immigrant Workers, New York City, 1881-1905.* Albany, NY: State University of New York Press.

_____. 2005. 'Tailors and Troublemakers: Jewish Militancy in the New York Garment Industry, 1889-1910.' In *A Coat of Many Colours,* edited by Daniel Soyer, 115-39. New York: Fortham University Press.

Krippner, Greta. 2002. 'The Elusive market: Embeddedness and the Paradigm of Economic Sociology.' *Theory and Society* 30 (6): 775–810.

Krippner, Greta, Mark Granovetter, Fred Block, Nicole Biggart, Tom Beamish, Youtien Hsing, Gillian Hart, Giovanni Arrighi, Margie Mendell, John Hall, Michael Burawoy, Steve Vogel, and Sean O'Riain. 2004. 'Polanyi Symposium: A Conversation on Embeddedness.' *Socio-Economic Review.* 2 (1): 109-135.

Krueger, Anne. O. 1974. 'The Political Economy of the Rent-seeking Society.' *American Economic Review* 64 (3): 291-303.

Krugman, Paul. 1992. 'Toward a Counter-Counterrevolution in Development Theory.' In *Proceedings of the World Bank Annual Conference on Development Economics*, 15-62. Washington, D.C.: International Bank for Reconstruction and Development/ World Bank.

Kudaisya, Medha. 2003. *The Life and Times of G.D. Birla.* New York: Oxford University Press.

Lakshman, Narayan. 2013. 'India disputes World Bank business ranking methodology.' *The Hindu,* 22 March.

Lazonick, W. and J. West. 1998. 'Organisational Integration and Competitive Advantage.' In *Technology, Organisation, and Competitiveness: Perspectives on Industrial and Corporate Change,* edited by G. Dosi, D. J. Teese, and D. J. Chytry, 247-88. Oxford: Oxford University Press.

LeVine, Robert A., Sarah LeVine, Beatrice Schnell-Anzola, Meredith L. Rowe, and Emily Dexter. 2012. *Literacy and Mothering: How Women's Schooling Changes the Lives of the World's Children.* New York: Oxford University Press.

Lindauer, David L. Jong-Gie Kim, Joung-Woo Lee, Hy-Sop Lim, Jae-Young Son, and Ezra F. Vogel. 1991. *Korea: The Strains of Economic Growth.* Cambridge, Massachusetts: Harvard Institute for International Development and Korea Development Institute.

Lynch, Caitrin. 2007. *Juki Girls, Good Girls: Gender and Cultural Politics in Sri Lanka's Global Garment Industry.* Ithaca and London: Cornell University Press.

Macfarlane, Alan. 1976. *Resources and Population: A Study of the Gurungs of Nepal.* Cambridge: Cambridge University Press.

Mahat, Ram Sharan. 2005. *In Defence of Democracy: Dynamics and Fault Lines of Nepal's Political Economy*. New Delhi: Adroit Publishers.

Maurice, M. 1979. 'For a Study of "the Societal Effect": Universality and Specificity in Organisation Research.' In *Organisations Alike and Unlike*, edited by C.J. Lammers and D.J. Hickson, Ch. 3. London: Routledge.

Mayhew, Henry. 1861. *London Labour and the London Poor*. Vol. I. London: London, Griffin, Bohn and Company. http://etext.virginia.edu/toc/modeng/public/MayLond.html.

Mcwandawire, Thandika. 2001. 'The Need to Rethink Development Economics.' Paper prepared for the discussion at the UNRISD meeting on the same topic, 7-8 September.

Messerschmidt, Donald. 1976a. 'Ecological Change and Adaptation among the Gurungs of the Nepal Himalaya.' *Human Ecology* 4 (2): 167-185.

_____. 1976b. *The Gurungs of Nepal: Conflict and Change in a Village Society*. Warminster: Aris & Phillips.

Mezzadri, Alessandra. 2014. 'Indian Garment Clusters and CSR Norms: Incompatible Agendas at the Bottom of the Garment Commodity Chain.' *Oxford Development Studies* 42 (2):217-37.

Mihaly, Eugene Bramer. (1965) 2009. *Foreign Aid and Politics in Nepal: A Case Study*. Reprint, Kathmandu: HIMAL Books.

Mirowski, Philip. 2013. *Never Let a Serious Crisis Go to Waste: How Neoliberalism Survived the Financial Meltdown*. London, New York: Verso.

Mishra. Chaitanya. 2014. *Poonjivaad ra Nepal [Capitalism and Nepal]*. Kathmandu: Phoenix Books.

Mollona, M. 2009. *Made in Sheffield: An Ethnography of Industrial Work and Politics*. Oxford: Berghahn Press.

Moore, Mick. 1999. 'Truth, Trust, and Market Transactions: What Do We Know?' *The Journal of Development Studies* 36 (1): 74-88.

Narotzky, Susana. 2005. 'Provisioning.' In *A Handbook of Economic Anthropology*, edited by James G. Carrier, 77-94. Cheltenham, UK and Northampton, USA: Edward Elgar.

Nelson, Andrew. 2011. '"No horn please." Sociality and self-governance in a Kathmandu housing colony.' In *Urban Navigations: Politics, Space, and the City in South Asia*, edited by Jonathan S. Anjaria and Colin McFarlane, 213-38. London: Routledge.

Neveling, Patrick. 2014. 'Three Shades of Embeddedness, State Capitalism as the Informal Economy, Emic Notions of the Anti-Market, and Counterfeit Garments in the Mauritian Export Processing Zone.' *Research in Economic Anthropology* 34 (1): 65-94.

North, Douglass. 1990. *Institutions, Institutional Change, and Economic Performance*. Cambridge: Cambridge University Press.

_____. 2005. *Understanding the Process of Economic Change*. New Jersey: Princeton University Press.

Nurkse, Ragnar. 1953. *Problems of Capital Formation in Underdeveloped Countries*. Oxford: Oxford University Press.

O'Neill, Tom. 2005. 'Ethnic Identity and Instrumentality in Tibeto-Nepalese Carpet Production.' *Asian Studies Review* 29 (3): 275-86.

Ong, Aihwa. 1997. *Spirits of Resistance and Capitalist Discipline: Factory Women in Malaysia.* New York: State University of New York Press.

Orru, Marco, Gary G. Hamilton, and Mariko Suzuki. 1989. 'Patterns of Inter-Firm Control in Japanese Business.' In *Organisation Studies* 10: 549-74.

Orru, Marco, Nicole Woolsey Biggart, and Gary Hamilton. 1991. 'Organisational Isomorphism in East Asia.' In *The New Institutionalism in Organisational Analysis,* edited by W. W. Powell and P. DiMaggio, 361-89. Chicago: University of Chicago Press.

Orru, Marco, Nicole Woolsey Biggart, and Gary Hamilton. eds. 1997. *The Economic Organisation of East Asian Capitalism.* California: Sage Publications.

Ortner, Sherry. 1999. *Life and Death on Mt. Everest: Sherpas and Himalayan Mountaineering.* New Delhi: Oxford University Press.

Ostrom, Elinor. 2005. 'Doing Institutional Analysis: Digging Deeper than Markets and Hierarchies.' In *Handbook of New Institutional Economics,* edited by C. Ménard and M. Shirley, 819-48. Berlin and Heidelberg: Springer.

Pack, Howard. 1992. 'New Perspectives on Industrial Growth in Taiwan.' In *Taiwan: From Developing to Mature Economy,* edited by Gustav Ranis. Boulder, Colorado: Westview.

Panday, Devendra Raj. 1999. *Nepal's Failed Development: Reflections on the Mission and the Maladies.* Kathmandu: Nepal South Asia Centre.

―――――. 2011. *Looking at Development and Donors: Essays from Nepal.* Kathmandu: Martin Chautari.

Parry, Jonathan, Jan Breman, and Karin Kapadia. eds. 1999. 'The Worlds of Indian Industrial Labour.' *Contributions to Indian Sociology* 3 (1-2): 1-431. Special Issue.

Peck, Jamie and Adam Tickell. 2002. 'Neoliberalizing Space.' *Antipode* 34 (3): 380-404.

Perroux, Francois. 1950. 'Economic Space: Theory and Applications.' *Quarterly Journal of Economics* 64 (1): 89-104.

Perry, Alex. 2010. *Falling Off the Edge: Globalization, World Peace, and other Lies.* Oxford: Pan Books.

Phelan, Craig. 2007. *Trade Union Revitalisation: Trends and Prospects in Thirty-Four Countries.* Berne: Peter Lang.

Piore, M. and C. Sabel. 1984. *The Second Industrial Divide: Possibilities for Prosperity.* New York: Basic Books.

Piot, Charles. 2010. *Nostalgia for the Future: West Africa after the Cold War.* Chicago: University of Chicago Press.

Polanyi. Karl. 1944. *The Great Transformation.* Boston: Beacon Press.

Porter, Michael. 1990. *The Competitive Advantage of Nations.* New York: The Free Press.

Pradhan, R.S. 1984. *Industrialisation in Nepal: A Macro and Micro Perspective.* Ahmedabad: NBO Publishers.

Prentice, Rebecca and Geert De Neve. 2017. *Unmaking the Global Sweatshop: Health and Safety of the World's Garment Workers.* Philadelphia: University of Pennsylvania Press.

Putnam, R. 1993. *Making Democracy Work: Civic Traditions in Modern Italy*. New Jersey: Princeton University Press.

————. 2000. *Bowling Alone: The Collapse and Revival of American Community*. New York: Simon and Schuster.

Quigley, Declan. 1984. *The Social Structure of a Newar Trading Community: East-Central Nepal*. PhD thesis, London School of Economics/Anthropology.

————. 1985. 'The Guthi Organisation of Dhulikhel Shresthas.' *Kailash* 12 (1-2): 5-61.

Rankin, Katharine. 2004. *The Cultural Politics of Markets: Economic Liberalisation and Social Change in Nepal*. London: Pluto Press.

Regmi, Mahesh Chandra. 1971. *A Study in Nepali Economic History*. New Delhi: Manjusri Publishing House.

Rodriguez-Clare, A. 2005. 'Coordination Failures, Clusters and Microeconomic Interventions.' *Economia* 6 (1): 1-42.

Rodrik, Dani. 2006. 'Goodbye Washington Consensus, Hello Washington Confusion?' *Journal of Economic Literature*. XLIV (December): 973-87.

————. 2011. *The Globalization Paradox: Democracy and the Future of the World Economy*. NY and London: W. W. Norton.

————. 2004. 'Industrial Policy for the Twenty-First Century.' *Harvard John F. Kennedy School of Government Faculty Research Working Paper Series*. RWP04-047.

Rosenstein-Rodan, Paul. 1943. 'Problems of industrialization in Eastern and South-Eastern Europe.' *Economic Journal* 53 (210/211): 202-11.

Ross, Andrew. ed. 1997. *No Sweat: Fashion, Free Trade, and the Rights of Garment Workers*. New York: Verso.

Rostow. Walt W. 1960. *The Stages of Economic Growth: A Non-Communist Manifesto*. Cambridge, Massachusetts: Harvard University Press.

Ruwanpura, Kanchana. 2013. 'Scripted Performances? Local Readings of "Global" Health and Safety Standards (The Apparel Sector in Sri Lanka).' *Global Labour Journal* 4 (2): 88-108.

Sabel, Charles. 2001. 'Bootstrapping Development: Rethinking the Role of Public Intervention in Promoting Growth.' Paper presented at the Protestant Ethic and Spirit of Capitalism Conference, Corness University, Ithaca, New York October 8-10, 2004 (revised in 2005).

Sabel, Charles and Jonathan Zeitlin. 1997. *World of Possibilities: Flexibility and Mass Production in Western Industrialization*. New York: Cambridge University Press.

Saxena, Sanchita. 2014. *Made in Bangladesh, Cambodia, and Sri Lanka: The Labor Behind the Global Garment and Textiles Industries*. New York: Cambria Press.

Schloss, A. 1980. 'Making Planning Relevant: Nepal's Experience, 1968-1976.' *Asian Survey* 20 (10): 1008-22.

Schmitz, Hubert. 1999. 'Collective Efficiency and Increasing Returns.' *Cambridge Journal of Economics* 23 (4): 465-83.

Schmitz, Hubert and Khalid Nadvi. 1999. 'Clustering and Industrialisation'. *World Development* 27 (9): 1503-14.

Schmitz, Hubert and Peter Knorringa. 2000. 'Learning from Global Buyers.' *Journal of Development Studies* 37 (2): 177-205.

Scott, Gregory Shawn. 1998. *Sewing with Dignity: Class Struggle and Ethnic Conflict in the Los Angeles Garment Industry.* PhD thesis, University of California.

Seddon, David, Piers Blaikie, and John Cameron. (1979) 2002. *Peasants and Workers in Nepal.* Reprint, Delhi: Adroit Publications.

Sehata, Samer S. 2009. *Shop Floor Culture and Politics in Egypt.* New York: State University of New York Press.

Shakya, Mallika. 2004. 'Nepalisation of an Indian Industry: The Fast Evolving (and Dismantling) Ready-Made Garment Industry of Nepal.' *Contributions to Nepalese Studies* 31: 265-91.

_____. 2007. 'Our Hymns are Different but Our Gods are the Same: Religious Rituals in Modern Garment Factories in Nepal.' *European Bulletin of Himalayan Research* 31: 67–82.

_____. 2008. 'In Search of Pragmatism within Politics: Capitalism, Culture and the Rising Wave of Communism in Nepal.' *HIMALAYA* 28 (1-2): 49-57.

_____. 2011a. 'Bridging the Design Gap: The Case of the Nepali Clothing Industry.' *The Journal of Modern Craft* 4 (3): 294-395.

_____. 2011b. 'Apparel Exports in Lesotho: The State's Role in Building Critical Mass for Competitiveness.' In *Yes Africa Can: Success Stories from a Dynamic Continent,* edited by P. Chuhan-Pole and M. Angwafo, 219-30. Washington, D.C.: World Bank.

_____. 2011c. 'The World Bank and Private Sector Development: Is "Doing Business" an Extension of the Structural Adjustment Programme or a Departure?' *St Antony's International Review: Special Edition on International Financial Institutions in an Age of Crisis* 7 (1): 30-47.

_____. 2013a. 'A Garment May Day.' *The Hindu.* May 1, 2013.

_____. 2013b. 'Nepali Economic History through the Ethnic Lens: Changing State Alliances with Business Elites.' In *Nationalism and Ethnic Conflict: Identities and Mobilization after 1990,* edited by Mahendra Lawoti and Susan Hangen, 58-82. Oxford and New York: Routledge.

_____. 2014. 'Marwari Traders between Hindu Neoliberalism and Democratic Socialism in Nepal.' In *People, Money and Power in the Economic Crisis: Perspectives from the Global South,* edited by Keith Hart and John Sharp, 190-206. New York and Oxford: Berghahn Books.

_____. 2016a. 'Country of Rumours: Making Sense of a Bollywood Controversy.' In *Political Change and Public Culture in Post-1990 Nepal,* edited by Michael Hutt and Pratyoush Onta, 56-74. Cambridge and Delhi: Cambridge University Press.

_____. 2016b. 'Labour Militancy in Neoliberal Times: A Preliminary Comparison of Nepal with South Africa.' In *World Anthropologies in Practice: Situated Perspectives, Global Knowledge,* edited by John Gledhill, Chapter 3. London and New York: Bloomsbury Academic.

————. 2017. 'An Anthropological Reading of the Policies of International Development: Export Competitiveness as a Conjunctural Case Study.' *Dialectical Anthropology* 41 (2): 113-28.

Shils, Edward. 1960. 'Political Development in the New States.' *Comparative Studies in Society and History* 2 (3): 265-92.

Shrestha, Badri Prasad. 1967. *The Economy of Nepal: Problems and Processes of Industrialization.* Bombay: Vosa & Co. Publishers.

Shrestha, Mona. 2013. *Exploring Gendered Work and Women's Empowerment: A Study of Hotels, Resorts and Casinos in Nepal.* PhD thesis, University of Warwick.

Shrestha, Nanda R. 2009 (1998). *In the Name of Development: A Reflection on Nepal.* Kathmandu: Educational Publishing House.

Shrestha, Shyamal Krishna. 2003. *Nepal's Carpet Industry in the Area of Globalization and Competition.* Masters in Development Studies thesis, Institute of Development Studies.

Sijapati, Bandita. 2013. 'In Pursuit of Recognition: Regionalism, Madhesi Identity and the Madhes Andolan.' In *Nationalism and Ethnic Conflict in Nepal: Identities and Mobilization after 1990*, edited by Mahendra Lawoti and Susan Hangen, 145-72. Oxford and New York: Routledge.

Singer, Milton. 1972. *When a Great Tradition Modernizes: An Anthropological Approach to Indian Civilisation.* New York: Praeger Publishers.

Slusser, M. S. 1982. *Nepal Mandala: A Cultural Study of the Kathmandu Valley*, Vol. 1&2. New Jersey: Princeton University Press.

Smith, Adam. 1776. *An Inquiry into the Nature and Causes of the Wealth of Nations.* London: W. Strahan and T. Cadell.

Smith, Jackie, Charles Chatfield, and Ron Pagnucco. eds. 1997. *Transnational Social Movements and Global Politics.* Syracuse, NY: Syracuse University Press.

Sorge, A. 1991. 'Strategic Fit and the Social Effect: Interpreting Cross-National Comparisons of Technology, Organisation, and Human Resources.' *Organisation Studies* 12 (2): 161-90.

Soyer, Daniel. 2005. 'Cockroach Capitalists: Jewish Contractors at the Turn of the Twentieth Century.' In *A Coat of Many Colours: Immigration, Globalization, and Reform in New York City's Garment Industry*, edited by Daniel Soyer, 91-114. New York: Fordham University Press.

Soyer, Daniel, ed. 2005. *A Coat of Many Colours: Immigration, Globalization, and Reform in New York City's Garment Industry.* New York: Fordham University Press.

Spinanger, Dean, 1999. 'Faking Liberalization and Finagling Protectionism: The ATC at its Best.' Background Paper presented at the ERF/IAI/World Bank Workshop, Cairo, 14-15 July.

Stein, Howard. 1995. 'Institutional Theories and Structural Adjustment in Africa.' In *The New Institutional Economics and Third World Development*, edited by John Harriss, Jane Hunter and Colin M. Lewis, 109-33. London: Routledge.

Stiglitz, Joseph. 2001. Foreword. *The Great Transformation: The Political and Economic Origins of Our Time.* Massachusetts: Beacon Press:

_____. 2002. *Globalization and Its Discontents*. New York: W.W. Norton & Company.

Strathern, Marilyn. 1985. 'Kinship and Economy: Constitutive Orders of a Provisional Kind.' *American Ethnologist* 12 (2): 191-209.

Subedi, Surya. 2005. *Dynamics of Foreign Policy and Law: A Study of Indo-Nepal Relations*. New Delhi: Oxford University Press.

Tam, Simon. 1990. 'Centrifugal Versus Centripetal Growth Processes: Contrasting Ideal Types for Conceptualising the Developmental Patterns of Chinese and Japanese Firms.' In *Capitalism in Contrasting Cultures*, edited by Stewart R. Clegg, Monica Cartner, and S. Gordon Redding, 153-83. Berlin: Walter de Gruyter.

Taylor, Frederick. W. 1947. *The Principles of Scientific Management*. New York: Norton Publications.

Teal, Francis and Simon Baptist. 2008. 'Why do Korean firms produce so much more output per worker than Ghanaian firms?'Working Paper, Centre for the Study of African Economies, Department of Economics, University of Oxford. .http://www.csae.ox.ac.uk/materials/data/28/2008-10text.pdf

Tewari, Meenu. 2008. 'Varieties of Global Integration: Navigating Institutional Legacies and Global Networks in India's Garment Industry.' *Competition and Change* 12 (1): 49-67.

Thompson. E.P. 1967. 'Time, Work-Discipline, and Industrial Capitalism.' *Past and Present* 38 (December): 56-97.

Thráinn, Eggertsson. 2005. *Imperfect Institutions: Possibilities and Limits of Reform*. Ann Arbor: University of Michigan Press.

Toye, John. 1995. 'The New Institutional Economics and Its Implications for Development Theory.' In *The New Institutional Economics and Third World Development*, edited by J. Harriss, Jane Hunter and Colin M. Lewis, 109-33. London: Routledge.

Tsing, Anna. 1993. *In the Realm of the Diamond Queen: Marginality in an Out-of-the-Way Place*. New Jersey: Princeton University Press.

van Heerden, Auret, Maria Prieto Berhouet, and Cathrine Caspari. 2003. 'Rags or Riches? Phasing Out the Multi-Fibre Arrangement (MFA).' ILO SEED Working Paper No 40. http://www.ilo.org/wcmsp5/groups/public/---ed_emp/---emp_ent/---ifp_seed/documents/publication/wcms_117697.pdf.

Wallerstein, I. 1974. *The Modern World-System: Capitalist Agriculture and the Origins of the European World-Economy in the Sixteenth Century*. New York: Academic Press.

Whitley, Richard. 1992. *Business Systems in East Asia: Firms, Markets, and Societies*. London: Sage Publications.

_____. 1999. *Divergent Capitalisms: The Social Structuring and Change of Business Systems*. London: Oxford University Press.

Wildavsky, Aaron. 1972. 'Why Planning Fails in Nepal.' *Administrative Science Quarterly* 17 (94): 508-28.

Wilks, S. 1990. 'The Embodiment of Industrial Culture in Bureaucracy and Management.' In *Capitalism in Contrasting Cultures*, edited by Stewart R. Clegg, Monica Cartner and S. Gordon Redding, 131-52. Berlin: Walter de Gruyter.

Williamson, John. 2004. 'The Strange History of the Washington Consensus.' *Journal of Post Keynesian Economics* 27 (2): 195-206.

Williamson, Oliver E. 1975. *Markets and Hierarchies: Analysis and Antitrust Implications.* New York: The Free Press.

_____. 1986. *Economic Organisation: Firms, Markets and Policy Control.* New York: New York University Press.

Zeng, Dougless Z. 2006. *Africa: Knowledge, Technology, and Cluster-Based Growth.* Washington, D.C.: World Bank Institute Development Study.

Zivetz, L. 1992. *Private Enterprises and the State in Modern Nepal.* Madras: Oxford University Press.

Zonaband, Francoise. 1993. *The Nuclear Peninsula.* Cambridge: Cambridge University Press.

Zucker, Lynn. 1986. 'Production of Trust: Institutional Sources of Economic Structure, 1840-1920.' *Research in Organisational Behaviour* 8 (1986): 53-111.

Index